Student Solutions Manual for
FUNDAMENTAL
Accounting Principles

ELEVENTH CANADIAN EDITION

Volume
1

CHAPTERS 1–11

Kermit D. Larson

University of Texas – Austin

Tilly Jensen

Northern Alberta Institute of Technology

McGraw-Hill
Ryerson

Toronto   Montréal   Boston   Burr Ridge, IL   Dubuque, IA   Madison, WI   New York
San Francisco   St. Louis   Bangkok   Bogotá   Caracas   Kuala Lumpur   Lisbon
London   Madrid   Mexico City   Milan   New Delhi   Santiago   Seoul   Singapore
Sydney   Taipei

**McGraw-Hill
Ryerson**

Student Solutions Manual for use with
Fundamental Accounting Principles
Volume 1
Eleventh Canadian Edition

ISBN: 0-07-095321-X

4 5 6 7 8 9 10 CP 0 9 8 7 6

Printed and bound in Canada

Care has been taken to trace ownership of copyright material contained in this text; however, the publisher will welcome any information that enables them to rectify any reference or credit for subsequent editions.

Executive Sponsoring Editor: Nicole Lukach
Marketing Manager: Kim Verhaeghe
Developmental Editor: Brook Nymark
Senior Production Coordinator: Madeleine Harrington
Cover Design: Dianna Little
Printer: Canadian Printco

Contents

Chapter 1 Accounting: The Key to Success

EXERCISES

Exercise 1-1 (10 minutes)

a. Corporation
b. Sole proprietorship
c. Corporation
d. Partnership
e. Sole proprietorship
f. Sole proprietorship
g. Corporation

Exercise 1-3 (15 minutes) (Answers will vary.)

External users and some questions they seek to answer with accounting information include:

a. Shareholders (investors), who seek answers for questions such as:
   1. Are resources owned by a business adequate to carry out plans?
   2. Are the debts owed excessive in amount?
   3. What is the current level of income?

b. Creditors, who seek answers for questions such as:
   1. Does the business have the ability to repay its debts?
   2. Can the business take on additional debt?
   3. Are resources sufficient to cover current amounts owed?

c. Employees, who seek answers to questions like:
   1. Is the business financially stable?
   2. Can the business afford to pay higher salaries?
   3. What are growth prospects for the organization?

Exercise 1-5 (20 minutes)

http://globeandmail.ca
- a Canadian newspaper online

http://www.canadianbusiness.com
- a Canadian business magazine online

http://www.PROFITguide.com
- a Canadian business magazine online

http://finance.yahoo.com
- a general business site

http://www.sedar.com
- an online database that has accounting information for thousands of public companies that operate in Canada

http://www.strategis.ic.gc.ca
- The Canadian Business Map provides access to international, national, provincial, territorial, and municipal business information

http://canada.gc.ca
- The Canada Site is very useful in keeping you abreast of changes in regulations and legislation that affect business

http://www.canadiancareers.com
- Canadian Careers provides information as to where the jobs in Canada are

Exercise 1-7 (5 minutes)

1. H
2. C
3. E
4. A
5. F

PROBLEMS

Problem 1-1B (5 minutes)

a) WestJet Airlines Ltd. is a corporation because it has shareholders.
b) Leon's Furniture is a corporation because it has shareholders.

Chapter 2   Financial Statements and Accounting Transactions

EXERCISES

Exercise 2-1 (10 minutes)

a) $80,000 – $65,000 = $\underline{15,000}$ net income

b) $92,000 – $149,000 = $\underline{57,000}$ net loss

c) $10,000 + 0 – 0 + x = $86,000
   x = $86,000 – $10,000
   x = $\underline{76,000}$ net income

d) $25,000 + $40,000 – 0 + x = $52,000
   x = 52,000 – 25,000 – 40,000
   x = –$13,000 or a $\underline{13,000}$ Net loss

Exercise 2-3 (15 minutes)

THE GRAYSON GROUP
Income Statement
For Month Ended November 30, 2005

Revenues:		
Consulting fees earned		$15,000
Operating expenses:		
Salaries expense..	$6,000	
Rent expense	2,550	
Utilities expenses	680	
Telephone expense	660	
Total operating expenses.........................		9,890
Net income...		$ 5,110

Exercise 2-5 (15 minutes)

THE GRAYSON GROUP
Balance Sheet
November 30, 2005

Assets		Liabilities	
Cash	$12,000	Accounts payable	$ 7,500
Accounts receivable	15,000		
Office supplies	2,250	*Owner's Equity*	
Automobiles	36,000	Joseph Grayson, capital	85,750
Office equipment	28,000	Total liabilities and	
Total assets	$93,250	owner's equity	$93,250

Exercise 2-6 (15 minutes)

TUTOR-RIGHT SERVICES
Income Statement
For Month Ended July 31, 2005

Revenues:		
Tutoring fees earned		$2,100
Textbook rental revenue		150
Total revenues		$ 2,250
Operating expenses:		
Office rent expense	$1,250	
Tutors wages expense	770	
Utilities expense	290	
Total operating expenses		2,310
Net loss		$ 60

Fundamental Accounting Principles, Eleventh Canadian Edition

Exercise 2-7 (15 minutes)

TUTOR-RIGHT SERVICES
Statement of Owner's Equity
For Month Ended July 31, 2005

Leena Mahan, capital, July 1		$ 3,700
Add: Investments by owner		600
Total		$ 4,300
Less: Withdrawals by owner	$ 500	
Net loss	60	560
Leena Mahan, capital, July 31		$ 3,740

Exercise 2-9 (10 minutes)

Description

B 1. Requires every business to be accounted for separately from its owner or owners.

D 2. Requires financial statement information to be supported by evidence other than someone's opinion or imagination.

A 3. Requires financial statement information to be based on costs incurred in transactions.

E 4. Requires financial statements to reflect the assumption that the business will continue operating instead of being closed or sold.

C 5. Requires revenue to be recorded only when the earnings process is complete.

Exercise 2-11 (10 minutes)

If assets decreased by $5,000 during August, then
$20,000 + $5,000 = $25,000 Assets at August 1, 2005.
Therefore, Owner's Equity at August 1, 2005 = $25,000 - $1,000 = $24,000

If liabilities increased by $3,000 during August, then
$1,000 + $3,000 = $4,000 Liabilities at August 31, 2005.
Therefore, Owner's Equity at August 31, 2005 = $20,000 - $4,000 = $16,000

Exercise 2-13 (20 minutes)

	Assets					Liabilities	+	Owner's Equity
	Cash	+ Accounts Receivable	+ Parts Supplies	+ Equipment	=	Accounts Payable	+	Janine Commry, Capital
a)	+ $7,000							+ $ 7,000
b)	- 2,500							- 2,500
Totals	$4,500							$ 4,500
c)			+ $1,200			+ $1,200		
Totals	$4,500		$1,200			$1,200		$ 4,500
d)		+ $3,400						+ $ 3,400
Totals	$4,500	$3,400	$1,200			$1,200		$7,900
e)	− $ 950			+ $950				
Totals	$3,550	$3,400	$1,200	$950		$1,200		$7,900
f)*								
Totals	$3,550	$3,400	$1,200	$950		$1,200		$ 7,900
g)	− $1,200					− $1,200		
Totals	$2,350	$3,400	$1,200	$950		$ 0		$7,900
h)	+ $1,400							+ $ 1,400
Totals	$3,750	$3,400	$1,200	$950		$ 0		$9,300
i)	− $2,700							− $ 2,700
Totals	$1,050	$3,400	$1,200	$950		$ 0		$6,600

$6,600 = $6,600

*Note: For (f), since no transaction has occurred, no entry is required.

Exercise 2-15 (10 minutes)

a) The business purchased land paying $3,000.

b) Office supplies were purchased on credit (or on account).

c) Revenue on account (or on credit) was earned.

d) A creditor (or liability) was paid.

e) A credit customer made a payment on their account (or the amount that was owing).

Exercise 2-17 (15 minutes) (Answers may vary.)

Possible examples include:

a. The business purchases office supplies (or some other asset) for cash.

b. The owner withdraws cash (or some other asset) from the business; also, the business incurs an expense paid with cash.

c. The business incurs an expense on credit.

d. The business purchases equipment (or some other asset) on credit.

e. The owner invests cash (or some other asset); or, the business earns a revenue and accepts cash or an account receivable.

f. The business pays an account payable (or some other liability) with cash.

Exercise 2-19 (25 minutes)

Bert Zimm – Freelance Writing Income Statement For Month Ended March 31, 2005		
Revenues:		
Freelance service revenue		$3,500
Operating expenses:		
Salaries expense	$900	
Rent expense	600	
Total operating expenses		1,500
Net income		$2,000

Bert Zimm – Freelance Writing Statement of Owner's Equity For Month Ended March 31, 2005		
Bert Zimm, capital, March 1		$ 0
Add: Investment by owner	$5,000	
Net income	2,000	
Bert Zimm, capital, March 31		$7,000

Bert Zimm – Freelance Writing Balance Sheet March 31, 2005				
Assets			*Liabilities*	
Cash	$1,000		Accounts payable	$ 300
Accounts receivable	1,000			
Supplies	300			
Equipment	5,000			
			Owner's Equity	
			Bert Zimm, capital	7,000
Total assets	$7,300		Total liabilities and owner's equity	$7,300

Fundamental Accounting Principles, Eleventh Canadian Edition

PROBLEMS

Problem 2-1B (20 minutes)

	2007	2006	2005
Beginning capital	146,000[1]	35,000[3]	0
+ Owner investment	0	0	50,000
+ Net income (loss)	183,000	163,000	(15,000)[5]
– Owner withdrawals	69,000	52,000	0
= Ending capital	260,000	146,000[2]	35,000 [4]

Note: The superscripts show the order in which the answers were calculated.

Calculations:
1. 260,000 + 69,000 – 183,000 = <u>146,000</u>
2. The beginning capital of 146,000 for 2007 is the ending capital from 2006.
3. 146,000 + 52,000 – 163,000 = <u>35,000</u>
4. The beginning capital of 35,000 for 2006 is the ending capital from 2005.
5. 35,000 – 50,000 = <u>-15,000</u>

Problem 2-2B (30 minutes)

FIREWORKS FANTASIA
Income Statement
For Year Ended December 31, 2005

Revenues:		
Fees earned..		$ 70,000
Rent revenue...		<u>33,000</u>
Total revenues...................................		$ 103,000
Operating expenses:		
Wages expense....................................	$46,000	
Fireworks supplies expense	41,000	
Utilities expense	17,800	
Advertising expense.................................	4,500	
Office supplies expense.............................	<u>1,800</u>	
Total operating expenses..........................		<u>111,100</u>
Net loss		<u>$ 8,100</u>

Problem 2-2B *(continued)*

FIREWORKS FANTASIA
Statement of Owner's Equity
For Year Ended December 31, 2005

Wes Gandalf, capital, January 1		$187,600
Add: Investments by owner		15,000
Total		$202,600
Less: Withdrawals by owner..........................	$26,000	
Net loss	8,100	34,100
Wes Gandalf, capital, December 31		$168,500

FIREWORKS FANTASIA
Balance Sheet
December 31, 2005

Assets		*Liabilities*	
Cash	$ 14,000	Accounts payable	$ 9,000
Accounts receivable...........	7,000		
Fireworks supplies.............	16,000		
Office supplies....................	1,500		
Tools.....................................	9,000		
Building................................	62,000	*Owner's Equity*	
Land......................................	56,000	Wes Gandalf, capital.........	168,500
Office equipment	12,000	Total liabilities and	
Total assets.........................	$177,500	owner's equity..............	$177,500

Fundamental Accounting Principles, Eleventh Canadian Edition

Problem 2-3B (60 minutes) *Part 1*

STILLER CO.
Balance Sheet
December 31, 2006

Assets		*Liabilities*	
Cash..............................	$ 14,000	Accounts payable........................	$ 5,000
Accounts receivable.........	25,000		
Office supplies..................	10,000		
Office equipment	60,000	*Owner's Equity*	
Machinery.........................	30,500	Joseph Stiller, capital...................	134,500[1]
		Total liabilities and	
Total assets......................	$139,500	owner's equity	$139,500

STILLER CO.
Balance Sheet
December 31, 2007

Assets		*Liabilities*	
Cash..............................	$ 10,000	Accounts payable	$ 15,000
Accounts receivable.........	30,000	Notes payable.......................	260,000
Office supplies..................	12,500	Total liabilities	275,000
Office equipment	60,000		
Machinery.........................	30,500		
Building.............................	260,000	*Owner's Equity*	
Land..................................	65,000	Joseph Stiller, capital	193,000[2]
		Total liabilities and	
Total assets......................	$468,000	owner's equity..................	$468,000

Calculations:
1. $139,500 – $5,000 = $134,500
2. $468,000 – $275,000 = $193,000

Problem 2-3B *(concluded) Part 2*

Calculation of net income for 2007:

Owner's equity, December 31, 2007	$193,000
Owner's equity, December 31, 2006	134,500
Increase in owner's equity during 2007	$ 58,500
Less: Additional investment	25,000
Net increase in owner's equity during 2007, apart from new investment	$ 33,500
Add: Withdrawals ($1,000 × 12)	12,000
Net income earned in 2007	$ 45,500

Problem 2-4B (40 minutes) *Part 1*

Company V:

(a) and (b)
   Calculation of owner's equity:

	12/31/05	12/31/06
Assets	$45,000	$49,000
Liabilities	–30,000	–26,000
Owner's equity	$15,000	$23,000

(c) Calculation of net income for 2006:

Owner's equity, December 31, 2005	$15,000
Add: Owner investments......................	6,000
Net income	?
Less: Owner withdrawals.....................	4,500
Owner's equity, December 31, 2006	$23,000

Therefore, the net income must have been $6,500.

Fundamental Accounting Principles, Eleventh Canadian Edition

Problem 2-4B *(continued)*

Part 2

Company W:

(a) Calculation of equity at December 31, 2005:

Assets	$70,000
Liabilities	−50,000
Owner's equity	$20,000

(b) Calculation of equity at December 31, 2006:

Owner's equity, December 31, 2005	$20,000
Add: Owner investments.........................	10,000
Net income	30,000
Less: Owner withdrawals	2,000
Owner's equity, December 31, 2006	$58,000

(c) Calculation of the amount of liabilities at December 31, 2006:

Assets	$90,000
Owner's equity	−58,000
Liabilities	$32,000

Part 3

Company X:

First, calculate the beginning and ending equity balances:

	12/31/05	12/31/06
Assets	$121,500	$136,500
Liabilities	−58,500	−55,500
Owner's equity	$ 63,000	$ 81,000

Then, find the amount of owner investments during 2006 by completing this table:

Owner's equity, December 31, 2005	$63,000
Add: Owner investments.........................	?
Net income	16,500
Less: Owner withdrawals	0
Owner's equity, December 31, 2006	$81,000

Therefore, the owner investments must have been $1,500.

Problem 2-4B *(continued)*

Part 4

Company Y:

First, calculate the beginning balance of equity:

	Dec. 31, 2005
Assets	$82,500
Liabilities	–61,500
Owner's equity	$21,000

Next, find the ending balance of equity by completing this table:

Owner's equity, December 31, 2005	$21,000
Add: Owner investments........................	38,100
Net income	24,000
Less: Owner withdrawals........................	18,000
Owner's equity, December 31, 2006	$65,100

Finally, find the ending amount of assets by adding the ending balance of equity to the ending balance of the liabilities:

	Dec. 31, 2006
Liabilities	$ 72,000
Owner's equity	65,100
Assets	$137,100

Problem 2-4B *(concluded) Part 5*

Company Z:

First, calculate the balance of equity as of December 31, 2006:

Assets	$160,000
Liabilities	−52,000
Owner's equity	$108,000

Next, find the beginning balance of equity by completing this table:

Owner's equity, December 31, 2005	$?
Add: Owner investments.......................	40,000
Net income	32,000
Less: Owner withdrawals	6,000
Owner's equity, December 31, 2006	$108,000

Therefore, the beginning balance of equity was $42,000.

Finally, find the beginning amount of liabilities by subtracting the beginning balance of equity from the beginning balance of the assets:

	Dec. 31, 2005
Assets	$124,000
Owner's equity	−42,000
Liabilities	$ 82,000

Problem 2-5B (45 minutes) Parts 1 and 2

	Assets					=	Liabilities		+	Owner's Equity	
	Cash	+ Accounts Receivable	+ Office Supplies	+ Office Equipment	+ Building	=	Accounts Payable	+ Notes Payable	+	Judith Grimm, Capital	Explanation of Changes
(a)	+$50,000			+ $5,000						+$55,000	Investment
(b)	− 10,000				+$120,000			+$110,000			
Bal.	$40,000			$5,000	$120,000			$110,000		$55,000	
(c)	− 9,000			+ 9,000							
Bal.	$31,000			$14,000	$120,000			$110,000		$55,000	
(d)			+$2,000	+ 3,200			+$5,200				
Bal.	$31,000		$2,000	$17,200	$120,000		$5,200	$110,000		$55,000	
(e)	− 1,500									− 1,500	Advertising Expense
Bal.	$29,500		$2,000	$17,200	$120,000		$5,200	$110,000		$53,500	
(f)		+$3,000								+ 3,000	Consulting Services Revenue
Bal.	$29,500	$3,000	$2,000	$17,200	$120,000		$5,200	$110,000		$56,500	
(g)	+ 5,400									+ 5,400	Consulting Services Revenue
Bal.	$34,900	$3,000	$2,000	$17,200	$120,000		$5,200	$110,000		$61,900	
(h)	− 2,750									− 2,750	Withdrawal
Bal.	$32,150	$3,000	$2,000	$17,200	$120,000		$5,200	$110,000		$59,150	
(i)*											
Bal.	$32,150	$3,000	$2,000	$17,200	$120,000		$5,200	$110,000		$59,150	
(j)	+ 1,200	− 1,200									
Bal.	$33,350	$1,800	$2,000	$17,200	$120,000		$5,200	$110,000		$59,150	
(k)	− 900						− 900				
Bal.	$32,450	$1,800	$2,000	$17,200	$120,000		$4,300	$110,000		$59,150	
(l)	− 1,900									− 1,900	Wages Expense
Bal.	$30,550 +	$1,800 +	$2,000 +	$17,200 +	$120,000 =		$4,300 +	$110,000 +		$57,250	

$171,550 = $171,550

Note: For (i), since no transaction has occurred, no entry is required.

Fundamental Accounting Principles, Eleventh Canadian Edition

Problem 2-5B (continued)   Part 3

Southwest Consulting Income Statement For Year Ended December 31, 2005		
Revenues:		
Consulting services revenue		$8,400
Operating expenses:		
Wages expense	$1,900	
Advertising expense	1,500	
Total operating expenses		3,400
Net income		$5,000

Southwest Consulting Statement of Owner's Equity For Year Ended December 31, 2005		
Judith Grimm, capital, January 1		$ 0
Add: Investment by owner	$55,000	
Net income	5,000	60,000
Total		$60,000
Less: Withdrawal by owner		2,750
Judith Grimm, capital, December 31		$57,250

Southwest Consulting Balance Sheet December 31, 2005				
Assets			**Liabilities**	
Cash	$ 30,550		Accounts payable	$ 4,300
Accounts receivable	1,800		Notes payable	110,000
Office supplies	2,000		Total liabilities	$114,300
Office equipment	17,200			
Building	120,000		**Owner's Equity**	
			Judith Grimm, capital	57,250
Total assets	$171,550		Total liabilities and owner's equity	$171,550

Problem 2-6B (60 minutes) Parts 1 and 2

	Assets			= Liabilities +	Owner's Equity	
June	Cash	+ Accounts Receivable	+ Cleaning Supplies	= Accounts Payable	+ Andrew Martin, Capital	Explanation of Change
1	+$120,000				+$120,000	Investment
1	– 4,500				– 4,500	Rent Expense
4	– 2,400		+$2,400			
6	– 2,250				– 2,250	Advertising Expense
8	+ 750				+ 750	Service Revenue
14		+$5,300			+ 5,300	Service Revenue
16	– 1,900				– 1,900	Salaries Expense
20	+ 5,300	– 5,300				
21		+ 3,500			+ 3,500	Service Revenue
22			+ 750	+$750		
24		+ 825			+ 825	Service Revenue
29	+ 3,500	– 3,500				
29	– 375			– 375		
30	– 120				– 120	Telephone Expense
30	– 525				– 525	Utilities Expense
30	– 1,900				– 1,900	Salaries Expense
30	– 2,000				– 2,000	Withdrawal
	$113,580	+ $ 825	+ $3,150	= $375	+ $117,180	

$117,555 = $117,555

Fundamental Accounting Principles, Eleventh Canadian Edition

Problem 2-6B *(concluded) Part 3*

UNIVERSAL MAINTENANCE CO.
Income Statement
For Month Ended June 30, 2005

Revenues:		
Maintenance services revenue		$10,375
Operating expenses:		
Rent expense	$4,500	
Salaries expense...	3,800	
Advertising expense..	2,250	
Utilities expense	525	
Telephone expense	120	
Total operating expenses............................		11,195
Net loss		$ 820

UNIVERSAL MAINTENANCE CO.
Statement of Owner's Equity
For Month Ended June 30, 2005

Andrew Martin, capital, June 1................................		$ 0
Add: Investments by owner		120,000
Total		$120,000
Less: Withdrawals by owner..................................	$2,000	
Net loss...	820	
Total		2,820
Andrew Martin, capital, June 30..............................		$117,180

UNIVERSAL MAINTENANCE CO.
Balance Sheet
June 30, 2005

	Assets		*Liabilities*	
Cash	$113,580	Accounts payable.........................	$	375
Accounts receivable.........	825			
Cleaning supplies.............	3,150	*Owner's Equity*		
		Andrew Martin, capital		117,180
		Total liabilities and		
Total assets......................	$117,555	owner's equity		$117,555

Problem 2-7B (50 minutes) Parts 1 and 2

	Assets					= Liab.	+ Owner's Equity	
Date	Cash	+ Accounts Receivable	+ Office Supplies	+ Office Equip.	+ Excavat. Equip.	= Accounts Payable	+ Robert Cantu, Capital	Explanation of Change
June 30	$ 6,000	$2,300	$780	$4,800	$17,000	$3,100	$27,780	
July 1	60,000						60,000	Investment
Bal.	$66,000						$87,780	
1	− 500						− 500	Rent Expense
Bal.	$65,500						$87,280	
1	− 800				+ 4,000	+ 3,200		
Bal.	$64,700				$21,000	$6,300	$87,280	
6	− 500		+ 500					
Bal.	$64,200		$1,280		$21,000	$6,300	$87,280	
8	+ 2,200						+ 2,200	Excavating Fees Earned
Bal.	$66,400		$1,280		$21,000	$6,300	$89,480	
10				+ 3,800		+ 3,800		
Bal.	$66,400		$1,280	$8,600	$21,000	$10,100	$89,480	
15		+ 2,400					+ 2,400	Excavating Fees Earned
Bal.	$66,400	$4,700	$1,280	$8,600	$21,000	$10,100	$91,880	
17			+ 1,920			+ 1,920		
Bal.	$66,400	$4,700	$3,200	$8,600	$21,000	$12,020	$91,880	
23	− 3,800					− 3,800		
Bal.	$62,600	$4,700	$3,200	$8,600	$21,000	$8,220	$91,880	
25		+ 5,000					+ 5,000	Excavating Fees Earned
Bal.	$62,600	$9,700	$3,200	$8,600	$21,000	$8,220	$96,880	
28	+ 2,400	− 2,400						
Bal.	$65,000	$7,300	$3,200	$8,600	$21,000	$8,220	$96,880	
31	− 1,260						− 1,260	Salaries Expense
Bal.	$63,740	$7,300	$3,200	$8,600	$21,000	$8,220	$95,620	
31	− 260						− 260	Utilities Expense
Bal.	$63,480	$7,300	$3,200	$8,600	$21,000	$8,220	$95,360	
31	− 1,200						− 1,200	Withdrawal
Bal.	$62,280	$7,300	$3,200	$8,600	$21,000	$8,220	$94,160	

$102,380 = $102,380

CANTU EXCAVATING CO.
Income Statement
For Month Ended July 31, 2005

Revenues:		
Excavating fees earned		$9,600
Operating expenses:		
Salaries expense..	$1,260	
Rent expense	500	
Utilities expense	260	
Total operating expenses............................		2,020
Net income..		$7,580

CANTU EXCAVATING CO.
Statement of Owner's Equity
For Month Ended July 31, 2005

Robert Cantu, capital, June 30.............................		$ 27,780
Add: Investments by owner	$60,000	
Net income	7,580	67,580
Total..		$95,360
Less: Withdrawals by owner................................		1,200
Robert Cantu, capital, July 31..............................		$94,160

Fundamental Accounting Principles, Eleventh Canadian Edition

CANTU EXCAVATING CO.
Balance Sheet
July 31, 2005

Assets		Liabilities	
Cash...............................	$62,280	Accounts payable	$ 8,220
Accounts receivable.........	7,300		
Office supplies..................	3,200		
Office equipment	8,600	Owner's Equity	
Excavating equipment......	21,000	Robert Cantu, capital	94,160
		Total liabilities and	
Total assets......................	$102,380	owner's equity.................	$102,380

Problem 2-8B (25 minutes)

		Balance Sheet			Income Stmnt
		Total Assets	Total Liab.	Equity	Net Income
1	Owner invests cash	+		+	
2	Pay wages with cash	–		–	–
3	Acquire services on credit		+	–	–
4	Buy store equipment for cash........	+/–			
5	Borrow cash with note payable	+	+		
6	Sell services for cash......................	+		+	+
7	Sell services on credit	+		+	+
8	Pay rent with cash...........................	–		–	–
9	Owner withdraws cash	–		–	
10	Collect receivable from (7)	+/–			

Fundamental Accounting Principles, Eleventh Canadian Edition

Chapter 3   Analyzing and Recording Transactions

EXERCISES

Exercise 3-1 (30 minutes)

Cash

(a)	12,750	375	(b)
(d)	1,500	7,050	(e)
(h)	1,125	525	(g)
		1,000	(i)
Balance	6,425		

Accounts Receivable

(f)	2,700	1,125	(h)
Balance	1,575		

Office Supplies

(b)	375	
Balance	375	

Office Equipment

(c)	7,050	
Balance	7,050	

Accounts Payable

(e)	7,050	7,050	(c)
		0	Balance

Steve Moore, Capital

		12,750	(a)
		12,750	Balance

Steve Moore, Withdrawals

(i)	1,000	
Balance	1,000	

Fees Earned

		1,500	(d)
		2,700	(f)
		4,200	Balance

Rent Expense

(g)	525	
Balance	525	

Exercise 3-3 (10 minutes)

Cash

Mar. 31	1,800	400	Apr. 10
Apr. 2	780	300	15
19	2,000	1,000	29
Bal.	2,880		

Accounts Receivable

Mar. 31	4,800	2,000	Apr. 19
Apr. 18	1,200		
Bal.	4,000		

Repair Supplies

Mar. 31	1,400	
Apr. 9	890	
Bal.	2,290	

Equipment

Mar. 31	7,400	
Apr. 15	300	
Bal.	7,700	

Accounts Payable

Apr. 10	400	500	Mar. 31
		890	Apr. 9
		250	25
		1,240	Bal.

Nels Sigurdsen, Capital

		2,350	Mar. 31
		2,350	Bal.

Nels Sigurdsen, Withdrawals

Mar. 31	500	
Apr. 29	1,000	
Bal.	1,500	

Repair Revenue

		14,000	Mar. 31
		780	Apr. 2
		1,200	18
		15,980	Bal.

Rent Expense

Mar. 31	950	
Apr. 25	250	
Bal.	1,200	

NOTE: There is no entry to be recorded for April 5

Fundamental Accounting Principles, Eleventh Canadian Edition

Exercise 3-5 (10 minutes)

Note: Students could choose any account number within the specified range.

Account Number	Account Name
110	Cash
115	Accounts Receivable
160	Office Equipment
210	Accounts Payable
215	Unearned Revenue
310	Bill Evans, Capital
320	Bill Evans, Withdrawals
410	Consulting Revenues
510	Salaries Expense
520	Rent Expense
530	Utilities Expense

Exercise 3-7 (25 minutes)

b. Paid $3,600 in advance for insurance.

c. Paid $600 for office supplies.

d. Acquired $200 of office supplies and $9,400 of equipment on credit.

e. Received $2,500 cash for services provided.

f. Paid $2,400 on accounts payable.

g. Paid $700 for gas and oil.

Exercise 3-9 (20 minutes)

2005

April 5	Cash..	1,500	
	Surgical Revenues...................................		1,500
	Performed surgery and collected cash.		
8	Supplies...	3,000	
	Accounts Payable.....................................		3,000
	Purchased surgical supplies on credit.		
15	Salaries Expense	57,000	
	Cash...		57,000
	Paid salaries.		
20	Accounts Payable...	3,000	
	Cash...		3,000
	Paid for the credit purchase of April 8.		
22	No entry.		
27	Accounts Receivable......................................	9,000	
	Surgical Revenues...................................		9,000
	Performed six surgeries on credit;		
	$1,500 x 6 = $9,000		
30	Utilities Expense...	1,800	
	Cash...		1,800
	Paid the April utilities.		

Exercise 3-11 (20 minutes)

b.	Salaries Expense...	1,125	
	Cash...		1,125
	Paid the salary of the receptionist.		
d.	Utilities Expense	930	
	Cash...		930
	Paid the utilities for the office.		

Expenses are outflows or using up of assets (or the creation of liabilities) that occur in the process of providing goods or services to customers. The transactions labelled a, c, and e were not expenses for the following reasons:

a. This transaction decreased assets in settlement of a previously existing liability. Thus, the using up of assets did not reduce owner's equity.

Fundamental Accounting Principles, Eleventh Canadian Edition

Exercise 3-11 (*continued*)

c. This transaction was the purchase of an asset. The form of the company's assets changed, but total assets did not change, and the equity did not decrease.

e. This transaction was a distribution of cash to the owner. Even though owner's equity decreased, the decrease did not occur in the process of providing goods or services to customers.

Exercise 3-13 (10 minutes)

	Cash		101			Accounts Receivable	106				Equipment		167
Bal	1,700	4,000	Jan. 20		Bal	600	10,000	Jan. 31		Bal	3,000		
Jan. 1	7,000	6,000	31		Jan. 12	18,000				Jan. 20	24,000		
31	10,000	1,500	31		Bal	8,600				Bal	27,000		
Bal	7,200												

	Accounts Payable	201			Alice Hay, Capital	301			Alice Hay, Withdrawals	302
		650	Bal			4,650	Bal	Bal	600	
		20,000	Jan. 20			7,000	Jan. 1	Jan. 31	1,500	
		20,650	Bal			11,650	Bal	Bal	2,100	

	Fees Earned	401			Salaries Expense	622	
		3,600	Bal	Bal	3,000		
		18,000	Jan. 12	Jan. 31	6,000		
		21,600	Bal	Bal	9,000		

Exercise 3-15 (30 minutes)

Cash — Account No. 101

Date		Explanation	PR	Debit	Credit	Balance
2005						
Aug.	1		G1	7,500		7,500
	1		G1		3,000	4,500
	5		G1		1,400	3,100
	20		G1	2,650		5,750
	31		G1		875	4,875

Office Supplies — Account No. 124

Date		Explanation	PR	Debit	Credit	Balance
2005						
Aug.	5		G1	1,400		1,400

Exercise 3-15 (continued)

Prepaid Rent — Account No. 131

Date	Explanation	PR	Debit	Credit	Balance
2005 Aug. 1		G1	3,000		3,000

Photography Equipment — Account No. 167

Date	Explanation	PR	Debit	Credit	Balance
2005 Aug. 1		G1	32,500		32,500

Hannah Young, Capital — Account No. 301

Date	Explanation	PR	Debit	Credit	Balance
2005 Aug. 1		G1		40,000	40,000

Photography Fees Earned — Account No. 401

Date	Explanation	PR	Debit	Credit	Balance
2005 Aug. 20		G1		2,650	2,650

Utilities Expense — Account No. 690

Date	Explanation	PR	Debit	Credit	Balance
2005 Aug. 31		G1	875		875

PHOTOFINISH CO.
Trial Balance
August 31, 2005

Acct No.	Account Title	Debit	Credit
101	Cash	$ 4,875	
124	Office supplies	1,400	
131	Prepaid rent	3,000	
167	Photography equipment	32,500	
301	Hannah Young, capital		$40,000
401	Photography fees earned		2,650
690	Utilities expense	875	
	Totals	$42,650	$42,650

Exercise 3-17 (20 minutes)

JenCo
Income Statement
For Month Ended March 31, 2005

Revenues:		
Service revenue		$1,900
Operating expenses:		
Salaries expense..	$ 800	
Interest expense...	10	
Total operating expenses..		810
Net income		$1,090

JenCo
Statement of Owner's Equity
For Month Ended March 31, 2005

Marie Jensen, capital, March 1		$ 0
Add: Investment by owner	$2,050	
Net income	1,090	$3,140
Total		$3,140
Less: Withdrawal by owner...		1,500
Marie Jensen, capital, March 31		$1,640

JenCo
Balance Sheet
March 31, 2005

Assets		Liabilities	
Cash...	$1,000	Accounts payable.............................	$ 260
Accounts receivable.............	950	Unearned service revenues..............	250
Prepaid insurance..................	300	Notes payable	800
Equipment	700	Total liabilities	$1,310
		Owner's Equity	
		Marie Jensen, capital	1,640
Total assets	$2,950	Total liabilities and owner's equity ..	$2,950

Exercise 3-19 (20 minutes)

	Description	(1) Difference between Debit and Credit Columns	(2) Column with the Larger Total	(3) Identify account(s) incorrectly stated	(4) Amount that account(s) is overstated or understated
a.	A $2,400 debit to Rent Expense was posted as a $1,590 debit.	$810	Credit	Rent Expense	Rent Expense is understated by $810
b.	A $42,000 debit to Machinery was posted as a debit to Accounts Payable.	$0	—	Machinery	Machinery is understated by $42,000 and
				Accounts Payable	Accounts Payable is understated by $42,000
c.	A $4,950 credit to Services Revenue was posted as a $495 credit.	$4,455	Debit	Services Revenue	Services Revenue is understated by $4,455
d.	A $1,440 debit to Store Supplies was not posted at all.	$1,440	Credit	Store Supplies	Store Supplies is understated by $1,440
e.	A $2,250 debit to Prepaid Insurance was posted as a debit to Insurance Expense.	$0	—	Prepaid Insurance	Prepaid Insurance is understated by $2,250 and Insurance
				Insurance Expense	Expense is overstated by $2,250
f.	A $4,050 credit to Cash was posted twice as two credits to the Cash account.	$4,050	Credit	Cash	Cash is understated by $4,050
g.	A $9,900 debit to the owner's withdrawals account was debited to the owner's capital account.	$0	—	Owner's Capital	Owner's Capital account is understated by $9,900
				Owner's Withdrawals	Owner's Withdrawals is understated by $9,900

Exercise 3-21 (15 minutes)

Case A:
1. Subtract total debits in the trial balance from total credits
   5,010 – 4,290 = 720
2. Divide the difference by 9
   720 ÷ 9 = 80
3. The quotient equals the difference between the two transposed numbers.
   The difference between the correct number and the incorrect number is 80.
4. The number of digits in the quotient tells us the location of the transposition.
   Look for a difference of 8 between the second number from the right and the third number from the right.

Through a process of elimination, the incorrect value is Accounts Payable of $190. The correct value must be $910.

Proof: Recalculate the trial balance replacing $910 for the incorrect $190 and the trial balance now balances at $5,010.

Case B:
1. Subtract total debits in the trial balance from total credits
   28,100 – 23,600 = 4,500
2. Divide the difference by 9
   4,500 ÷ 9 = 500
3. The quotient equals the difference between the two transposed numbers.
   The difference between the correct number and the incorrect number is 500.
4. The number of digits in the quotient tells us the location of the transposition.
   Look for a difference of 5 between the third number from the right and the fourth number from the right.

Through a process of elimination, the incorrect value is Capital for $16,150. The correct value must be $11,650.

Proof: Recalculate the trial balance replacing $11,650 for the incorrect $16,150 and the trial balance now balances at $23,600.

Case C:
1. Subtract total debits in the trial balance from total credits
   942 – 906 = 36
2. Divide the difference by 9
   36 ÷ 9 = 4
3. The quotient equals the difference between the two transposed numbers.
   The difference between the correct number and the incorrect number is 4.
4. The number of digits in the quotient tells us the location of the transposition.

Exercise 3-21 (*continued*))

Look for a difference of 4 between the first number from the right and the second number from the right.

Through a process of elimination, the incorrect value is Cash for $59. The correct value must be <u>$95</u>.

Proof: Recalculate the trial balance replacing $95 for the incorrect $59 and the trial balance now balances at $942.

PROBLEMS

Problem 3-1B (40 minutes) *Parts 1 and 2*

Cash

(a)	23,000	15,000	(b)
(g)	2,700	800	(f)
(m)	1,000	430	(h)
		600	(i)
		2,400	(j)
		800	(l)
		1,050	(n)
Balance	5,620		

Accounts Receivable

(k)	2,400	1,000	(m)
Balance	1,400		

Office Supplies

(c)	600	

Automobiles

(d)	7,000	

Office Equipment

(a)	12,000	1,600	(j)
(e)	1,100		
(j)	4,000		
Balance	15,500		

Building

(b)	33,000	

Land

(b)	8,000	

Accounts Payable

(i)	600	600	(c)
		1,100	(e)
		1,100	Balance

Long-Term Notes Payable

	26,000	(b)

Susan West, Capital

	35,000	(a)
	7,000	(d)
	42,000	Balance

Susan West, Withdrawals

(n)	1,050	

Fees Earned

	2,700	(g)
	2,400	(k)
	5,100	Balance

Salaries Expense

(f)	800	
(l)	800	
Balance	1,600	

Utilities Expense

(h)	430	

Problem 3-2B

Date	General Journal Accounts Titles and Explanations	Debit	Page 1 Credit
2005			
March 1	Building...	750,000	
	Cash..		250,000
	Note Payable..		500,000
	Purchased new building paying cash and signing		
	a five-year note payable.		
1	Prepaid Insurance..	7,200	
	Cash..		7,200
	Purchased six months of insurance to begin March 1.		
3	Cash..	5,000	
	Consulting Revenue.......................................		5,000
	Provided consulting services and collected cash.		
4	Cleaning Supplies	750	
	Accounts Payable..		750
	Purchased cleaning supplies on account.		
10	Accounts Receivable..	55,000	
	Consulting Revenue.......................................		55,000
	Performed work for a client on account.		
11	No entry.		
15	Accounts Payable...	750	
	Cash..		750
	Paid for the March 4 purchase.		

Problem 3-2B *(continued)*

March	20	Cash..	10,000	
		Unearned Revenue.....................................		10,000
		Collected cash from a customer for work to be		
		done in April.		
	28	Hotel Expense or Travel Expense	180	
		Cash..		180
		Paid for a hotel regarding a business meeting.		
	30	Salaries Expense...	49,000	
		Cash		49,000
		Paid month end salaries.		
	30	Telephone Expense...	1,300	
		Accounts Payable		1,300
		March telephone bill to be paid on April 14.		
	30	Cash..	27,500	
		Accounts Receivable		27,500
		Collected half of the amount owed by the customer		
		of March 10.		

Note: Assume all entries were journalized on Page 1 of the General Journal.

Fundamental Accounting Principles, Eleventh Canadian Edition

Problem 3-3B (60 minutes)

General Journal

Page 1

Date	Account Titles and Explanations	PR	Debit	Credit
2005				
Sept. 1	Cash	101	4,200	
	Office Equipment..................................	163	4,800	
	Adam Uppe, Capital	301		9,000
	Investment by owner.			
1	Prepaid Rent	131	1,800	
	Cash	101		1,800
	Paid two months' rent.			
2	Office Supplies	124	75	
	Office Equipment..................................	163	420	
	Accounts Payable	210		495
	Purchased items on credit.			
4	Cash	101	180	
	Accounting Fees Earned	401		180
	Sold accounting services for cash.			
8	Accounts Receivable	106	700	
	Accounting Fees Earned	401		700
	Sold accounting services on credit.			
10	Accounts Payable	210	495	
	Cash	101		495
	Paid for credit purchase.			
14	Prepaid Insurance	128	750	
	Cash	101		750
	Paid insurance premium.			
15	Professional Development Expense........	680	250	
	Cash	101		250
	Paid for seminar.			

Problem 3-3B *(concluded)*

Sept.	18	Cash	101	700	
		Accounts Receivable	106		700
		Received cash from credit customer.			
	20	No entry.			
	24	Accounts Receivable	106	500	
		Accounting Fees Earned	401		500
		Sold accounting services on credit.			
	28	Adam Uppe, Withdrawals	302	300	
		Cash	101		300
		Owner withdrew cash.			
	29	Office Supplies	124	45	
		Accounts Payable	210		45
		Purchased supplies on credit.			
	30	Utilities Expense	690	165	
		Cash	101		165
		Paid utilities bill.			

Note: The account numbers in the PR column above would be included only when these journal entries are being posted in Problem 3-4B. Assume that all entries were journalized on Page 1 of the General Journal.

Problem 3-4B

Parts 1 and 2

Cash   Acct. No. 101

Date		Explanation	PR	Debit	Credit	Balance
2005						
Sept.	1		G1	4,200		4,200
	1		G1		1,800	2,400
	4		G1	180		2,580
	10		G1		495	2,085
	14		G1		750	1,335
	15		G1		250	1,085
	18		G1	700		1,785
	28		G1		300	1,485
	30		G1		165	1,320

Accounts Receivable   Acct. No. 106

Date		Explanation	PR	Debit	Credit	Balance
2005						
Sept.	8		G1	700		700
	18		G1		700	0
	24		G1	500		500

Office Supplies   Acct. No. 124

Date		Explanation	PR	Debit	Credit	Balance
2005						
Sept.	2		G1	75		75
	29		G1	45		120

Prepaid Insurance   Acct. No. 128

Date		Explanation	PR	Debit	Credit	Balance
2005						
Sept.	14		G1	750		750

Prepaid Rent   Acct. No. 131

Date		Explanation	PR	Debit	Credit	Balance
	2005					
Sept.	1		G1	1,800		1,800

Office Equipment   Acct. No. 163

Date		Explanation	PR	Debit	Credit	Balance
2005						
Sept.	1		G1	4,800		4,800
	2		G1	420		5,220

Problem 3-4B *(continued) Parts 1 and 2*

Accounts Payable — Acct. No. 210

Date		Explanation	PR	Debit	Credit	Balance
2005						
Sept.	2		G1		495	495
	10		G1	495		0
	29		G1		45	45

Adam Uppe, Capital — Acct. No. 301

Date		Explanation	PR	Debit	Credit	Balance
2005						
Sept.	1		G1		9,000	9,000

Adam Uppe, Withdrawals — Acct. No. 302

Date		Explanation	PR	Debit	Credit	Balance
2005						
Sept.	28		G1	300		300

Accounting Fees Earned — Acct. No. 401

Date		Explanation	PR	Debit	Credit	Balance
2005						
Sept.	4		G1		180	180
	8		G1		700	880
	24		G1		500	1,380

Professional Development Expense — Acct. No. 680

Date		Explanation	PR	Debit	Credit	Balance
2005						
Sept.	15		G1	250		250

Utilities Expense — Acct. No. 690

Date		Explanation	PR	Debit	Credit	Balance
2005						
Sept.	30		G1	165		165

Problem 3-4B *(concluded) Part 3*

ADAM UPPE, PUBLIC ACCOUNTANT
Trial Balance
September 30, 2005

Acct. No.	Account Title	Debit	Credit
101	Cash	$ 1,320	
106	Accounts receivable	500	
124	Office supplies	120	
128	Prepaid insurance	750	
131	Prepaid rent	1,800	
163	Office equipment	5,220	
201	Accounts payable		$ 45
301	Adam Uppe, capital		9,000
302	Adam Uppe, withdrawals	300	
401	Accounting fees earned		1,380
680	Professional development expense	250	
690	Utilities expense	165	
	Totals	$10,425	$10,425

Problem 3-5B (30 minutes)
Parts 1 and 2

Cash   101

Sept. 1	4,200	Sept. 1	1,800
4	180	10	495
18	700	14	750
		15	250
		28	300
		30	165
Bal.	1,320		

Accounts Receivable   106

Sept. 8	700	Sept. 18	700
		24	500
Bal.	500		

Prepaid Insurance   128

Sept. 14	750		

Office Supplies   124

Sept. 2	75		45
29	45		
Bal.	120		

Prepaid Rent   131

Sept. 1	1,800		

Office Equipment   163

Sept. 1	4,800		
2	420		
Bal.	5,220		

Accounts Payable   201

Sept. 10	495	Sept. 2	495
	45	29	45
		Bal.	45

Adam Uppe, Capital   301

		9,000	Sept. 1

Adam Uppe, Withdrawals   302

Sept. 28	300		

Accounting Fees Earned   401

		180	Sept. 4
		700	8
		500	24
		1,380	Bal.

Prof. Development Expense   680

Sept. 15	250		

Utilities Expense   690

Sept. 30	165		

Note: No entry for September 20 as it is not a transaction.

   Fundamental Accounting Principles, Eleventh Canadian Edition

Problem 3-5B *(concluded)*

Part 3

ADAM UPPE, PUBLIC ACCOUNTANT
Trial Balance
September 30, 2005

Acct. No.	Account Title	Debit	Credit
101	Cash	$ 1,320	
106	Accounts receivable	500	
124	Office supplies	120	
128	Prepaid insurance	750	
131	Prepaid rent	1,800	
163	Office equipment	5,220	
201	Accounts payable		$ 45
301	Adam Uppe, capital		9,000
302	Adam Uppe, withdrawals	300	
401	Accounting fees earned		1,380
680	Professional development expense	250	
690	Utilities expense	165	
	Totals	$10,425	$10,425

Problem 3-6B (90 minutes) *Part 1*

General Journal

Page 1

Date 2005	Account Titles and Explanations		Debit	Credit
Nov. 1	Cash	101	48,000	
	Office Equipment	163	25,000	
	Arthur Leonard, Capital..................	301		73,000
	Owner invested in the business.			
2	Prepaid Rent................................	131	10,500	
	Cash...	101		10,500
	Prepaid three months' rent.			
4	Office Equipment	163	9,000	
	Office Supplies............................	124	1,200	
	Accounts Payable..............................	201		10,200
	Purchased equipment and supplies on credit.			
8	Cash	101	2,600	
	Service Fees Earned...........................	401		2,600
	Received cash from client for completed work.			
12	Accounts Receivable	106	3,400	
	Service Fees Earned...........................	401		3,400
	Billed client for completed work.			
13	Accounts Payable	201	10,200	
	Cash...	101		10,200
	Paid balance due on accounts payable.			
19	Prepaid Insurance	128	5,200	
	Cash...	101		5,200
	Paid annual premium for insurance.			
22	Cash	101	1,800	
	Accounts Receivable............................	106		1,800
	Collected part of the amount owed by a client.			
24	Accounts Receivable	106	1,900	
	Service Fees Earned...........................	401		1,900
	Billed client for completed work.			

Fundamental Accounting Principles, Eleventh Canadian Edition

Problem 3-6B (continued) Part 1

Nov.	28	Arthur Leonard, Withdrawals	302	5,300	
		Cash	101		5,300
		Owner withdrew cash for personal use.			
	29	Office Supplies	124	1,700	
		Accounts Payable	201		1,700
		Purchased supplies on credit.			
	30	Wages Expense	680	8,000	
		Cash	101		8,000
		Paid wages.			
	30	Utilities Expense	690	1,460	
		Cash	101		1,460
		Paid monthly utility bill.			

Note: Assume all entries were journalized on Page 1 of the General Journal.

Problem 3-6B (continued)

Parts 2 and 3

Cash   Acct. No. 101

Date	Explanation	PR	Debit	Credit	Balance
2005					
Nov. 1		G1	48,000		48,000
2		G1		10,500	37,500
8		G1	2,600		40,100
13		G1		10,200	29,900
19		G1		5,200	24,700
22		G1	1,800		26,500
28		G1		5,300	21,200
30		G1		8,000	13,200
30		G1		1,460	11,740

Accounts Receivable   Acct. No. 106

Date	Explanation	PR	Debit	Credit	Balance
2005					
Nov. 12		G1	3,400		3,400
22		G1		1,800	1,600
24		G1	1,900		3,500

Office Supplies   Acct. No. 124

Date	Explanation	PR	Debit	Credit	Balance
2005					
Nov. 4		G1	1,200		1,200
29		G1	1,700		2,900

Prepaid Insurance   Acct. No. 128

Date	Explanation	PR	Debit	Credit	Balance
2005					
Nov. 19		G1	5,200		5,200

Prepaid Rent   Acct. No. 131

Date	Explanation	PR	Debit	Credit	Balance
2005					
Nov. 2		G1	10,500		10,500

Fundamental Accounting Principles, Eleventh Canadian Edition

Problem 3-6B (continued) Parts 2 and 3

Office Equipment   Acct. No. 163

Date	Explanation	PR	Debit	Credit	Balance
2005 Nov. 1		G1	25,000		25,000
4		G1	9,000		34,000

Accounts Payable   Acct. No. 201

Date	Explanation	PR	Debit	Credit	Balance
2005 Nov. 4		G1		10,200	10,200
13		G1	10,200		0
29		G1		1,700	1,700

Arthur Leonard, Capital   Acct. No. 301

Date	Explanation	PR	Debit	Credit	Balance
2005 Nov. 1		G1		73,000	73,000

Arthur Leonard, Withdrawals   Acct. No. 302

Date	Explanation	PR	Debit	Credit	Balance
2005 Nov. 28		G1	5,300		5,300

Service Fees Earned   Acct. No. 401

Date	Explanation	PR	Debit	Credit	Balance
2005 Nov. 8		G1		2,600	2,600
12		G1		3,400	6,000
24		G1		1,900	7,900

Wages Expense   Acct. No. 680

Date	Explanation	PR	Debit	Credit	Balance
2005 Nov. 30		G1	8,000		8,000

Utilities Expense   Acct. No. 690

Date	Explanation	PR	Debit	Credit	Balance
2005 Nov. 30		G1	1,460		1,460

Problem 3-6B *(continued)* *Part 4*

LEONARD MANAGEMENT SERVICES
Trial Balance
November 30, 2005

Acct. No.	Account Title	Debit	Credit
101	Cash	$ 11,740	
106	Accounts receivable	3,500	
124	Office supplies	2,900	
128	Prepaid insurance	5,200	
131	Prepaid rent	10,500	
163	Office equipment	34,000	
201	Accounts payable		$ 1,700
301	Arthur Leonard, capital		73,000
302	Arthur Leonard, withdrawals	5,300	
401	Service fees earned		7,900
680	Wages expense	8,000	
690	Utilities expense	1,460	
	Totals	$82,600	$82,600

Fundamental Accounting Principles, Eleventh Canadian Edition

Problem 3-7B (30 minutes)

Part 1

Date		General Journal Account Titles and Explanations		Debit	Page 1 Credit
2005					
Nov.	1	Cash	101	48,000	
		Office Equipment..	163	25,000	
		Arthur Leonard, Capital........................	301		73,000
		Owner invested in the business.			
	2	Prepaid Rent...	131	10,500	
		Cash	101		10,500
		Prepaid three months' rent.			
	4	Office Equipment..	163	9,000	
		Office Supplies	124	1,200	
		Accounts Payable	201		10,200
		Purchased equipment and supplies on credit.			
	8	Cash	101	2,600	
		Service Fees Earned...........................	401		2,600
		Received cash from client for completed work.			
	12	Accounts Receivable	106	3,400	
		Service Fees Earned...........................	401		3,400
		Billed client for completed work.			
	13	Accounts Payable	201	10,200	
		Cash..	101		10,200
		Paid balance due on accounts payable.			
	19	Prepaid Insurance	128	5,200	
		Cash..	101		5,200
		Paid annual premium for insurance.			
	22	Cash	101	1,800	
		Accounts Receivable..........................	106		1,800
		Collected part of the amount owed by a client.			

Problem 3-7B *(continued) Part 1*

Nov.	24	Accounts Receivable	106	1,900	
		Service Fees Earned............................	401		1,900
		Billed client for completed work.			
	28	Arthur Leonard, Withdrawals	302	5,300	
		Cash...	101		5,300
		Owner withdrew cash for personal use.			
	29	Office Supplies..	124	1,700	
		Accounts Payable..................................	201		1,700
		Purchased supplies on credit.			
	30	Wages Expense...	680	8,000	
		Cash...	101		8,000
		Paid wages.			
	30	Utilities Expense	690	1,460	
		Cash...	101		1,460
		Paid monthly utility bill.			

Note: Assume all entries were journalized on Page 1 of the General Journal.

Problem 3-7B (continued)

Parts 2 and 3

Cash 101

	Debit		Credit
Nov. 1	48,000	Nov. 2	10,500
8	2,600	13	10,200
22	1,800	19	5,200
		28	5,300
		30	8,000
		30	1,460
Bal.	11,740		

Prepaid Rent 131

	Debit		Credit
Nov. 2	10,500		

Arthur Leonard, Withdrawals 302

	Debit		Credit
Nov. 28	5,300		

Accounts Receivable 106

	Debit		Credit
Nov. 12	3,400	Nov. 22	1,800
24	1,900		
Bal.	3,500		

Office Equipment 163

	Debit		Credit
Nov. 1	25,000		
4	9,000		
Bal.	34,000		

Service Fees Earned 401

	Debit		Credit
		Nov. 8	2,600
		12	3,400
		24	1,900
		Bal.	7,900

Office Supplies 124

	Debit		Credit
Nov. 4	1,200		
29	1,700		
Bal.	2,900		

Accounts Payable 201

	Debit		Credit
Nov. 13	10,200	Nov. 4	10,200
		29	1,700
		Bal.	1,700

Wages Expense 680

	Debit		Credit
Nov. 30	8,000		

Prepaid Insurance 128

	Debit		Credit
Nov. 19	5,200		

Arthur Leonard, Capital 301

	Debit		Credit
		Nov. 1	73,000

Utilities Expense 690

	Debit		Credit
Nov. 30	1,460		

Problem 3-7B *(continued)*

Part 4

LEONARD MANAGEMENT SERVICES
Trial Balance
November 30, 2005

Acct. No.	Account Title	Debit	Credit
101	Cash	$ 11,740	
106	Accounts receivable...........................	3,500	
124	Office supplies....................................	2,900	
128	Prepaid insurance	5,200	
131	Prepaid rent	10,500	
163	Office equipment................................	34,000	
201	Accounts payable...............................		$ 1,700
301	Arthur Leonard, capital......................		73,000
302	Arthur Leonard, withdrawals............	5,300	
401	Service fees earned...........................		7,900
680	Wages expense	8,000	
690	Utilities expense................................	1,460	
	Totals...	$82,600	$82,600

Fundamental Accounting Principles, Eleventh Canadian Edition

Problem 3-8B (25 minutes)

LEONARD MANAGEMENT SERVICES
Income Statement
For Month Ended November 30, 2005

Service fees earned		$7,900
Operating expenses:		
Wages expense.................................	$8,000	
Utilities expense...............................	1,460	
Total operating expenses........................		9,460
Net loss..		$ 1,560

LEONARD MANAGEMENT SERVICES
Statement of Owner's Equity
For Month Ended November 30, 2005

Arthur Leonard, capital, November 1		$ 0
Add: Investments by owner...........................		73,000
Total...		73,000
Less: Withdrawals by owner.........................	$ 5,300	
Net loss..	1,560	6,860
Arthur Leonard, capital, July 31		$66,140

LEONARD MANAGEMENT SERVICES
Balance Sheet
November 30, 2005

Assets		Liabilities	
Cash..	$ 11,740	Accounts payable..........................	$ 1,700
Accounts receivable..............	3,500		
Office supplies.......................	2,900		
Prepaid insurance	5,200	**Owner's Equity**	
Prepaid rent...........................	10,500	Arthur Leonard, capital	66,140
Office equipment	34,000	Total liabilities and	
Total assets	$ 67,840	owner's equity............................	$67,840

Problem 3-9B (90 minutes)

Part 1

Date	General Journal Account Titles and Explanations	PR	Debit	Page 1 Credit
2005				
July 1	Office Equipment	163	4,500	
	Computer Equipment......................................	167	28,000	
	Accounts Payable	201		32,500
	Purchased equipment on credit.			
2	Land	183	24,000	
	Cash	101		4,800
	Long-Term Notes Payable........................	251		19,200
	Purchased land.			
3	Building	173	21,000	
	Cash	101		21,000
	Purchased a building.			
5	Prepaid Insurance..	128	6,600	
	Cash	101		6,600
	Purchased two one-year insurance policies.			
9	Cash	101	3,200	
	Fees Earned...	401		3,200
	Performed services for cash.			
12	Computer equipment.....................................	167	3,500	
	Cash	101		700
	Long-Term Notes Payable........................	251		2,800
	Purchased computer equipment.			
15	Accounts Receivable	106	3,750	
	Fees Earned...	401		3,750
	Performed services on credit.			
16	Office Equipment	163	750	
	Accounts Payable	201		750
	Purchased equipment on credit.			
20	Accounts Receivable	106	9,200	
	Fees Earned...	401		9,200
	Performed services on credit.			

Problem 3-9B *(continued)*

Part 1

		General Journal Account Titles and Explanations	PR	Debit	Page 2 Credit
Date					
2005					
July	21	Computer Rental Expense..............................	645	320	
		Accounts Payable	201		320
		Rented computer on credit.			
	22	Cash	101	4,600	
		Accounts Receivable	106		4,600
		Collected cash from credit customer.			
	23	Wages Expense......................................	623	1,600	
		Cash	101		1,600
		Paid wages to assistant.			
	24	Accounts Payable	201	750	
		Cash	101		750
		Paid for July 16 purchase.			
	25	Repairs Expense	684	425	
		Cash	101		425
		Paid for computer repairs.			
	26	Avery Wilson, Withdrawals	302	3,875	
		Cash	101		3,875
		Owner withdrawal.			
	27	Wages Expense......................................	623	1,600	
		Cash	101		1,600
		Paid wages to assistant.			
	28	Advertising Expense.................................	655	800	
		Cash	101		800
		Paid for advertising in local newspaper.			
	29	Cash	101	1,400	
		Unearned Fees	233		1,400
		Received cash for services to be performed in August.			

Problem 3-9B *(continued)*

Parts 2 and 3

Cash   Account No. 101

Date		Explanation	PR	Debit	Credit	Balance
2005						
June	30	Beginning balance				51,175
July	2		G1		4,800	46,375
	3		G1		21,000	25,375
	5		G1		6,600	18,775
	9		G1	3,200		21,975
	12		G1		700	21,275
	22		G2	4,600		25,875
	23		G2		1,600	24,275
	24		G2		750	23,525
	25		G2		425	23,100
	26		G2		3,875	19,225
	27		G2		1,600	17,625
	28		G2		800	16,825
	29		G2	1,400		18,225

Accounts Receivable   Account No. 106

Date		Explanation	PR	Debit	Credit	Balance
2005						
June	30	Beginning balance				950
July	15		G1	3,750		4,700
	20		G1	9,200		13,900
	22		G2		4,600	9,300

Prepaid Insurance   Account No. 128

Date		Explanation	PR	Debit	Credit	Balance
2005						
June	30	Beginning balance				275
July	5		G1	6,600		6,875

Office Equipment   Account No. 163

Date		Explanation	PR	Debit	Credit	Balance
2005						
June	30	Beginning balance				1,200
July	1		G1	4,500		5,700
	16		G1	750		6,450

Problem 3-9B *(continued)*

Parts 2 and 3

Computer Equipment — Account No. 167

Date		Explanation	PR	Debit	Credit	Balance
2005						
June	30	Beginning balance				800
July	1		G1	28,000		28,800
	12		G1	3,500		32,300

Building — Account No. 173

Date		Explanation	PR	Debit	Credit	Balance
2005						
June	30	Beginning balance				14,000
July	3		G1	21,000		35,000

Land — Account No. 183

Date		Explanation	PR	Debit	Credit	Balance
2005						
June	30	Beginning balance				6,000
July	2		G1	24,000		30,000

Accounts Payable — Account No. 201

Date		Explanation	PR	Debit	Credit	Balance
2005						
June	30	Beginning balance				725
July	1		G1		32,500	33,225
	16		G1		750	33,975
	21		G2		320	34,295
	24		G2	750		33,545

Unearned Fees — Account No. 233

Date		Explanation	PR	Debit	Credit	Balance
2005						
June	30	Beginning balance				0
July	29		G2		1,400	1,400

Long-Term Notes Payable — Account No. 251

Date		Explanation	PR	Debit	Credit	Balance
2005						
June	30	Beginning balance				7,000
July	2		G1		19,200	26,200
	12		G1		2,800	29,000

Problem 3-9B *(continued)*

Parts 2 and 3

Avery Wilson, Capital — Account No. 301

Date		Explanation	PR	Debit	Credit	Balance
2005						
June	30	Beginning balance				60,000

Avery Wilson, Withdrawals — Account No. 302

Date		Explanation	PR	Debit	Credit	Balance
2005						
June	30	Beginning balance				600
July	26		G2	3,875		4,475

Fees Earned — Account No. 401

Date		Explanation	PR	Debit	Credit	Balance
2005						
June	30	Beginning balance				8,400
July	9		G1		3,200	11,600
	15		G1		3,750	15,350
	20		G1		9,200	24,550

Wages Expense — Account No. 623

Date		Explanation	PR	Debit	Credit	Balance
2005						
June	30	Beginning balance				780
July	23		G2	1,600		2,380
	27		G2	1,600		3,980

Computer Rental Expense — Account No. 645

Date		Explanation	PR	Debit	Credit	Balance
2005						
June	30	Beginning balance				230
July	21		G2	320		550

Advertising Expense — Account No. 655

Date		Explanation	PR	Debit	Credit	Balance
2005						
June	30	Beginning balance				75
July	28		G2	800		875

Repairs Expense — Account No. 684

Date		Explanation	PR	Debit	Credit	Balance
2005						
June	30	Beginning balance				40
July	25		G2	425		465

Fundamental Accounting Principles, Eleventh Canadian Edition

Problem 3-9B *(concluded)*

Part 4

SOFTOUCH CO.
Trial Balance
July 31, 2005

Acct. No.	Account Title	Debit	Credit
101	Cash	$ 18,225	
106	Accounts receivable	9,300	
128	Prepaid insurance	6,875	
163	Office equipment	6,450	
167	Computer equipment	32,300	
173	Building	35,000	
183	Land	30,000	
201	Accounts payable		$ 33,545
233	Unearned fees		1,400
251	Long-term notes payable		29,000
301	Avery Wilson, capital		60,000
302	Avery Wilson, withdrawals	4,475	
401	Fees earned		24,550
623	Wages expense	3,980	
645	Computer rental expense	550	
655	Advertising expense	875	
684	Repairs expense	465	
	Totals	$148,495	$148,495

PROBLEM 3-10B (90 minutes)

Part 1

General Journal   Page 1

Date	Account Titles and Explanations	PR	Debit	Credit
2005				
July 1	Office Equipment	163	4,500	
	Computer Equipment.....................................	167	28,000	
	Accounts Payable	201		32,500
	Purchased equipment on credit.			
2	Land	183	24,000	
	Cash	101		4,800
	Long-Term Notes Payable.......................	251		19,200
	Purchased land.			
3	Building	173	21,000	
	Cash	101		21,000
	Purchased a building.			
5	Prepaid Insurance...	128	6,600	
	Cash	101		6,600
	Purchased two one-year insurance policies.			
9	Cash	101	3,200	
	Fees Earned...	401		3,200
	Performed services for cash.			
12	Computer equipment......................................	167	3,500	
	Cash	101		700
	Long-Term Notes Payable.......................	251		2,800
	Purchased computer equipment.			
15	Accounts Receivable	106	3,750	
	Fees Earned...	401		3,750
	Performed services on credit.			
16	Office Equipment	163	750	
	Accounts Payable	201		750
	Purchased equipment on credit.			
20	Accounts Receivable	106	9,200	
	Fees Earned...	401		9,200
	Performed services on credit.			

Problem 3-10B *(continued)*

Part 1

Date		General Journal Account Titles and Explanations	PR	Debit	Page 2 Credit
2005					
July	21	Computer Rental Expense............................	645	320	
		Accounts Payable	201		320
		Rented computer on credit.			
	22	Cash	101	4,600	
		Accounts Receivable	106		4,600
		Collected cash from credit customer.			
	23	Wages Expense..	623	1,600	
		Cash	101		1,600
		Paid wages to assistant.			
	24	Accounts Payable	201	750	
		Cash	101		750
		Paid for July 16 purchase.			
	25	Repairs Expense	684	425	
		Cash	101		425
		Paid for computer repairs.			
	26	Avery Wilson, Withdrawals	302	3,875	
		Cash	101		3,875
		Owner withdrawal.			
	27	Wages Expense..	623	1,600	
		Cash	101		1,600
		Paid wages to assistant.			
	28	Advertising Expense...................................	655	800	
		Cash	101		800
		Paid for advertising in local newspaper.			
	29	Cash	101	1,400	
		Unearned Fees	233		1,400
		Received cash for services to be performed in August.			

Problem 3-10B (continued)

Parts 2 and 3

Cash 101

Debit		Credit	
Bal Jun 30	51,175	Jul 2	4,800
Jul 9	3,200	3	21,000
22	4,600	5	6,600
29	1,400	12	700
		23	1,600
		24	750
		25	425
		26	3,875
		27	1,600
		28	800
Bal Jul 31	18,225		

Accounts Receivable 106

Debit		Credit	
Bal Jun 30	4,600	Jul 22	950
Jul 15	3,750		
20	9,200		
Bal Jul 31	9,300		

Computer Equipment 167

Debit		Credit	
Bal Jun 30	800		
Jul 1	28,000		
12	3,500		
Bal Jul 31	32,300		

Prepaid Insurance 128

Debit		Credit	
Bal Jun 30	275		
Jul 5	6,600		
Bal Jul 31	6,875		

Building 173

Debit		Credit	
Bal Jun 30	14,000		
Jul 3	21,000		
Bal Jul 31	35,000		

Land 813

Debit		Credit	
Bal Jun 30	6,000		
Jul 2	24,000		
Bal Jul 31	30,000		

Office Equipment 163

Debit		Credit	
Bal Jun 30	1,200		
Jul 1	4,500		
16	750		
Bal Jul 31	6,450		

Accounts Payable 201

Debit		Credit	
Jul 24	750	Bal Jun 30	725
		Jul 1	32,500
		16	750
		21	320
		Bal Jul 31	33,545

Unearned Fees 233

Debit		Credit	
		Bal Jun 30	-0-
		Jul 29	1,400
		Bal Jul 31	1,400

Long-Term Notes Payable 251

Debit		Credit	
		Bal Jun 30	7,000
		Jul 2	19,200
		12	2,800
		Bal Jul 31	29,000

Avery Wilson, Capital 301

Debit		Credit	
		Bal Jun 30	60,000
		Bal Jul 31	60,000

Avery Wilson, Withdrawals 302

Debit		Credit	
Bal Jun 30	600		
Jul 26	3,875		
Bal J ul 31	4,475		

Problem 3-10B (continued)
Parts 2 and 3

Fees Earned — 401

Debit		Credit	
		Bal Jun 30	8,400
		Jul 9	3,200
		15	3,750
		20	9,200
		Bal Jul 31	24,550

Wages Expense — 623

Bal Jun 30	780		
Jul 23	1,600		
27	1,600		
Bal Jul 31	3,980		

Computer Rental Expense — 645

Bal Jun 30	230		
Jul 21	320		
Bal Jul 31	550		

Advertising Expense — 655

Bal Jun 30	75		
Jul 28	800		
Bal Jul 31	875		

Repairs Expense — 684

Bal Jun 30	40		
Jul 25	425		
Bal Jul 31	465		

Problem 3-10B (*concluded*)

Part 4

SOFTOUCH CO.
Trial Balance
July 31, 2005

Acct. No.	Account Title	Debit	Credit
101	Cash	$ 18,225	
106	Accounts receivable	9,300	
128	Prepaid insurance	6,875	
163	Office equipment	6,450	
167	Computer equipment	32,300	
173	Building	35,000	
183	Land	30,000	
201	Accounts payable		$ 33,545
233	Unearned fees		1,400
251	Long-term notes payable		29,000
301	Avery Wilson, capital		60,000
302	Avery Wilson, withdrawals	4,475	
401	Fees earned		24,550
623	Wages expense	3,980	
645	Computer rental expense	550	
655	Advertising expense	875	
684	Repairs expense	465	
	Totals	$148,495	$148,495

Fundamental Accounting Principles, Eleventh Canadian Edition

Problem 3-11B

SOFTOUCH CO.
Income Statement
For Two Months Ended July 31, 2005

Fees earned		$24,550
Operating expenses:		
Wages expense	$3,980	
Advertising expense	875	
Computer rental expense	550	
Repairs expense	465	
Total operating expenses		5,870
Net income		$18,680

SOFTOUCH CO.
Statement of Owner's Equity
For Two Months Ended July 31, 2005

Avery Wilson, capital, May 1		$ 0
Add: Investments by owner	$60,000	
Net income	18,680	78,680
Total		78,680
Less: Withdrawals by owner		4,475
Avery Wilson, capital, July 31		$74,205

SOFTOUCH CO.
Balance Sheet
July 31, 2005

Assets		Liabilities	
Cash	$ 18,225	Accounts payable	$ 33,545
Accounts receivable	9,300	Unearned fees	1,400
Prepaid insurance	6,875	Long-term notes payable	29,000
Office equipment	6,450	Total liabilities	$ 63,945
Computer equipment	32,300		
Building	35,000	**Owner's Equity**	
Land	30,000	Avery Wilson, capital	74,205
		Total liabilities and	
Total assets	$138,150	owner's equity	$138,150

Problem 3-12B

THE PARTY PLACE
Trial Balance
December 31, 2005

Account Title	Debit	Credit
Cash ($37,175[a] - $30,540[a])	$ 6,635	
Accounts receivable ($7,900 - $275[b])	7,625	
Office supplies ($2,650 + 400[c])	3,050	
Office equipment	20,500	
Accounts payable ($9,465 + 400[c])		$ 9,865
Jan Taylor, capital (a credit balance account)		16,745
Services revenue ($23,250[d] not $22,350)		23,250
Wages expense (a debit balance account)	6,000	
Rent expense (a debit balance account)	4,800	
Advertising expense (a debit balance account)	1,250	
Totals	$49,860	$49,860

Note: The superscripts (a) to (d) are references to items (a) to (d) listed in Problem 3-12B.

Chapter 4 Adjusting Accounts for Financial Statements

EXERCISES

Exercise 4-1 (10 minutes)

1.	f.	4.	b.
2.	d.	5.	e.
3.	a.	6.	c.

Exercise 4-3 (20 minutes)

2005

a) Dec. 31 Unearned Revenue... 32,000
      Revenue..   32,000
      To record earned revenue;
      $37,000 - $5,000 = $32,000.

b)   31 Amortization Expense, Building 21,000
      Accumulated Amortization, Building   21,000
      To record amortization expense.

c)   31 Spare Parts Expense 700
      Spare Parts Inventory   700
      To record the use of spare parts inventory;
      $900 - $200 = $700.

d)   31 Accounts Receivable.. 7,100
      Revenue..   7,100
      To record accrued revenue.

e)   31 Utilities Expense 2,600
      Utilities Payable (or Accounts Payable).............   2,600
      To record accrued utilities.

2006

f) Jan. 4 Cash.. 7,100
      Accounts Receivable   7,100
      To record collection of accrued revenues.

g)   14 Utilities Payable (or Accounts Payable).................... 2,600
      Cash   2,600
      To record payment of accrued utilities.

Exercise 4-5 (25 minutes)

2005

a)	Mar.	31	Unearned Rent	7,500	
			Rent Earned		7,500
			Earned five months' rent previously paid in advance; *$1,500 x 5 = $7,500.*		
b)		31	Rent Receivable..	2,700	
			Rent Earned		2,700
			Earned two months' rent that has not yet *been collected; $1,350 x 2 = $2,700.*		
c)	Apr.	2	Cash..	4,050	
			Rent Receivable...		2,700
			Rent Earned		1,350
			Collected rent for February, March, and April.		

Exercise 4-7 (15 minutes)

a. $1,650 (300 + 2,100 − 750 = 1,650)
b. $5,700 (1,600 + 5,400 − 1,300 = 5,700)
c. $10,080 (9,600 + 1,840 − 1,360 = 10,080)
d. $1,375 (6,575 + 800 − 6,000 = 1,375)

Proof:

	(a)	(b)	(c)	(d)
Supplies on hand—January 1	$ 300	$1,600	$ 1,360	$1,375
Supplies purchased during the year.............	2,100	5,400	10,080	6,000
Total supplies available	$2,400	$7,000	$11,440	$7,375
Supplies on hand—December 31..................	(750)	(5,700)	(1,840)	(800)
Supplies expense for the year......................	$1,650	$1,300	$ 9,600	$6,575

Fundamental Accounting Principles, Eleventh Canadian Edition

Exercise 4-9 (25 minutes)

2005

a) Apr. 30 Interest Expense 2,080
                    Interest Payable   2,080
                    To record accrued interest expense;
                    0.8% × $780,000 × 10/30.

    May 20 Interest Payable 2,080
                  Interest Expense 4,160
                    Cash   6,240
                    To record payment of accrued and current
                    expense; 0.8% × $780,000 × 20/30.

2005

b) Apr. 30 Salaries Expense... 3,600
                    Salaries Payable...   3,600
                    To record accrued salaries;
                    $9,000/5 days = $1,800/day;
                    2 days x $1,800 = $3,600.

2005

    May 3 Salaries Payable.. 3,600
                  Salaries Expense.. 5,400
                    Cash   9,000
                    To record payment of accrued and current salaries;
                    3 days x $1,800 = $5,400.

2005

c) Apr. 30 Legal Fees Expense... 2,500
                    Legal Fees Payable...   2,500
                    To record accrued legal fees.

    May 12 Legal Fees Payable.. 2,500
                  Cash   2,500
                    To pay accrued legal fees.

Exercise 4-11 (25 minutes)

Ayotte Music
Partial Work Sheet
February 28, 2005

Account	Unadjusted Trial Balance Debit	Credit	Adjustments Debit	Credit	Adjusted Trial Balance Debit	Credit
Cash..............................	5,000				5,000	
Accounts receivable....................	4,500		c) 1,400		5,900	
Prepaid insurance.......................	700			b) 250	450	
Equipment.................................	12,000				12,000	
Accumulated amortization, equipment...................		6,000		a) 2,400		8,400
Accounts payable......................		1,200				1,200
Jane Adams, capital		9,000				9,000
Jane Adams, withdrawals..............	3,000				3,000	
Revenues...................................		45,000		c) 1,400		46,400
Amortization expense, equipment	0		a) 2,400		2,400	
Salaries expense........................	29,000				29,000	
Insurance expense	7,000		b) 250		7,250	
Totals......................................	61,200	61,200	4,050	4,050	65,000	65,000

*Exercise 4-13

a)	Cash...	1,800	
	Accounts Payable.............................		1,800
	To correct the original entry.		
	OR		
	Cash	1,800	
	Office Supplies		1,800
	To reverse the incorrect entry.		
	Office Supplies	1,800	
	Accounts Payable.............................		1,800
	To journalize the correct entry.		

Exercise 4-13 (*continued*)

b)

| Revenue | 4,500 | |
| Accounts Receivable | | 4,500 |

To correct the original entry.

OR

| Revenue | 4,500 | |
| Cash | | 4,500 |

To reverse the incorrect entry.

| Cash | 4,500 | |
| Accounts Receivable | | 4,500 |

To journalize the correct entry.

c)

| Withdrawals | 1,500 | |
| Salaries Expense | | 1,500 |

To correct the original entry.

OR

| Cash | 1,500 | |
| Salaries Expense | | 1,500 |

To reverse the incorrect entry.

| Withdrawals | 1,500 | |
| Cash | | 1,500 |

To journalize the correct entry.

d)

| Accounts Receivable | 750 | |
| Revenue | | 750 |

To correct the original entry.

OR

| Accounts Receivable | 750 | |
| Cash | | 750 |

To reverse the incorrect entry.

| Cash | 750 | |
| Revenue | | 750 |

To journalize the correct entry.

*Exercise 4-15 (25 minutes)

a) Initial credit recorded in Unearned Fees account:

July	1	Cash	2,000	
		Unearned Fees		2,000
		Received fees for work to be done.		
	6	Cash	8,400	
		Unearned Fees		8,400
		Received fees for work to be done.		
	12	Unearned Fees	2,000	
		Fees Earned		2,000
		Completed work for customer.		
	18	Cash	7,500	
		Unearned Fees		7,500
		Received fees for work to be done.		
	27	Unearned Fees	8,400	
		Fees Earned		8,400
		Completed work for customer.		
	31	No entry.		

b) Initial credit recorded in Fees Earned account:

July	1	Cash	2,000	
		Fees Earned		2,000
		Received fees for work to be done.		
	6	Cash	8,400	
		Fees Earned		8,400
		Received fees for work to be done.		
	12	No entry.		
	18	Cash	7,500	
		Fees Earned		7,500
		Received fees for work to be done.		
	27	No entry.		
	31	Fees Earned..	7,500	
		Unearned Fees		7,500
		Adjusting entry to reflect unearned fees for unfinished job.		

Fundamental Accounting Principles, Eleventh Canadian Edition

Exercise 4-15 (*continued*)

c) Under the first method:
    Unearned fees = $2,000 + $8,400 – $2,000 + $7,500 – $8,400 = $7,500
    Fees earned = $2,000 + $8,400 = $10,400

    Under the second method:
    Unearned fees = $7,500
    Fees earned = $2,000 + $8,400 + $7,500 – $7,500 = $10,400

PROBLEMS

Problem 4-1B (15 minutes)

	2005				
a)	Apr.	30	Equipment Rental Expense...	2,500	
			Prepaid Equipment Rental		2,500
			To record expired prepaid equipment rental;		
			9,000/18 months = 500/month × 5 months =		
			2,500.		
b)		30	Warehouse Rental Expense...	3,000	
			Prepaid Warehouse Rental......................................		3,000
			To record expired rent		
c)		30	Insurance Expense	1,800	
			Prepaid Insurance..		1,800
			To record the use of insurance.		
d)		30	Cleaning Supplies Expense	1,200	
			Cleaning Supplies..		1,200
			To record the use of cleaning supplies.		

Problem 4-2B (15 minutes)

2005

a) Nov. 30 Amortization Expense, Furniture................................... 10,200
                  Accumulated Amortization, Furniture.....................   10,200
                  To record amortization on the furniture;
                  30,600/3 years = 10,200/year.

b) 30 Amortization Expense, Equipment............................. 14,850
                  Accumulated Amortization, Equipment...................   14,850
                  To record amortization on the equipment;
                  210,000 – 12,000 = 198,000/10 years = 19,800/year;
                  19,800/year × 9/12 = 14,850.

c) 30 Amortization Expense, Building................................... 1,320
                  Accumulated Amortization, Building......................   1,320
                  To record amortization on the building;
                  307,600 – 70,000 = 237,600/15 years = 15,840/year;
                  15,840/year × 1/12 = 1,320.

Problem 4-3B (15 minutes)

2005

a) Jan. 31 *No entry required on January 31, 2005.*

b) 31 Unearned Tour Package Revenue 397,000
                  Tour Package Revenue...............................   397,000
                  To record tour revenue earned.

c) 31 Unearned Scuba Diving Revenue................... 97,000
                  Scuba Diving Revenue   97,000
                  To record scuba diving revenue;
                  133,000 – 36,000 = 97,000.

d) 31 Unearned Kayaking Tour Revenue................. 55,650
                  Kayaking Tour Revenue   55,650
                  To record kayaking tour revenue earned;
                  64,000 – 8,350 = 55,650 earned.

Problem 4-4B (30 minutes)

Adjusting Entries

a.

Sept 30	Interest Expense	3,800	
	Interest Payable...........		3,800
	To record accrued interest.		

b.

Sept 30	Wages Expense...............	27,000	
	Wages Payable...........		27,000
	To record accrued wages expense.		

c.

Sept 30	Cell Phone Expense...............	180	
	Accounts Payable...........		180
	To record accrued cell phone expense.		

d.

Sept 30	Cable Expense...............	390	
	Accounts Payable...........		390
	To record accrued expense.		

e.

Sept 30	Property Tax Expense	1,950	
	Property Tax Payable...........		1,950
	To record accrued expense.		

Subsequent Entries

a.

Oct 2	Interest Payable...............	3,800	
	Cash		3,800
	To record payment of accrued interest.		

b.

Oct 4	Wages Payable...............	27,000	
	Wages Expense	18,000	
	Cash		45,000
	To record payment of wages.		

c.

Oct 5	Accounts Payable...............	180	
	Cash		180
	To record payment of accrual.		

d.

Oct 2	Accounts Payable...............	390	
	Cash		390
	To record payment of accrual.		

e.

Oct 15	Property Tax Payable...............	1,950	
	Cash		1,950
	To record payment of accrual.		

Problem 4-5B (30 minutes)

Adjusting Entries

a.
Mar 31	Interest Receivable	650	
	Interest Revenue		650
	To record accrued interest revenue.		

b.
Mar 31	Accounts Receivable	5,400	
	Consulting Fees		5,400
	To record accrued revenue.		

c.
Mar 31	Accounts Receivable	6,800	
	Web Design Revenue		6,800
	To record accrued revenue.		

d.
Mar 31	Rent Receivable	350	
	Rent Revenue		350
	To record accrued rent for March.		

Subsequent Entries

a.
Apr 5	Cash	780	
	Interest Receivable		650
	Interest Revenue		130
	To record collection of interest; 650/25 = 26/day x 5 days = 130.		

b.
Apr 6	Cash	5,400	
	Accounts Receivable		5,400
	To record collection of accrued revenue.		

c.
Apr 13	Cash	6,800	
	Accounts Receivable		6,800
	To record collection of accrued revenue.		

d.
Apr 27	Cash	700	
	Rent Receivable		350
	Rent Revenue		350
	To record collection of March and April rent.		

Fundamental Accounting Principles, Eleventh Canadian Edition

Problem 4-6B (30 minutes)

1. Preparation Component

2005

a)	Dec.	31	Insurance Expense	6,400	
			Prepaid Insurance		6,400

To record the cost of insurance expired during the year.

b)		31	Teaching Supplies Expense	57,500	
			Teaching Supplies		57,500

To record the cost of supplies used during the year; $60,000 - $2,500 = $57,500.

c)		31	Amortization Expense, Equipment	4,000	
			Accumulated Amortization, Equipment		4,000

To record equipment amortization expense.

d)		31	Amortization Expense, Prof. Library	2,000	
			Accumulated Amortization, Professional Library		2,000

To record professional library amortization expense.

e)		31	Unearned Extension Fees	9,200	
			Extension Fees Earned		9,200

To record extension fees earned that were collected in advance; $4,600 x 2 months.

f)		31	Accounts Receivable	5,500	
			Tuition Fees Earned		5,500

To record the amount of tuition fees earned; $2,200 x 2.5 months.

g)		31	Salaries Expense	540	
			Salaries Payable		540

To accrue salaries expense.

Problem 4-6B (*concluded*)

h) Dec. 31 Rent Expense 2,600

               Prepaid Rent...   2,600

            To record the expiration of prepaid rent.

2. Analysis Component

Account	DESIGN INSTITUTE Trial Balances December 31, 2005					
	Unadjusted Trial Balance		Adjustments		Adjusted Trial Balance	
	Debit	Credit	Debit	Credit	Debit	Credit
Cash.............................	$50,000				$ 50,000	
Accounts receivable	-0-		f) $5,500		5,500	
Teaching supplies....................	60,000			b) $57,500	2,500	
Prepaid insurance...................	18,000			a) 6,400	11,600	
Prepaid rent..........................	2,600			h) 2,600	-0-	
Professional library.................	10,000				10,000	
Accum. amort., professional library........................		$ 1,500		d) 2,000		$ 3,500
Equipment	30,000				30,000	
Accum. amort., equipment........		16,000		c) 4,000		20,000
Accounts payable		12,200				12,200
Salaries payable.....................		-0-		g) 540		540
Unearned extension fees..........		27,600	e) 9,200			18,400
Jay Stevens, capital................		68,500				68,500
Jay Stevens, withdrawals..........	20,000				20,000	
Tuition fees earned..................		105,000		f) 5,500		110,500
Extension fees earned..............		62,000		e) 9,200		71,200
Amort. expense, equipment......	-0-		c) 4,000		4,000	
Amort. expense, professional library..........................	-0-		d) 2,000		2,000	
Salaries expense.....................	43,200		g) 540		43,740	
Insurance expense...................	-0-		a) 6,400		6,400	
Rent expense.........................	28,600		h) 2,600		31,200	
Teaching supplies expense.......	-0-		b) 57,500		57,500	
Advertising expense.................	18,000				18,000	
Utilities expense.....................	12,400				12,400	
Totals..................................	$292,800	$292,800	$87,740	$87,740	$304,840	$304,840

3. If the adjusting entries were not recorded, net income would be overstated by $58,340
(4,000 + 2,000 + 540 + 6,400 + 2,600 + 57,500 − 5,500 − 9,200).

4. It is unethical to ignore adjusting entries because it misrepresents assets, liabilities, and equity.

Problem 4-7B (35 minutes)

2005

a) **May 31** Amortization Expense, Machinery 2,625
          Accumulated Amortization, Machinery 2,625
          To record amortization on the machinery;
          21,000/6 yrs = 3,500/yr × 9/12 = 2,625.

b) **31** Unearned Revenue 3,000
          Revenue 3,000
          To record revenue earned.

c) **31** Insurance Expense 11,250
          Prepaid Insurance 11,250
          To record expired insurance;
          90,000/2 yrs = 45,000/yr × 3/12 = 11,250 or
          90,000 x 3/24 = 11,250.

d) **31** Salaries Expense 5,000
          Salaries Payable 5,000
          To record accrued salaries.

e) **31** Interest Expense 2,520
          Interest Payable 2,520
          To record accrued interest.

f) **31** Accounts Receivable 1,700
          Revenue 1,700
          To record accrued revenues.

g) **31** Advertising Expense 12,000
          Prepaid Advertising 12,000
          To record the use of prepaid advertising.

h) **31** Amortization Expense, Office Equipment 1,800
          Accumulated Amortization, Office Equipment 1,800
          To record amortization on the office equipment.

i) **31** Interest Receivable 350
          Interest Revenue 350
          To record accrued interest revenue.

j) **31** Office Supplies Expense 5,500
          Office Supplies 5,500
          To record the use of office supplies.

Problem 4-8B (30 minutes)

1.	b.	7.	h.
2.	d.	8.	f.
3.	e.	9.	f.
4.	g.	10.	c.
5.	a.	11.	i.
6.	i.	12.	a.

Problem 4-9B (30 minutes) *Part 1*

2007

a) Oct. 31   Office Supplies Expense   3,450

               Office Supplies   3,450

               To record the cost of supplies used during the year; $500 + $3,650 – $700.

b) 31   Insurance Expense...   2,365

               Prepaid Insurance   2,365

               To record the cost of insurance coverage that expired during the year.

Policy	Cost per Month	No. of Months	Current Year
1	$125	12	$1,500
2	100	7	700
3	55	3	165
Total			$2,365

c) 31   Salaries Expense   2,400

               Salaries Payable   2,400

               To record accrued but unpaid wages; 3 days × $800/day.

d) 31   Amortization Expense, Building.....................   1,350

               Accumulated Amortization, Building.....   1,350

               To record amortization expense. Annual amortization = ($155,000 – $20,000)/25 = $5,400; amortization for three months = $5,400 × 3/12.

e) 31   Rent Receivable   600

               Rent Earned   600

               To record earned but unpaid rent.

         Fundamental Accounting Principles, Eleventh Canadian Edition

Problem 4-9B *(concluded) Part 1*

f)	Oct.	31	Unearned Rent...	1,050	
			Rent Earned..		1,050
			To record the amount of rent earned;		
			2 × $525.		

Part 2

2007

c.	Nov.	5	Salaries Payable.......................................	2,400	
			Salaries Expense.....................................	1,600	
			Cash		4,000
			To record payment of accrued and current		
			salaries; 2 × $800 = $1,600.		
e.		15	Cash	1,200	
			Rent Receivable		600
			Rent Earned.......................................		600
			To record past due rent for two months.		

Problem 4-10B (30 minutes)

	Date 2005	General Journal Account Titles and Explanations	PR	Debit	Page G7 Credit

a)	Dec. 31	Amortization Expense, Surveying Equipment ....
		  Accumulated Amortization, Surveying Equipment...
		  To record amortization for December.
				167	167

b)	31	Unearned Surveying Fees.................................
		  Surveying Fees Earned.................................
		  To record earned surveying fees;
		  2,400 – 2,000 = 400 earned.
				400	400

c)	31	Rent Expense...
		  Prepaid Rent ....
		  To record expired rent;
		  13,500 ÷ 6 months = 2,250.
				2,250	2,250

d)	31	Wages Expense ....
		  Wages Payable ....
		  To record accrued wages.
				5,000	5,000

e)	31	Interest Expense..
		  Interest Payable ....
		  To record accrued interest.
				105	105

f)	31	Accounts Receivable....................................
		  Surveying Fees Earned ....
		  To record accrued fees.
				790	790

g)	31	Advertising Expense ....
		  Prepaid Advertising....................................
		  To record used advertising;
		  2,800 ÷ 4 months = 700/month ÷ 2 = 350 for
		  half of December.
				350	350

h)	31	Supplies Expense..
		  Supplies ....
		  To record supplies used.
				150	150

i)	31	Utilities Expense...
		  Accounts Payable.......................................
		  To record accrued utilities.
				540	540

Fundamental Accounting Principles, Eleventh Canadian Edition

Problem 4-11B (60 minutes)

Parts 1 and 2

Note: The solution to Parts 1 and 2 is also done using T-accounts and can be found immediately following the balance column format.

Cash — Account No. 101

Date		Explanation	PR	Debit	Credit	Balance
2005						
Dec.	31	Unadjusted balance				2,800

Accounts Receivable — Account No. 106

Date		Explanation	PR	Debit	Credit	Balance
2005						
Dec.	31	Unadjusted balance				3,955
	31		G7	790		4,745

Supplies — Account No. 126

Date		Explanation	PR	Debit	Credit	Balance
2005						
Dec.	31	Unadjusted balance				320
	31		G7		150	170

Prepaid Advertising — Account No. 128

Date		Explanation	PR	Debit	Credit	Balance
2005						
Dec.	31	Unadjusted balance				2,800
	31		G7		350	2,450

Prepaid Rent — Account No. 131

Date		Explanation	PR	Debit	Credit	Balance
2005						
Dec.	31	Unadjusted balance				13,500
	31		G7		2,250	11,250

Surveying Equipment — Account No. 167

Date		Explanation	PR	Debit	Credit	Balance
2005						
Dec.	31	Unadjusted balance				29,000

Problem 4-11B (continued)

Accumulated Amortization - Surveying Equipment   Account No. 168

Date		Explanation	PR	Debit	Credit	Balance
2005						
Dec.	31	Unadjusted balance				3,674
	31		G7		167	3,841

Accounts Payable   Account No. 201

Date		Explanation	PR	Debit	Credit	Balance
2005						
Dec.	31	Unadjusted balance				1,900
	31		G7		540	2,440

Interest Payable   Account No. 203

Date		Explanation	PR	Debit	Credit	Balance
2005						
Dec.	31		G7		105	105

Wages Payable   Account No. 210

Date		Explanation	PR	Debit	Credit	Balance
2005						
Dec.	31		G7		5,000	5,000

Unearned Surveying Fees   Account No. 233

Date		Explanation	PR	Debit	Credit	Balance
2005						
Dec.	31	Unadjusted balance				2,400
	31		G7	400		2,000

Notes Payable   Account No. 251

Date		Explanation	PR	Debit	Credit	Balance
2005						
Dec.	31	Unadjusted balance				18,000

Alissa Kay, Capital   Account No. 301

Date		Explanation	PR	Debit	Credit	Balance
2005						
Dec.	31	Unadjusted balance				14,326

Fundamental Accounting Principles, Eleventh Canadian Edition

Problem 4-11B (continued)

Alissa Kay, Withdrawals   Account No. 302

Date			Explanation	PR	Debit	Credit	Balance
2005							
Dec.	31		Unadjusted balance				2,150

Surveying Fees Earned   Account No. 401

Date			Explanation	PR	Debit	Credit	Balance
2005							
Dec.	31		Unadjusted balance				67,049
	31			G7		400	67,449
	31			G7		790	68,239

Amortization Expense, Surveying Equipment   Account No. 601

Date			Explanation	PR	Debit	Credit	Balance
2005							
Dec.	31		Unadjusted balance				1,837
	31			G7	167		2,004

Wages Expense   Account No. 622

Date			Explanation	PR	Debit	Credit	Balance
2005							
Dec.	31		Unadjusted balance				19,863
	31			G7	5,000		24,863

Interest Expense   Account No. 633

Date			Explanation	PR	Debit	Credit	Balance
2005							
Dec.	31		Unadjusted balance				945
	31			G7	105		1,050

Rent Expense   Account No. 640

Date			Explanation	PR	Debit	Credit	Balance
2005							
Dec.	31		Unadjusted balance				22,000
	31			G7	2,250		24,250

Problem 4-11B *(continued)*

Supplies Expense   Account No. 650

Date		Explanation	PR	Debit	Credit	Balance
2005						
Dec.	31	Unadjusted balance				1,479
	31		G7	150		1,629

Advertising Expense   Account No. 655

Date		Explanation	PR	Debit	Credit	Balance
2005						
Dec.	31	Unadjusted balance				500
	31		G7	350		850

Utilities Expense   Account No. 690

Date		Explanation	PR	Debit	Credit	Balance
2005						
Dec.	31	Unadjusted balance				6,200
	31		G7	540		6,740

Problem 4-11B (continued)

Parts 1 and 2 (in T-account format)

NOTE: AJE = Adjusting Journal Entry

Cash — 101

Unadj Bal Dec 31 2,800	

Accounts Receivable — 106

Unadj Bal Dec 31 3,955	
AJE 790	
Adj Bal Dec 31 4,745	

Supplies — 126

Unadj Bal Dec 31 320	AJE Dec 31 150
Adj Bal Dec 31 170	

Prepaid Advertising — 128

Unadj Bal Dec 31 2,800	AJE Dec 31 350
Adj Bal Dec 31 2,450	

Prepaid Rent — 131

Unadj Bal Dec 31 13,500	AJE Dec 31 2,250
Adj Bal Dec 31 11,250	

Surveying Equipment — 167

Unadj Bal Dec 31 29,000	

Accum. Amort., Surveying Equipment — 168

	Unadj Bal Dec 31 3,674
	AJE Dec 31 167
	Adj Bal Dec 31 3,841

Accounts Payable — 201

	Unadj Bal Dec 31 1,900
	AJE Dec 31 540
	Adj Bal Dec 31 2,440

Interest Payable — 203

	AJE Dec 31 105

Wages Payable — 210

	AJE Dec 31 5,000

Unearned Surveying Fees — 233

AJE Dec 31 400	Unadj Bal Dec 31 2,400
	Adj Bal Dec 31 2,000

Notes Payable — 251

	Unadj Bal Dec 31 18,000

Problem 4-11B (continued)

Alissa Kay, Capital 301

Unadj Bal Dec 31		14,326

Alissa Kay, Withdrawals 302

Unadj Bal Dec 31	2,150	

Surveying Fees Earned 401

Unadj Bal Dec 31		67,049
AJE Dec 31		400
AJE Dec 31		790
Adj Bal Dec 31		68,239

Amort. Expense, Surveying Equipment 601

Unadj Bal Dec 31	1,837	
AJE Dec 31	167	
Adj Bal Dec 31	2,004	

Wages Expense 622

Unadj Bal Dec 31	19,863	
AJE Dec 31	5,000	
Adj Bal Dec 31	24,863	

Interest Expense 633

Unadj Bal Dec 31	945	
AJE Dec 31	105	
Adj Bal Dec 31	1,050	

Rent Expense 640

Unadj Bal Dec 31	22,000	
AJE Dec 31	2,250	
Adj Bal Dec 31	24,250	

Supplies Expense 650

Unadj Bal Dec 31	1,479	
AJE Dec 31	150	
Adj Bal Dec 31	1,629	

Advertising Expense 655

Unadj Bal Dec 31	500	
AJE Dec 31	350	
Adj Bal Dec 31	850	

Utilities Expense 690

Unadj Bal Dec 31	6,200	
AJE Dec 31	540	
Adj Bal Dec 31	6,740	

Fundamental Accounting Principles, Eleventh Canadian Edition

Problem 4-11B *(concluded)*

NOTE: After posting the December 31, 2005 adjusting entries, the general journal PR column would appear as follows to show that the posting has been done.

General Journal Page G7

Date 2005		Account Titles and Explanations	PR	Debit	Credit
		Adjusting entries:			
a) Dec.	31	Amortization Expense, Surveying Equipment	601	167	
		Accumulated Amortization, Surveying Equipment .	168		167
		To record amortization for December.			
b)	31	Unearned Surveying Fees..	233	400	
		Surveying Fees Earned	401		400
		To record earned surveying fees;			
		2,400 – 2,000 = 400 earned.			
c)	31	Rent Expense...	640	2,250	
		Prepaid Rent	131		2,250
		To record expired rent;			
		13,500 ÷ 6 months = 2,250.			
d)	31	Wages Expense	622	5,000	
		Wages Payable..	210		5,000
		To record accrued wages.			
e)	31	Interest Expense...	633	105	
		Interest Payable	203		105
		To record accrued interest.			
f)	31	Accounts Receivable..	106	790	
		Surveying Fees Earned	401		790
		To record accrued fees.			
g)	31	Advertising Expense	655	350	
		Prepaid Advertising..	128		350
		To record used advertising;			
		2,800 ÷ 4 months = 700/month ÷ 2 = 350 for			
		half of December.			
h)	31	Supplies Expense..	650	150	
		Supplies..	126		150
		To record supplies used.			
i)	31	Utilities Expense...	690	540	
		Accounts Payable...	201		540
		To record accrued utilities.			

Problem 4-11B *(continued)*

Part 3

Colt Surveying Services
Adjusted Trial Balance
December 31, 2005

Acct. No.	Account	Debit	Credit
101	Cash	$ 2,800	
106	Accounts receivable	4,745	
126	Supplies	170	
128	Prepaid advertising	2,450	
131	Prepaid rent	11,250	
167	Surveying equipment	29,000	
168	Accumulated amortization, surveying equipment		$ 3,841
201	Accounts payable		2,440
203	Interest payable		105
210	Wages payable		5,000
233	Unearned surveying fees		2,000
251	Notes payable		18,000
301	Alissa Kay, capital		14,326
302	Alissa Kay, withdrawals	2,150	
401	Surveying fees earned		68,239
601	Amortization expense	2,004	
622	Wages expense	24,863	
633	Interest expense	1,050	
640	Rent expense	24,250	
650	Supplies expense	1,629	
655	Advertising expense	850	
690	Utilities expense	6,740	
	Totals	$113,951	$113,951

Fundamental Accounting Principles, Eleventh Canadian Edition

Problem 4-11B *(continued)*

Part 4

Colt Surveying Services
Income Statement
For Year Ended December 31, 2005

Revenues:		
Service revenue		$68,239
Operating expenses:		
Wages expense	$24,863	
Rent expense	24,250	
Utilities expense	6,740	
Amortization expense, surveying equipment............................	2,004	
Supplies expense	1,629	
Interest expense	1,050	
Advertising expense...	850	
Total operating expenses		61,386
Net income		$ 6,853

Colt Surveying Services
Statement of Owner's Equity
For Year Ended December 31, 2005

Alissa Kay, capital, January 1...		$12,326*
Add: Investment by owner...	$2,000	
Net income	6,853	8,853
Total..		$21,179
Less: Withdrawal by owner		2,150
Alissa Kay, capital, December 31		$19,029

Calculation: The adjusted balance of $68,239 is <u>after</u> the owner invested $2,000 during the year. Therefore, the balance at the beginning of the year was $66,239 ($68,239 - $2,000).

Problem 4-11B (*concluded*)

Part 4

Colt Surveying Services
Balance Sheet
December 31, 2005

Assets

Cash		$ 2,800
Accounts receivable		4,745
Supplies		170
Prepaid advertising		2,450
Prepaid rent		11,250
Surveying equipment	$29,000	
Less: Accumulated amortization	3,841	25,159
Total assets		$46,574

Liabilities

Accounts payable	$ 2,440
Interest payable	105
Wages payable	5,000
Unearned surveying fees	2,000
Notes payable	18,000
Total liabilities	$27,545

Owner's Equity

Alissa Kay, capital	19,029
Total liabilities and owner's equity	$46,574

Problem 4-12B (25 minutes)

	2005				
a)	June	30	Arena Rental Expense	65,000	
			Prepaid Arena Rental....................................		65,000

To record rent;
91,000/7 months = 13,000/month × 5 months = 65,000.

b)		30	Repair Supplies Expense	950	
			Repair Supplies...		950

To record the use of repair supplies.

c)		30	Amortization Expense, Hockey Equipment	41,000	
			Accumulated Amortization, Hockey Equipment...		41,000

To record amortization of hockey equipment.

d)		30	Unearned Ticket Revenue	3,500	
			Ticket Revenue...		3,500

To record revenues earned;
9,800 – 6,300 = 3,500.

e)		30	Salaries Expense...	29,000	
			Salaries Payable..		29,000

To record accrued salaries.

f)		30	Interest Expense	900	
			Interest Payable		900

To record accrued interest.

g)		30	Ticket Revenue..	46,000	
			Unearned Ticket Revenue		46,000

To record ticket revenue not yet earned.

Problem 4-13B (45 minutes) *Part 1*

Orca Bay Hockey Holdings
Trial Balances
June 30, 2005

Account	Unadjusted Trial Balance Debit	Credit	Adjustments Debit		Credit		Adjusted Trial Balance Debit	Credit
Cash	56,000						56,000	
Accounts receivable	14,000						14,000	
Repair supplies	1,400				b)	950	450	
Prepaid arena rental	91,000				a)	65,000	26,000	
Hockey equipment	214,000						214,000	
Accumulated amort., hockey equip.		82,000			c)	41,000		123,000
Accounts payable		2,700						2,700
Unearned ticket revenue		9,800	d)	3,500	g)	46,000		52,300
Notes payable		80,000						80,000
Ben Gibson, capital		225,700						225,700
Ben Gibson, withdrawals	36,000						36,000	
Ticket revenue		275,000	g)	46,000	d)	3,500		232,500
Salaries expense	175,000		e)	29,000			204,000	
Arena rental expense	84,000		a)	65,000			149,000	
Other expenses	3,800						3,800	
Totals	675,200	675,200						
Repair supplies expense			b)	950			950	
Amortization expense, hockey equip.			c)	41,000			41,000	
Salaries payable					e)	29,000		29,000
Interest expense			f)	900			900	
Interest payable					f)	900		900
Totals				186,350		186,350	746,100	746,100

Fundamental Accounting Principles, Eleventh Canadian Edition

Problem 4-13B *(continued)*

Part 2

Orca Bay Hockey Holdings
Income Statement
For Year Ended June 30, 2005

Revenues:		
Ticket revenue		$232,500
Operating expenses:		
Salaries expense..	$204,000	
Arena rental expense	149,000	
Amortization expense, hockey equipment	41,000	
Other expenses...	3,800	
Repair supplies expense...	950	
Interest expense	900	
Total operating expenses		399,650
Net loss		$167,150

Orca Bay Hockey Holdings
Statement of Owner's Equity
For Year Ended June 30, 2005

Ben Gibson, capital, July 1		$215,700*
Add: Investment by owner...		10,000
Total..		$225,700
Less: Withdrawal by owner	$36,000	
Net loss	167,150	203,150
Ben Gibson, capital, June 30...		$ 22,550

Calculation: The adjusted balance of $225,700 is <u>after</u> the owner invested $10,000 during the year. Therefore, the balance at the beginning of the year was $215,700 ($225,700 - $10,000).

Problem 4-13B *(concluded)*

Orca Bay Hockey Holdings
Balance Sheet
June 30, 2005

Assets

Cash		$ 56,000
Accounts receivable...		14,000
Prepaid arena rental		26,000
Repair supplies..		450
Hockey equipment...	$214,000	
Less: Accumulated amortization	123,000	91,000
Total assets...		$187,450

Liabilities

Accounts payable...	$ 2,700
Interest payable	900
Salaries payable	29,000
Unearned ticket revenue..	52,300
Notes payable	80,000
Total liabilities	$164,900

Owner's Equity

Ben Gibson, capital..	22,550
Total liabilities and owner's equity	$187,450

Fundamental Accounting Principles, Eleventh Canadian Edition

Problem 4-14B (50 minutes) *Part 1*

HORIZON COURIER
Income Statement
For Year Ended December 31, 2005

Revenues:		
Delivery fees earned	$580,000	
Interest earned	24,000	
Total revenues		$604,000
Operating Expenses:		
Wages expense	$290,000	
Salaries expense	64,000	
Amortization expense, equipment...........................	46,000	
Repairs expense, trucks..	34,600	
Office supplies expense...	33,000	
Advertising expense..	26,400	
Interest expense	25,000	
Amortization expense, trucks..................................	24,000	
Total operating expenses		543,000
Net income		$ 61,000

Part 2

HORIZON COURIER
Statement of Owner's Equity
For Year Ended December 31, 2005

Kim Ainesworth, capital, January 1		$ 95,000*
Add: Investment by owner..	$ 20,000	
Net income	61,000	81,000
Total		$176,000
Less: Withdrawal by owner..		40,000
Kim Ainesworth, capital, December 31		$136,000

Calculation: The adjusted balance of $115,000 is after the owner invested $20,000 during the year. Therefore, the balance at the beginning of the year was $95,000 ($115,000 - $20,000).

HORIZON COURIER
Balance Sheet
December 31, 2005

Assets

Cash		$ 48,000
Accounts receivable		110,000
Interest receivable		6,000
Notes receivable (due in 90 days)		200,000
Office supplies		12,000
Trucks	$124,000	
Less: Accumulated amortization	48,000	76,000
Equipment	$260,000	
Less: Accumulated amortization	190,000	70,000
Land		90,000
Total assets		$612,000

Liabilities

Accounts payable	$124,000	
Interest payable	22,000	
Salaries payable	30,000	
Unearned delivery fees	110,000	
Long-term notes payable	190,000	
Total liabilities		$476,000

Owner's Equity

Kim Ainesworth, capital		136,000
Total liabilities and owner's equity		$612,000

*Problem 4-15B

		2005				
a.	May	31	Accounts Receivable	12,000	
			Advertising Expense............................		12,000

To reverse incorrect entry.

AND

		31	Repairs Expense	12,000	
			Cash		12,000

To record repairs paid in cash.

b.		31	Accounts Payable	8,000	
			Computer Equipment.............................		8,000

To reverse incorrect entry.

AND

		31	Office Furniture	8,000	
			Note Payable...		8,000

To record the purchase of office furniture by issuing a note payable.

c.		31	Telemarketing Fees Earned.........................	10,000	
			Unearned Fees......................................		10,000

To correct an incorrect entry.

OR

		31	Telemarketing Fees Earned.........................	10,000	
			Cash		10,000

To reverse incorrect entry.

AND

		31	Cash	10,000	
			Unearned Fees......................................		10,000

To record cash collected in advance.

d.		31	Delivery Expense.......................................	1,800	
			Telephone Expense...............................		1,800

To correct an incorrect entry.

e.		31	Telemarketing Fees Earned.........................	450	
			Interest Revenue		450

To correct an incorrect entry.

MELI JANITORIAL SERVICES
Trial Balances
October 31, 2005

Account	Unadjusted Trial Balance Debit	Unadjusted Trial Balance Credit	Adjustments Debit	Adjustments Credit	Adjusted Trial Balance Debit	Adjusted Trial Balance Credit
Cash	$ 29,000				$ 29,000	
Accounts receivable	18,000				18,000	
Prepaid advertising	-0-		e) $5,000		5,000	
Cleaning supplies	-0-		a) 3,100		3,100	
Equipment	62,000				62,000	
Accumulated amortization, equipment		$ 3,000		b) $3,000		$ 6,000
Unearned window washing fees		-0-		d) 5,000		5,000
Unearned office cleaning fees		-0-		c) 8,500		8,500
Joel Meli, capital		18,300				18,300
Window washing fees earned		76,000	d) 5,000			71,000
Office cleaning fees earned		138,000	c) 8,500			129,500
Advertising expense	7,300			e) 5,000	2,300	
Salaries expense	97,000				97,000	
Amortization expense, equipment	-0-		b) 3,000		3,000	
Cleaning supplies expense	22,000			a) 3,100	18,900	
Totals	$235,300	$235,300	$24,600	$24,600	$238,300	$238,300

*Problem 4-17B (40 minutes) *Part 1*

Entries that initially recognize assets and liabilities:

2005				
Apr.	1	Prepaid Consulting Fees..................................	3,450	
		Cash		3,450
		Paid for future consulting services.		
	1	Prepaid Insurance	2,700	
		Cash		2,700
		Paid insurance for one year.		
	30	Cash..	7,500	
		Unearned Service Fees		7,500
		Received fees in advance.		
May	1	Prepaid Advertising....................................	3,450	
		Cash		3,450
		Paid for future advertising.		
	23	Cash..	9,450	
		Unearned Service Fees		9,450
		Received fees in advance.		

Year-end adjusting entries:

2005				
May	31	Consulting Services Expense	1,500	
		Prepaid Consulting Fees		1,500
		To adjust prepaid consulting fees.		

May 31	Insurance Expense		450	
	Prepaid Insurance			450
	To adjust prepaid insurance;			
	2,700 x 2/12 = 450 used.			
31	Unearned Service Fees		3,900	
	Service Fees Earned			3,900
	To adjust unearned service fees;			
	7,500 – 3,600 = 3,900 earned.			
31	Advertising Expense		2,400	
	Prepaid Advertising.................................			2,400
	To adjust prepaid advertising;			
	3,450 – 1,050 = 2,400 used.			
31	Unearned Service Fees		4,500	
	Service Fees Earned			4,500
	To adjust unearned service fees.			

Note: The entries for Part 1 have been posted to T-accounts to help the student see the effects more clearly. The entries for Part 2 have also been posted to T-accounts in Part 2 of this question to help the student see that the results are the same regardless of which approach is used.

Prepaid Advertising							
May 1	3,450	2,400	May 31				
Bal.	1,050						

Prepaid Insurance			
Apr. 1	2,700	450	May 31
Bal.	2,250		

Prepaid Consulting Fees			
Apr. 1	3,450	1,500	May 31
Bal.	1,950		

Unearned Service Fees			
May 31	3,900	7,500	Apr. 30
31	4,500	9,450	May 23
		8,550	Bal.

Service Fees Earned			
		3,900	May 31
		4,500	31
		8,400	Bal.

Advertising Expense		
May 31	2,400	
Bal.	2,400	

Insurance Expense		
May 31	450	
Bal.	450	

Consulting Services Expense		
May 31	1,500	
Bal.	1,500	

*Problem 4-17B *(continued)*

Part 2

Entries that initially recognize expenses and revenues:

2005

Apr.	1	Consulting Services Expense.........................	3,450	
		Cash..		3,450
		Paid for future consulting services.		
	1	Insurance Expense	2,700	
		Cash..		2,700
		Paid insurance for one year.		
	30	Cash...	7,500	
		Service Fees Earned.....................................		7,500
		Received fees in advance.		
May	1	Advertising Expense	3,450	
		Cash..		3,450
		Paid for future advertising.		
	23	Cash...	9,450	
		Service Fees Earned.....................................		9,450
		Received fees in advance.		

Year-end adjusting entries:

2005

May	31	Prepaid Consulting Fees...............................	1,950	
		Consulting Services Expense................		1,950
		To adjust for prepaid consulting fees;		
		3,450 – 1,500 = 1,950 prepaid.		
	31	Prepaid Insurance...	2,250	
		Insurance Expense.................................		2,250
		To adjust for prepaid insurance;		
		2,700 – 450 = 2,250 prepaid.		
	31	Service Fees Earned......................................	3,600	
		Unearned Service Fees		3,600
		To adjust for unearned service fees.		

*Problem 4-17B *(continued)* Part 2

```
31 Prepaid Advertising.......................................................  1,050
         Advertising Expense....................................                    1,050
         To adjust for prepaid advertising.

   31   Service Fees Earned...............................................  4,950
         Unearned Service Fees ...........................                     4,950
         To adjust for unearned service fees;
         9,450 – 4,500 earned  = 4,950 unearned.
```

Note: The entries for Part 2 have been posted to T-accounts to help the student see the effects more clearly. The entries for Part 1 have also been posted to T-accounts in Part 1 of this question to help the student see that the results are the same regardless of which approach is used.

Prepaid Advertising		
May 31	1,050	
Bal.	1,050	

Prepaid Insurance		
May 31	2,250	
Bal.	2,250	

Prepaid Consulting Fees		
May 31	1,950	
Bal.	1,950	

Unearned Service Fees			
		3,600	May 31
		4,950	31
		8,550	Bal.

Service Fees Earned			
May 31	3,600	7,500	Apr. 30
31	4,950	9,450	May 23
		8,400	Bal.

Advertising Expense			
May 1	3,450	1,050	May 31
Bal.	2,400		

*Problem 4-17B *(concluded)*

Part 2

Insurance Expense			
Apr. 1	2,700	2,250	May 31
Bal.	450		

Consulting Services Expense			
Apr. 1	3,450	1,950	May 31
Bal.	1,500		

Part 3

There are no differences between the two methods in terms of the amounts that appear on the financial statements. In both cases, the financial statements reflect the following:

Prepaid consulting fees as of May 31	$1,950
Consulting fees expense for two months	1,500
Insurance expense for two months	450
Prepaid insurance as of May 31	2,250
Unearned service fees as of May 31 ($3,600 + $4,950)	8,550
Service fees earned for two months ($3,900 + $4,500)	8,400
Prepaid advertising as of May 31	1,050
Advertising expense for two months	2,400

When prepaid expenses and unearned revenues are recorded in balance sheet accounts, the related adjusting entries are designed to generate the correct asset, expense, liability, and revenue account balances. When prepaid expenses and unearned revenues are recorded in income statement accounts, the related adjusting entries are designed to accomplish exactly the same result.

Chapter 5   Completing the Accounting Cycle and Classifying Accounts

EXERCISES

Exercise 5-1 (15 minutes)

1.	C	5.	C	9.	C	13.	C
2.	B	6.	A	10.	C	14.	A
3.	D	7.	A	11.	D	15.	A
4.	B	8.	D	12.	D	16.	C

Exercise 5-3 (25 minutes) Parts 1, 2, and 3

Musical Sensations
Work Sheet
For Year Ended December 31, 2005

Account	Unadjusted Trial Balance Debit	Unadjusted Trial Balance Credit	Adjustments Debit	Adjustments Credit	Adjusted Trial Balance Debit	Adjusted Trial Balance Credit	Income Statement Debit	Income Statement Credit	Balance Sheet & Statement of Owner's Equity Debit	Balance Sheet & Statement of Owner's Equity Credit
Cash...............................	14,000				14,000				14,000	
Accounts receivable........	26,000				26,000				26,000	
Office supplies................	950			d) 430	520				520	
Musical equipment...........	212,000				212,000				212,000	
Accum. amort. musical equip.		16,200		b) 16,200		32,400				32,400
Accounts payable............		3,350				3,350				3,350
Unearned revenue performance		12,400	a) 10,600			1,800				1,800
Jim Daley, capital...........		272,000				272,000				272,000
Jim Daley, withdrawals.....	52,000				52,000				52,000	
Performance revenue		119,000		a) 10,600		129,600		129,600		
Salaries expense.............	76,000		c) 13,800		89,800		89,800			
Travelling expense..........	42,000				42,000		42,000			
Totals	422,950	422,950								
Amortization musical equip. expense, ...			b) 16,200		16,200		16,200			
Salaries payable..............				c) 13,800		13,800				13,800
Office supplies expense ...			d) 430		430		430			
Totals			41,030	41,030	452,950	452,950	148,430	129,600	304,520	323,350
Net loss.......................								18,830	18,830	
Totals							148,430	148,430	323,350	323,350

Exercise 5-3 (*concluded*)

Part 4

$272,000 - $52,000 - $18,830 = \underline{$201,170}$

or

Jim Daley, Capital

		272,000	(Beg. bal.)
(With.)	52,000		
(Net Loss)	18,830		
		201,170	(End. bal.)

Exercise 5-5 (15 minutes)

1.   Net Income = $36,800

2.

Mar. 31	Income Summary	36,800
	Pat Beck, Capital	36,800
	To close the income summary account to capital.	

3.

$63,000 + $36,800 - $17,000 = \underline{$82,800}$ OR

Pat Beck, Capital

			63,000	(Beg. bal.)
(With.)	17,000		36,800	(Net income)
			82,800	(End. bal.)

Fundamental Accounting Principles, Eleventh Canadian Edition

Exercise 5-7 (30 minutes)

	Debit	Credit
Rent earned		99,000
Salaries expense	35,300	
Insurance expense	4,400	
Dock rental expense	12,000	
Boat supplies expense	6,220	
Amortization expense, boats	21,500	
Totals	79,420	99,000
Net income	19,580	
Totals	99,000	99,000

2005	*Closing entries:*		
Dec. 31	Rent Earned	99,000	
	Income Summary		99,000
	To close the revenue account.		
31	Income Summary	79,420	
	Salaries Expense		35,300
	Insurance Expense		4,400
	Dock Rental Expense		12,000
	Boat Supplies Expense		6,220
	Amortization Expense, Boats		21,500
	To close the expense accounts.		
31	Income Summary	19,580	
	Carl Winston, Capital		19,580
	To close Income Summary.		
31	Carl Winston, Capital	18,000	
	Carl Winston, Withdrawals		18,000
	To close the withdrawals account.		

Exercise 5-9 (20 minutes)

2005	Closing entries:		
January 31	Subscription Revenues...............................	62,000	
	Interest Revenue.......................................	450	
	Income Summary....................................		62,450
	To close revenues to the income summary.		
31	Income Summary...	65,400	
	Amortization Expense, Equipment		2,000
	Rent Expense.......................................		7,400
	Salaries Expense...................................		56,000
	To close expense accounts to income summary.		
31	Kate Goldberg, Capital...................................	2,950	
	Income Summary....................................		2,950
	To close income summary to capital.		
31	Kate Goldberg, Capital...................................	4,000	
	Kate Goldberg, Withdrawals.......................		4,000
	To close withdrawals to capital.		

Exercise 5-11 (20 minutes)

2005	Closing entries:		
Sept. 30	Consulting Fees Earned..................................	136,000	
	Income Summary....................................		136,000
	To close revenues to the income summary.		
30	Income Summary...	37,500	
	Amortization Expense, Office Equipment...		7,000
	Rent Expense.......................................		3,500
	Wages Expense		27,000
	To close expense accounts to income summary.		
30	Income Summary...	98,500	
	Sandra Sloley, Capital		98,500
	To close income summary to capital.		
30	Sandra Sloley, Capital	38,000	
	Sandra Sloley, Withdrawals		38,000
	To close withdrawals to capital.		

Exercise 5-13 (10 minutes)

Jones' Consulting
Post-Closing Trial Balance
December 31, 2005

Account	Debit	Credit
Assets	$ 80,000	
Liabilities		$ 38,100
Marcy Jones, Capital		41,900
Totals	$80,000	$80,000

Exercise 5-15 (15 minutes)

a.

	Account Title	Adjusted Trial Balance Debit	Adjusted Trial Balance Credit
	Accounts payable		$ 11,000
	Accounts receivable...	$ 59,000	
	Accumulated amortization, equipment		9,000
	Accumulated amortization, truck.......................		21,000
X	Amortization expense	3,800	
	Cash	29,000	
	Equipment	13,000	
	Franchise	17,800	
X	Gas and oil expense	7,500	
X	Interest expense..	4,500	
	Interest payable...		750
	Land not currently used in business operations ..	52,000	
	Long-term notes payable[Note 1]		35,000
	Notes payable, due February 1, 2006		7,000
	Notes receivable[Note 2]	6,000	
	Patent	7,000	
	Prepaid rent	14,000	
X	Rent expense...	39,000	
X	Repair revenue		247,000
	Repair supplies	17,000	
X	Repair supplies expense	14,000	
X	Sid Whimsly, capital...		24,050
X	Sid Whimsly, withdrawals.................................	49,000	
	Truck	26,000	
	Unearned repair revenue		3,800
	Totals..	$358,600	$358,600

Exercise 5-15 (*continued*)

b. $24,050 -$3,800 - $7,500 - $4,500 - $39,000 + $247,000 - $14,000 - $49,000 = $153,250.

c.   Amortization expense, gas and oil expense, interest expense, rent expense, repair revenue, repair supplies expense, and withdrawals are all temporary accounts and do not appear on the post-closing trial balance because their balances were transferred to capital during the closing process leaving each with a zero post-closing balance. The adjusted balance of $24,050 in capital is the balance *prior to closing* all temporary accounts into it. A capital account balance does appear on the post-closing trial balance but it is the post-closing balance of $153,250 as determined in part (b) above. Therefore, the adjusted capital balance of $24,050 will not appear on the post-closing trial balance

Note to instructor: reinforce to the student that the question asks which account balances from the adjusted trial balance will not appear on the post-closing trial balance.

Exercise 5-17 (30 minutes)

WILSHIRE ATLANTIC TOURS
Balance Sheet
November 30, 2005

Assets

Current assets:

Cash	$ 10,000	
Accounts receivable	26,000	
Prepaid insurance	1,400	
Prepaid rent	18,000	
Supplies	4,500	
Current portion of notes receivable............................	15,000	
Total current assets		$ 74,900

Long-term investments:

Notes receivable, less $15,000 current portion...........		26,000

Property, plant and equipment:

Vehicles...	$128,000		
Less: Accumulated amortization.............................	34,000	$94,000	
Office furniture	$ 13,000		
Less: Accumulated amortization.............................	7,200	5,800	
Total property, plant and equipment			99,800

Intangible assets:

Copyright...		2,000
Total assets...		$202,700

Liabilities

Current liabilities:

Accounts payable..	$ 22,000	

Fundamental Accounting Principles, Eleventh Canadian Edition

Salaries payable	1,800	
Unearned touring revenue	46,000	
Notes payable	8,000	
Current portion of long-term notes payable	20,000	
Total current liabilities		$ 97,800
Long-term liabilities:		
Long-term notes payable, less $20,000 current portion		21,000
Total liabilities		$118,800

Owner's Equity

George Wilshire, capital*		83,900
Total liabilities and owner's equity		$202,700

Calculated as Total assets of $202,700 less Total liabilities of $118,800 = $83,900.

Exercise 5-19 (20 minutes)

HANSON TRUCKING COMPANY
Balance Sheet
December 31, 2005

Assets

Current assets:

Cash	$ 7,000	
Accounts receivable	16,500	
Office supplies	2,000	
Total current assets		$ 25,500

Property, plant and equipment:

Land		$ 75,000	
Trucks	$170,000		
Less: Accumulated amortization.................	35,000	135,000	
Total property, plant and equipment			$210,000
Total assets...			$235,500

Liabilities

Current liabilities:

Accounts payable...............................	$ 11,000		
Interest payable..................................	3,000		
Total current liabilities		$ 14,000	
Long-term notes payable		52,000	
Total liabilities....................................			$ 66,000

Owner's Equity

Stanley Hanson, capital	169,500
Total liabilities and owner's equity	$235,500

Exercise 5-21 (10 minutes)

Reversing entries are appropriate for adjustments (a) and (e):

2005

Sept. 1	Service Fees Earned	5,000	
	Accounts Receivable..............................		5,000
	To reverse accrued revenues.		
1	Salaries Payable..................................	2,400	
	Salaries Expense		2,400
	To reverse accrued salaries.		

*Exercise 5-22 (30 minutes)

1.   Adjusting entries:

2005

Oct. 31	Rent Expense..	3,200	
	Rent Payable		3,200
	To record accrued rent expense.		
31	Rent Receivable..	750	
	Rent Earned..		750
	To record accrued rent revenue.		

2.   Subsequent entries without reversing:

Nov. 5	Rent Payable..	3,200	
	Rent Expense...	3,200	
	Cash...		6,400
	To record payment of two months' rent.		
8	Cash	1,500	
	Rent Receivable		750
	Rent Earned..		750
	To record collection of two months' rent.		

3.   Reversing entries and subsequent entries:

Nov. 1	Rent Payable..	3,200	
	Rent Expense		3,200
	To reverse the accrual of rent expense.		
1	Rent Earned	750	
	Rent Receivable		750
	To reverse the accrual of rent revenue.		
5	Rent Expense..	6,400	
	Cash...		6,400
	To record payment of two months' rent.		
8	Cash	1,500	
	Rent Earned..		1,500
	To record collection of two months' rent.		

*Exercise 5-23 (15 minutes)

	Current Assets		Current Liabilities		Current Ratio	F/U
Case 1	$ 78,000	/	$31,000	=	2.52	F
Case 2	104,000	/	75,000	=	1.39	F
Case 3	44,000	/	48,000	=	0.92	U
Case 4	84,500	/	80,600	=	1.05	U

Landmark Tours
Work Sheet
For Month Ended July 31, 2005

Account Number	Account	Unadjusted Trial Balance Debit	Unadjusted Trial Balance Credit	Adjustments Debit	Adjustments Credit	Adjusted Trial Balance Debit	Adjusted Trial Balance Credit	Income Statement Debit	Income Statement Credit	Balance Sheet & Statement of Owner's Equity Debit	Balance Sheet & Statement of Owner's Equity Credit
101	Cash	17,800				17,800				17,800	
106	Accounts receivable	42,500		(g) 23,800		66,300				66,300	
111	Notes receivable	28,000				28,000				28,000	
128	Prepaid insurance	21,000			(d) 2,625	18,375				18,375	
161	Furniture	13,500				13,500				13,500	
201	Accounts payable		13,850		(b) 650		14,500				14,500
230	Unearned tour revenue		28,000	(f) 18,200			9,800				9,800
301	Jan Rider, capital		121,950				121,950				121,950
302	Jan Rider, withdrawals	0				0				0	
403	Tour revenue		31,000		(f) 18,200 (g)23,800**		73,000		73,000		
623	Wages expense	72,000		(e) 1,008		73,008		73,008			
	Totals	194,800	194,800								
109	Interest receivable			(a) 400		400				400	
409	Interest revenue				(a) 400		400		400		
690	Utility expense			(b) 650		650		650			
601	Amortization expense, furniture			(c) 350		350		350			
162	Accumulated amortization, furniture				(c) 350		350				350
637	Insurance expense			(d) 2,625		2,625		2,625			
210	Wages payable			(e) 1,008	(e) 1,008*		1,008				1,008
	Totals			47,033	47,033	221,008	221,008	76,633	73,400	144,375	147,608
	Net loss								3,233	3,233	
	Totals							76,633	76,633	147,608	147,608

*$630/5 days per week = $126/day × 2 days × 4 employees = $1,008

**40 children × $35/day × 17 days = $23,800

Fundamental Accounting Principles, Eleventh Canadian Edition

Problem 5-2B (25 minutes)

Parts 1, 2, and 3

Family Photographers
Work Sheet
For Month Ended December 31, 2005

Account	Unadjusted Trial Balance Debit	Unadjusted Trial Balance Credit	Adjustments Debit	Adjustments Credit	Adjusted Trial Balance Debit	Adjusted Trial Balance Credit	Income Statement Debit	Income Statement Credit	Balance Sheet & Statement of Owner's Equity Debit	Balance Sheet & Statement of Owner's Equity Credit
Cash	14,000				14,000				14,000	
Accounts receivable	3,100				3,100				3,100	
Prepaid equipment rental	1,930			a) 1,240	690				690	
Automobile	26,000				26,000				26,000	
Accumulated amort., automobile		0		b) 275		275				275
Accounts payable		960		c) 980		1,940				1,940
Unearned fees		2,870	d) 250			2,620				2,620
Jim Tucker, capital		39,400				39,400				39,400
Jim Tucker, withdrawals	700				700				700	
Fees earned		4,200		d) 250		4,450		4,450		
Amort., expense, automobile	0		b) 275		275		275			
Equipment rental expense	1,700		a) 1,240		2,940		2,940			
Utilities expense			c) 980		980		980			
Totals	47,430	47,430	2,745	2,745	48,685	48,685	4,195	4,450	44,490	44,235
Net income							255			255
Totals							4,450	4,450	44,490	44,490

Part 4

$$\$39{,}400 - \$700 + \$255 = \$38{,}955 \quad \text{OR}$$

	Jim Tucker, Capital	
(With.) 700	39,400	(Beg. bal.)
	255	(Net income)
	38,955	(End. bal.)

Problem 5-3B (90 minutes) Part 1

BOOMER DEMOLITION COMPANY
Work Sheet
For Year Ended June 30, 2005

No.	Title	Unadjusted Trial Balance Debit	Unadjusted Trial Balance Credit	Adjustments Debit	Adjustments Credit	Adjusted Trial Balance Debit	Adjusted Trial Balance Credit	Income Statement Debit	Income Statement Credit	Balance Sheet and Statement of Owner's Equity Debit	Balance Sheet and Statement of Owner's Equity Credit
101	Cash	9,000				9,000				9,000	
126	Supplies	18,000			(a) 9,900	8,100				8,100	
128	Prepaid insurance	14,600			(b) 11,500	3,100				3,100	
167	Equipment	140,000				140,000				140,000	
168	Accumulated amort., equipment		10,000		(c) 18,000		28,000				28,000
201	Accounts payable		16,000		(d) 700		16,700				16,700
203	Interest payable				(f) 200		200				200
210	Wages payable				(e) 2,200		2,200				2,200
251	Long-term notes payable		90,000				90,000				90,000
301	Rusty Boomer, capital		66,900				66,900				66,900
302	Rusty Boomer, withdrawals	4,000				4,000				4,000	
401	Demolition fees earned		137,000				137,000		137,000		
612	Amortization expense, equipment			(c) 18,000		18,000		18,000			
623	Wages expense	51,400		(e) 2,200		53,600		53,600			
633	Interest expense	2,200		(f) 200		2,400		2,400			
637	Insurance expense			(b) 11,500		11,500		11,500			
640	Rent expense	48,800				48,800		48,800			
652	Supplies expense			(a) 9,900		9,900		9,900			
683	Business tax expense	8,400				8,400		8,400			
684	Repairs expense	6,700				6,700		6,700			
690	Utilities expense	16,800		(d) 700		17,500		17,500			
	Totals	319,900	319,900	42,500	42,500	341,000	341,000	176,800	137,000	164,200	204,000
	Net loss								39,800	39,800	
	Totals							176,800	177,000	204,000	204,000

Problem 5-3B *(continued) Part 2*

	2005		*Adjusting entries:*		
(a)	June	30	Supplies Expense..	9,900	
			Supplies		9,900
			To record consumption of supplies.		
(b)		30	Insurance Expense..	11,500	
			Prepaid Insurance		11,500
			To record consumption of insurance coverage.		
(c)		30	Amortization Expense, Equipment..........................	18,000	
			Accumulated Amortization, Equipment...........		18,000
			To record amortization.		
(d)		30	Utilities Expense..	700	
			Accounts Payable...		700
			To record accrued utilities costs.		
(e)		30	Wages Expense	2,200	
			Wages Payable		2,200
			To record accrued wages.		
(f)		30	Interest Expense	200	
			Interest Payable..		200
			To record accrued interest expense.		

Fundamental Accounting Principles, Eleventh Canadian Edition

Problem 5-3B *(continued) Part 2*

2005   *Closing entries:*

June 30	Demolition Fees Earned	137,000	
	Income Summary		137,000
	To close the revenue account.		
30	Income Summary	176,800	
	Amortization Expense, Equipment		18,000
	Wages Expense		53,600
	Interest Expense		2,400
	Insurance Expense		11,500
	Rent Expense		48,800
	Supplies Expense		9,900
	Business Tax Expense		8,400
	Repairs Expense		6,700
	Utilities Expense		17,500
	To close the expense accounts.		
30	Rusty Boomer, Capital	39,800	
	Income Summary		39,800
	To close the Income Summary account.		
30	Rusty Boomer, Capital	4,000	
	Rusty Boomer, Withdrawals		4,000
	To close the withdrawals account.		

Part 3

BOOMER DEMOLITION COMPANY
Income Statement
For Year Ended June 30, 2005

Revenue:		
Demolition fees earned		$137,000
Operating expenses:		
Wages expense	$53,600	
Rent expense	48,800	
Amortization expense, equipment	18,000	
Utilities expense	17,500	
Insurance expense	11,500	
Supplies expense	9,900	
Business tax expense	8,400	
Repairs expense	6,700	
Interest expense	2,400	
Total operating expenses		176,800
Net loss		$ 39,800

Problem 5-3B *(continued) Part 3*

BOOMER DEMOLITION COMPANY
Statement of Owner's Equity
For Year Ended June 30, 2005

Rusty Boomer, capital, July 1		$ 36,900
Add: Investments by owner		30,000
Total		$ 66,900
Less: Withdrawals by owner	$ 4,000	
Net loss	39,800	43,800
Rusty Boomer, capital, June 30		$ 23,100

BOOMER DEMOLITION COMPANY
Balance Sheet
June 30, 2005

Assets

Current assets:			
Cash		$ 9,000	
Supplies		8,100	
Prepaid insurance		3,100	
Total current assets			$ 20,200
Property, plant and equipment:			
Equipment		$140,000	
Less: Accumulated amortization, equipment		28,000	112,000
Total assets			$132,200

Liabilities

Current liabilities:			
Accounts payable	$16,700		
Interest payable	200		
Wages payable	2,200		
Current portion of long-term note payable	4,000		
Total current liabilities		$ 23,100	
Long-term liabilities:			
Long-term note payable (less current portion)		86,000	
Total liabilities			$109,100

Owner's Equity

Rusty Boomer, capital			23,100
Total liabilities and owner's equity			$132,200

Fundamental Accounting Principles, Eleventh Canadian Edition

Problem 5-3B *(concluded) Part 4*

(a)   This error enters the wrong amount in the correct accounts. The ending balance of the Prepaid Insurance account should be $3,100, but the entry reduces that account by $3,100. Because its unadjusted balance was $14,600, the adjusted balance will be $11,500 (= $14,600 – $3,100), which is $8,400 greater than the correct $3,100 balance. In addition, the Insurance Expense account balance will be only $3,100 instead of $11,500.

The adjusted trial balance columns in the work sheet will be equal, but the error will cause the work sheet's net income to be overstated by $8,400 because of the understatement of the expense. In addition, the balance sheet columns will include the overstated balance for the Prepaid Insurance account. The Rusty Boomer, Capital account will also be overstated.

This error is not likely to be detected as a result of completing the work sheet. If it is not, the income statement will overstate net income by $8,400, and the balance sheet will overstate the cost of the unexpired insurance and owner's equity by $8,400.

(b)   This error inserts a debit in the balance sheet columns instead of the income statement columns. In the unlikely event that this error is not immediately detected, it will cause the work sheet measure of net income to be overstated because the total debits will incorrectly omit the $6,700 expense for repairs.

In all likelihood, the error will be discovered in the process of drafting the balance sheet because the accountant will realize that repairs expense is not an asset. If it is detected and corrected, the financial statements will be unaffected. However, if the repairs expense is erroneously included on the balance sheet, the reported net income will be overstated by $6,700. On the balance sheet, a nonexistent asset will be reported for the repairs expense and owner's equity will be overstated by $6,700.

Problem 5-4B (25 minutes)

Part 1

2005		*Closing* entries:		
Dec. 31	Sewing Fees Earned...		62,000	
	Income Summary			62,000
	To close the revenue.			
31	Income Summary...		38,060	
	Amortization Expense, Equipment			3,000
	Wages Expense...			28,400
	Insurance Expense...			1,100
	Rent Expense...			2,400
	Store Supplies Expense.................................			1,300
	Utilities Expense...			1,860
	To close the expense accounts.			
31	Income Summary...		23,940	
	Anne Taylor, Capital......................................			23,940
	To close the Income Summary account.			
31	Anne Taylor, Capital...		16,000	
	Anne Taylor, Withdrawals			16,000
	To close the withdrawals account.			

Part 2

Anne's Tailoring Services
Post-Closing Trial Balance
December 31, 2005

Acct. No.	Account	Debit	Credit
101	Cash..	$13,450	
125	Store supplies.....................................	4,140	
128	Prepaid insurance................................	2,200	
167	Equipment	33,000	
168	Accumulated amortization, equipment.......		$ 9,000
201	Accounts payable.................................		1,000
210	Wages payable....................................		3,200
301	Anne Taylor, capital*		39,590
	Totals..	$52,790	$52,790

Beginning capital $31,650 + Net income $23,940 – Withdrawals $16,000 = Ending capital $39,590

Fundamental Accounting Principles, Eleventh Canadian Edition

Problem 5-5B (90 minutes) *Part 1*

ANNE'S TAILORING SERVICES
Income Statement
For Year Ended December 31, 2005

Revenue:		
Sewing fees earned		$62,000
Operating expenses:		
Wages expense..	$28,400	
Amortization expense, equipment	3,000	
Rent expense	2,400	
Utilities expense	1,860	
Store supplies expense....................................	1,300	
Insurance expense	1,100	
Total operating expenses.............................		38,060
Net income..		$23,940

ANNE'S TAILORING SERVICES
Statement of Owner's Equity
For Year Ended December 31, 2005

Anne Taylor, capital, January 1............................	$31,650
Add: Net income..	23,940
Total	$55,590
Less: Withdrawals...	16,000
Anne Taylor, capital, December 31	$39,590

Problem 5-5B *(concluded)*

ANNE'S TAILORING SERVICES
Balance Sheet
December 31, 2005

Assets
Current assets:

Cash	$13,450	
Store supplies	4,140	
Prepaid insurance	2,200	
Total current assets		$19,790

Property, plant and equipment:

Equipment	$33,000	
Less: Accumulated amortization	9,000	24,000
Total assets		$43,790

Liabilities
Current liabilities:

Accounts payable	$ 1,000	
Wages payable	3,200	
Total current liabilities		$ 4,200

Owner's Equity

Anne Taylor, capital	39,590
Total liabilities and owner's equity	$43,790

Fundamental Accounting Principles, Eleventh Canadian Edition

Problem 5-6B (25 minutes)

2005		*Closing entries:*		
Dec. 31	Photography Fees Earned		47,000	
	Dividends Earned.................................		500	
	Income Summary................................			47,500
	To close the revenue account.			
31	Income Summary...................................		26,266	
	Amortization Expense, Building			2,000
	Amortization Expense, Equipment			1,000
	Amortization Expense, franchise			500
	Wages Expense.....................................			17,000
	Interest Expense....................................			1,200
	Insurance Expense..................................			1,425
	Supplies Expense...................................			900
	Telephone Expense.................................			421
	Utilities Expense....................................			1,820
	To close expense accounts.			
31	Income Summary...................................		21,234	
	Bea Jones, Capital................................			21,234
	To close the income summary to capital.			
31	Bea Jones, Capital.................................		6,000	
	Bea Jones, Withdrawals			6,000
	To close withdrawals to capital.			

Problem 5-7B (50 minutes)

BEA'S PHOTO STUDIO
Income Statement
For Year Ended December 31, 2005

Revenues:		
Photography fees earned................................	$47,000	
Dividends earned..	500	
Total revenues..		$47,500
Operating expenses:		
Wages expense..	$17,000	
Amortization expense, building......................	2,000	
Utilities expense	1,820	
Insurance expense	1,425	
Interest expense	1,200	
Amortization expense, equipment	1,000	
Supplies expense	900	
Amortization expense, franchise....................	500	
Telephone expense	421	
Total operating expenses.........................		26,266
Net income..		$21,234

BEA'S PHOTO STUDIO
Statement of Owner's Equity
For Year Ended December 31, 2005

Bea Jones, capital, January 1..........................		$67,316
Add: Investments by owner.............................	$ 20,000	
Net income..	21,234	41,234
Total		$108,550
Less: Withdrawals..		6,000
Bea Jones, capital, December 31		$102,550

Fundamental Accounting Principles, Eleventh Canadian Edition

Problem 5-7B *(concluded)*

BEA'S PHOTO STUDIO
Balance Sheet
December 31, 2005

Assets

Current assets:

Cash...		$ 6,400
Temporary investments		10,200
Supplies..		3,600
Total current assets...			$20,200

Long-term investments:

Notes receivable	35,000

Property, plant and equipment:

Land		$ 28,500	
Building	$60,000		
Less: Accumulated amortization	29,000	31,000	
Equipment	$18,000		
Less: Accumulated amortization	3,000	15,000	
Total property, plant and equipment..................			74,500

Intangible assets:

Franchise...	8,000
Total assets..	$137,700

Liabilities

Current liabilities:

Accounts payable...	$ 2,500	
Unearned professional fees	650	
Current portion of long-term notes payable	6,400	
Total current liabilities..		$ 9,550

Long-term liabilities:

Long-term notes payable (less current portion)	25,600
Total liabilities..	$35,150

Owner's Equity

Bea Jones, capital..	102,550
Total liabilities and owner's equity	$137,700

Problem 5-8B (20 minutes)

2005		*Closing entries:*		
Dec.	31	Consulting Fees Earned	97,000	
		Dividends Earned..	2,300	
		Income Summary		99,300
		To close the revenue accounts.		
	31	Income Summary	108,310	
		Amortization Expense, Equipment		2,000
		Amortization Expense, Office Furniture..........		900
		Amortization Expense, Copyright....................		500
		Insurance Expense...		1,200
		Interest Expense..		720
		Supplies Expense		4,300
		Telephone Expense..		940
		Utilities Expense		21,750
		Wages Expense..		76,000
		To close expense accounts.		
	31	Abby Dehara, Capital	9,010	
		Income Summary		9,010
		To close the income summary to capital.		
	31	Abby Dehara, Capital	8,000	
		Abby Dehara, Withdrawals		8,000
		To close withdrawals to capital.		

Fundamental Accounting Principles, Eleventh Canadian Edition

Problem 5-9B (40 minutes)

Wellness Consulting Services
Income Statement
For Year Ended December 31, 2005

Revenues:		
Consulting fees earned	$97,000	
Dividends earned	2,300	
Total revenues		$ 99,300
Operating expenses:		
Wages expense	$76,000	
Utilities expense...	21,750	
Supplies expense..	4,300	
Amortization expense, equipment...............................	2,000	
Insurance expense..	1,200	
Telephone expense...	940	
Amortization expense, office furniture.........................	900	
Interest expense...	720	
Amortization expense, copyright	500	
Total operating expenses		108,310
Net loss..		$ 9,010

Problem 5-9B (concluded)

Wellness Consulting Services
Statement of Owner's Equity
For Year Ended December 31, 2005

Abby Dehara, capital, April 1		$61,360
Less: Withdrawals by owner..	$8,000	
Net loss..	9,010	17,010
Abby Dehara, capital, March 31		$44,350

Wellness Consulting Services
Balance Sheet
December 31, 2005

Assets
Current assets:

Cash...	$ 3,500	
Temporary investments	14,000	
Supplies...	1,500	
Current portion of notes receivable	3,000	
Total current assets...		$22,000

Long-term investments:

Notes receivable (less $3,000 current portion)..	7,000

Property, plant and equipment:

Equipment	$32,000	
Less: Accumulated amortization........................	17,000	$15,000
Office furniture...	10,200	
Less: Accumulated amortization........................	6,900	3,300
Total property, plant and equipment....................		18,300

Intangible assets:

Copyright...	7,000
Total assets	**$54,300**

Liabilities
Current liabilities:

Accounts payable	$ 1,200	
Unearned professional fees....................................	750	
Current portion of long-term notes payable........	5,000	
Total current liabilities		$ 6,950

Long-term liabilities: ....

Long-term notes payable (less current portion) ...	3,000	
Total liabilities..		$ 9,950

Owner's Equity

Abby Dehara, capital	44,350
Total liabilities and owner's equity	$54,300

Problem 5-10B (20 minutes)

1.

Enviro Gardening Services
Income Statement
For Year Ended October 31, 2005

Revenues:		
Service revenue		$74,000
Operating expenses:		
Wages expense	$56,000	
Supplies expense	12,400	
Amortization expense, vehicles	5,300	
Amortization expense, gardening equipment	4,800	
Fuel expense	4,600	
Insurance expense	3,600	
Utilities expense	900	
Telephone expense	850	
Interest expense	680	
Total operating expenses		89,130
Net loss		$15,130

Grant Craig, Capital

			38,000	(Beg. bal.)
2. $38,000 – $15,130 – $5,000 = $17,870 OR	(Net loss)	15,130		
	(With.)	5,000		
			17,870	(End. bal.)

Problem 5-11B (50 minutes)

TelsCo Drill Servicing
Income Statement
For Year Ended August 31, 2005

Revenues:		
Drill servicing revenue	$106,000	
Interest earned	1,300	
Total revenues		$107,300
Operating expenses:		
Wages expense	$ 71,000	
Insurance expense	8,340	
Telephone expense	1,400	
Amortization expense, furniture	1,030	
Utilities expense	230	
Total operating expenses		82,000
Net income		$ 25,300

Problem 5-11B *(concluded)*

TelsCo Drill Servicing
Statement of Owner's Equity
For Year Ended August 31, 2005

Angela Telsco, capital, September 1		$24,210
Add: Owner investments	$25,000	
Net income	25,300	50,300
Total		$74,510
Less: Withdrawals by owner		17,000
Angela Telsco, capital, August 31, 2005		$57,510

TelsCo Drill Servicing
Balance Sheet
August 31, 2005

Assets

Current assets:		
Cash	$10,000	
Accounts receivable	28,000	
Interest receivable	140	
Office supplies	850	
Total current assets		$38,990
Long-term investments:		
Investment in Nortel shares		29,000
Property, plant and equipment:		
Furniture	$38,000	
Less: Accumulated amortization	21,750	$16,250
Intangible assets:		
Franchise		6,320
Total assets		$90,560

Liabilities

Current liabilities:		
Accounts payable	$14,950	
Short-term notes payable	1,600	
Unearned servicing revenue	2,500	
Current portion of long-term notes payable	9,000	
Total current liabilities		$28,050
Long-term liabilities:		
Long-term notes payable (less current portion)		5,000
Total liabilities		$33,050

Owner's Equity

Angela Telsco, capital		57,510
Total liabilities and owner's equity		$90,560

Problem 5-12B (30 minutes)

Part 1

Jan Rider, capital = $121,950 - $3,233* = $\underline{118,717}$ OR

Jan Rider, Capital	
	121,950
3,233*	
	118,717

*Net loss = Revenues – Expenses
= (73,000 + 400) – (350 + 2,625 + 650 + 73,008)
= 73,400 – 76,633
= 3,233 net loss

Part 2

Landmark Tours
Balance Sheet
July 31, 2005

Assets

Current assets:

Cash	$17,800	
Accounts receivable	66,300	
Interest receivable	400	
Notes receivable	28,000	
Prepaid insurance	18,375	
Total current assets		$130,875

Property, plant and equipment:

Furniture	$13,500	
Less: Accumulated amortization	350	13,150
Total assets		$144,025

Liabilities

Current liabilities:

Accounts payable	$14,500	
Wages payable	1,008	
Unearned tour revenue	9,800	
Total liabilities		$ 25,308

Owner's Equity

Jan Rider, capital	118,717
Total liabilities and owner's equity	$144,025

Problem 5-13B (90 minutes)

NOTE: The general ledger accounts are shown at the end of the solution (in both balance column and T-account format) as they would appear after all entries have been posted.

Part 2
Transactions for July:

Date 2005	General Journal Account Titles and Explanations	PR	Debit	Page G1 Credit
July 1	Cash	101	20,000	
	Buildings...	173	120,000	
	Cindy Tucker, Capital	301		140,000
	Owner invested in the business.			
2	Equipment Rental Expense.......................	640	1,800	
	Cash..	101		1,800
	Paid one month's rent.			
5	Office Supplies...	124	2,300	
	Cash..	101		2,300
	Acquired office supplies.			
10	Prepaid Insurance.....................................	128	5,400	
	Cash..	101		5,400
	Paid one year's premium in advance.			
14	Salaries Expense..	622	900	
	Cash..	101		900
	Paid two weeks' salary.			
24	Cash	101	8,800	
	Storage Fees Earned	401		8,800
	Collected fees from customers.			
28	Salaries Expense..	622	900	
	Cash..	101		900
	Paid two weeks' salary.			
29	Telephone Expense	688	300	
	Cash..	101		300
	Paid the telephone bill.			
30	Repairs Expense	684	850	
	Cash..	101		850
	Repaired the roof.			
31	Cindy Tucker, Withdrawals	302	1,600	
	Cash..	101		1,600
	Owner withdrew cash.			

Fundamental Accounting Principles, Eleventh Canadian Edition

Part 3

General Journal   Page G2

Date	Account Titles and Explanations	PR	Debit	Credit
2005	*Adjusting entries:*			
July 31	Insurance Expense.............................	637	300	
	Prepaid Insurance.........................	128		300
	To record expired insurance			
	($5,400/12 = $450/month; 2/3 × $450 per month).			
31	Office Supplies Expense	650	750	
	Office Supplies.............................	124		750
	To record the cost of consumed supplies			
	($2,300 – $1,550).			
31	Amortization Expense, Buildings	606	1,200	
	Accumulated Amortization, Buildings	174		1,200
	To record amortization.			
31	Salaries Expense.............................	622	180	
	Salaries Payable...........................	209		180
	To record accrued salaries.			
31	Accounts Receivable	106	950	
	Storage Fees Earned	401		950
	To record accrued storage fees.			

Part 4

LOCKIT CO.
Income Statement
For Month Ended July 31, 2005

Revenue:		
Storage fees earned		$9,750
Operating expenses:		
Salaries expense.....................................	$1,980	
Equipment rental expense	1,800	
Amortization expense, buildings.....................	1,200	
Repairs expense	850	
Office supplies expense..............................	750	
Insurance expense	300	
Telephone expense	300	
Total operating expenses.........................		7,180
Net income..		**$2,570**

LOCKIT CO.
Statement of Owner's Equity
For Month Ended July 31, 2005

Cinty Tucker, capital, July 1		$ 0
Add: Investments by owner	$140,000	
Net income...	2,570	$142,570
Total...		$142,570
Less: Withdrawals by owner		1,600
Cindy Tucker, capital, July 31		$140,970

LOCKIT CO.
Balance Sheet
July 31, 2005

Assets

Current assets:		
Cash	$ 14,750	
Accounts receivable	950	
Office supplies	1,550	
Prepaid insurance	5,100	
Total current assets		$ 22,350
Property, plant and equipment:		
Buildings...	$120,000	
Less: Accumulated amortization............................	1,200	118,800
Total assets		$141,150

Liabilities

Current liabilities:		
Salaries payable		$ 180

Owner's Equity

Cindy Tucker, capital...		140,970
Total liabilities and owner's equity		$141,150

Fundamental Accounting Principles, Eleventh Canadian Edition

Problem 5-13B (continued) Part 5

	General Journal			Page G3
Date	Account Titles and Explanations	PR	Debit	Credit
2005	*Closing entries:*			
July 31	Storage Fees Earned...............................	401	9,750	
	Income Summary	901		9,750
	To close the revenue account.			
31	Income summary..	901	7,180	
	Amortization Expense, Buildings	606		1,200
	Salaries Expense	622		1,980
	Insurance Expense	637		300
	Equipment Rental Expense................	640		1,800
	Office Supplies Expense	650		750
	Repairs Expense	684		850
	Telephone Expense	688		300
	To close the expense accounts.			
31	Income Summary	901	2,570	
	Cindy Tucker, Capital	301		2,570
	To close the Income Summary account.			
31	Cindy Tucker, Capital.............................	301	1,600	
	Cindy Tucker, Withdrawals	302		1,600
	To close the withdrawals account.			

Part 6

LOCKIT CO.
Post-Closing Trial Balance
July 31, 2005

Acct. No.	Account	Debit	Credit
101	Cash	$ 14,750	
106	Accounts receivable	950	
124	Office supplies	1,550	
128	Prepaid insurance	5,100	
173	Buildings...	120,000	
174	Accumulated amortization, buildings.......		$ 1,200
209	Salaries payable		180
301	Cindy Tucker, capital		140,970
	Totals...	$142,350	$142,350

Problem 5-13B *(continued)*

Parts 1, 2, 3, 5:

Ledger as of July 31 (using balance column format):

Cash — Acct. No. 101

Date	Explanation	PR	Debit	Credit	Balance
2005					
July 1		G1	20,000		20,000
2		G1		1,800	18,200
5		G1		2,300	15,900
10		G1		5,400	10,500
14		G1		900	9,600
24		G1	8,800		18,400
28		G1		900	17,500
29		G1		300	17,200
30		G1		850	16,350
31		G1		1,600	14,750

Accounts Receivable — Acct. No. 106

Date	Explanation	PR	Debit	Credit	Balance
2005					
July 31		G2	950		950

Office Supplies — Acct. No. 124

Date	Explanation	PR	Debit	Credit	Balance
2005					
July 5		G1	2,300		2,300
31		G2		750	1,550

Prepaid Insurance — Acct. No. 128

Date	Explanation	PR	Debit	Credit	Balance
2005					
July 10		G1	5,400		5,400
31		G2		300	5,100

Buildings — Acct. No. 173

Date	Explanation	PR	Debit	Credit	Balance
2005					
July 1		G1	120,000		120,000

Accumulated Amortization, Buildings — Acct. No. 174

Date	Explanation	PR	Debit	Credit	Balance
2005					
July 31		G2		1,200	1,200

Salaries Payable — Acct. No. 209

Date	Explanation	PR	Debit	Credit	Balance
2005					
July 31		G2		180	180

Cindy Tucker, Capital — Acct. No. 301

Date	Explanation	PR	Debit	Credit	Balance
2005					
July 1		G1		140,000	140,000
31		G3		2,570	142,570
31		G3	1,600		140,970

Cindy Tucker, Withdrawals — Acct. No. 302

Date	Explanation	PR	Debit	Credit	Balance
2005					
July 31		G1	1,600		1,600
31		G3		1,600	0

Storage Fees Earned — Acct.No. 401

Date	Explanation	PR	Debit	Credit	Balance
2005					
July 24		G1		8,800	8,800
31		G2		950	9,750
31		G3	9,750		0

Amortization Expense, Buildings — Acct. No. 606

Date	Explanation	PR	Debit	Credit	Balance
2005					
July 31		G2	1,200		1,200
31		G3		1,200	0

Salaries Expense — Acct. No. 622

Date	Explanation	PR	Debit	Credit	Balance
2005					
July 14		G1	900		900
28		G1	900		1,800
31		G2	180		1,980
31		G3		1,980	0

Insurance Expense — Acct. No. 637

Date	Explanation	PR	Debit	Credit	Balance
2005					
July 31		G2	300		300
31		G3		300	0

Problem 5-13B (concluded)

Equipment Rental Expense   Acct. No. 640

Date	Explanation	PR	Debit	Credit	Balance
2005					
July 2		G1	1,800		1,800
31		G3		1,800	0

Office Supplies Expense   Acct. No. 650

Date	Explanation	PR	Debit	Credit	Balance
2005					
July 31		G2	750		750
31		G3		750	0

Repairs Expense   Acct. No. 684

Date	Explanation	PR	Debit	Credit	Balance
2005					
July 30		G1	850		850
31		G3		850	0

Telephone Expense   Acct. No. 688

Date	Explanation	PR	Debit	Credit	Balance
2005					
July 29		G1	300		300
31		G3		300	0

Income Summary   Acct. No. 901

Date	Explanation	PR	Debit	Credit	Balance
2005					
July 31		G3		9,750	9,750
31		G3	7,180		2,570
31		G3	2,570		0

Problem 5-13B (continued) Parts 1, 2, 3, 5

Ledger as of July 31 (using the T-account format):

Cash   101

Jul	1	20,000	Jul	2	1,800
	24	8,800		5	2,300
				10	5,400
				14	900
				28	900
				29	300
				30	850
				31	1,600
Bal.		14,750			

Accounts Receivable   106

Jul 31	950	

Office Supplies   124

Jul 5	2,300	Jul 31	750
Bal.	1,550		

Prepaid Insurance   128

Jul 10	5,400	Jul 31	300
Bal.	5,100		

Buildings   173

Jul 1	120,000	

Accum. Amort., Building   174

	Jul 31	1,200

Salaries Payable   209

	Jul 31	180

Cindy Tucker, Capital   301

Jul 31	1,600	Jul 1	140,000
		31	2,570
		Bal.	140,970

Cindy Tucker, Withdrawals   302

Jul 31	1,600	Jul 31	1,600
Bal.	-0-		

Problem 5-13B (continued) Parts 1, 2, 3, 5

Storage Fees Earned 401

Jul 31	9,750	Jul 24	8,800
		Jul 31	950
		-0-	Bal.

Amort. Expense, Building 606

Jul 31	1,200	Jul 31	1,200
Bal.	-0-		

Salaries Expense 622

Jul 14	900	Jul 31	1,980
28	900		
31	180		
Bal.	-0-		

Insurance Expense 637

Jul 31	300	Jul 31	300
Bal.	-0-		

Equipment Rental Expense 640

Jul 2	1,800	Jul 31	1,800
Bal.	-0-		

Office Supplies Expense 650

Jul 31	750	Jul 31	750
Bal.	-0-		

Repairs Expense 684

Jul 30	850	Jul 31	850
Bal.	-0-		

Telephone Expense 688

Jul 29	300	Jul 31	300
Bal.	-0-		

Income Summary 901

Jul 31	7,180	Jul 31	9,750
31	2,570	2,570	Bal.
		-0-	Bal.

Fundamental Accounting Principles, Eleventh Canadian Edition

*Problem 5-14B (30 minutes)

Part 1

	2005		*Adjusting entries:*		
a)	Dec.	31	Salaries Expense.......................................	5,250	
			Salaries Payable....................................		5,250
			To record accrued salaries.		
b)		31	Rent Receivable.......................................	675	
			Rent Revenue		675
			To record accrued rent revenue;		
			$1,125 – $450.		
c)		31	Office Supplies Expense...........................	3,525	
			Office Supplies		3,525
			To record supplies used;		
			$4,200 – $675 left on hand = $3,525 used.		
d)		31	Insurance Expense...................................	450	
			Insurance Payable................................		450
			To record insurance payable.		
e)		31	Interest Expense	2,250	
			Interest Payable....................................		2,250
			To record accrued interest;		
			$900 + $900 + $450.		
f)		31	Unearned Service Fees	11,700	
			Service Fees Earned		11,700
			To record fees earned;		
			$18,000 – $6,300 still unearned = $11,700 earned.		
g)		31	Interest Receivable...................................	175	
			Interest Revenue		175
			To record accrued interest.		
h)		31	Accounts Receivable	8,250	
			Service Fees Earned		8,250
			To record accrued service fees.		

*Problem 5-14B *(continued)*
Part 2

2006		Reversing entries:		
Jan.	1	Salaries Payable..	5,250	
		Salaries Expense....................................		5,250
		To reverse accrued salaries.		
	1	Rent Revenue	675	
		Rent Receivable		675
		To reverse accrued rent revenue.		
	1	Insurance Payable..	450	
		Insurance Expense		450
		To reverse accrued insurance.		
	1	Interest Payable...	2,250	
		Interest Expense		2,250
		To reverse accrued interest expense.		
	1	Interest Revenue	175	
		Interest Receivable		175
		To reverse accrued interest revenue.		
	1	Service Fees Earned	8,250	
		Accounts Receivable...............................		8,250
		To reverse accrued service fees.		

Part 3
January 2006 transactions:

2006				
Jan.	4	Salaries Expense...	7,500	
		Cash		7,500
		To record payment of salaries.		
	12	Cash	1,800	
		Rent Revenue		1,800
		To record receipt of rent revenue; $675 + $1,125.		
	12	Insurance Expense..	450	
		Cash		450
		To record payment of insurance.		

Fundamental Accounting Principles, Eleventh Canadian Edition

*Problem 5-14B *Part 3 (concluded)*

2006

Jan.	15	Interest Expense	2,700	
		Cash		2,700
		To record payment of interest.		
	22	Cash	38,075	
		Note Receivable		37,500
		Interest Revenue		575
		To record receipt of note plus interest; $37,500 + $575.		
	24	Cash	11,350	
		Service Fees Earned		11,350
		To record receipt of service fees; $8,250 + $3,100.		

EXERCISES

Exercise 6-1 (15 minutes)

	a	b	c	d
Sales	$ 240,000	$ 75,000	$462,000	$85,000
Cost of goods sold	126,000	42,000	268,000	46,000
Gross profit from sales	$ 114,000	$33,000	$194,000	$ 39,000
Operating expenses..........................	95,000	41,000	146,000	53,000
Net Income (Loss).............................	$ 19,000	($ 8,000)	$ 48,000	($ 14,000)

Exercise 6-3 (30 minutes)

2005

Mar.	2	Merchandise Inventory	3,600	
		Accounts Payable — Blanton Company ...		3,600
		Purchased merchandise on credit.		
	3	Merchandise Inventory	200	
		Cash		200
		Paid shipping charges on purchased merchandise.		
	4	Accounts Payable — Blanton Company	600	
		Merchandise Inventory		600
		Returned unacceptable merchandise.		
	17	Accounts Payable — Blanton Company	3,000	
		Merchandise Inventory		60
		Cash		2,940
		Paid balance within the discount period; 3,600 – 600 = 3,000; 3,000 x 2% = 60.		
	18	Merchandise Inventory	7,500	
		Accounts Payable — Fleming Corp.		7,500
		Purchased merchandise on credit.		
	21	Accounts Payable — Fleming Corp.	2,100	
		Merchandise Inventory		2,100
		Received an allowance on purchase.		
	28	Accounts Payable — Fleming Corp.	5,400	
		Merchandise Inventory		108
		Cash		5,292
		Paid balance within the discount period; 7,500 – 2,100 = 5,400; 5,400 x 2% = 108.		

Exercise 6-5 (30 minutes)

Feb.	1	Accounts Receivable..	2,400	
		Sales		2,400
		To record sale; terms 2/10, n30, FOB destination.		
	1	Cost of Goods Sold	2,000	
		Merchandise Inventory.....................................		2,000
		To record cost of sales.		
	2	Delivery Expense or Freight-Out............................	150	
		Cash..		150
		To record delivery expenses for goods sold.		
	3	Sales Returns and Allowances...............................	1,200	
		Accounts Receivable..		1,200
		To record return of merchandise.		
	3	Merchandise Inventory..	1,000	
		Cost of Goods Sold		1,000
		To return merchandise to inventory.		
	4	Accounts Receivable...	3,800	
		Sales		3,800
		To record sale; terms 2/10, n30, FOB destination.		
	4	Cost of Goods Sold...	3,100	
		Merchandise Inventory.....................................		3,100
		To record cost of sales.		
	11	Cash..	1,176	
		Sales Discounts...	24	
		Accounts Receivable..		1,200
		To record collection, less return and discount;		
		$2,400 - $1,200 = $1,200 x 2% = $24 discount.		
	23	Cash..	1,200	
		Sales		1,200
		To record cash sale.		
	23	Cost of Goods Sold	950	
		Merchandise Inventory.....................................		950
		To record cost of sales.		
	28	Cash..	3,800	
		Accounts Receivable..		3,800
		To record collection.		

Exercise 6-7 (25 minutes)

a.

2005

May	11	Merchandise Inventory	30,000	
		Accounts Payable – Hostel Sales..............		30,000
		Purchased merchandise on credit.		
	11	Merchandise Inventory	335	
		Cash...		335
		Paid shipping charges on purchased merchandise.		
	12	Accounts Payable – Hostel Sales	1,200	
		Merchandise Inventory		1,200
		Returned unacceptable merchandise.		
	20	Accounts Payable – Hostel Sales	28,800	
		Merchandise Inventory.................................		864
		Cash...		27,936
		Paid balance within the discount period;		
		30,000 – 1,200 = 28,800; 28,800 x 3% = 864.		

b.

2005

May	11	Accounts Receivable – Wilson Purchasing	30,000	
		Sales		30,000
		Sold merchandise on account.		
	11	Cost of Goods Sold..	20,000	
		Merchandise Inventory.................................		20,000
		To record cost of sale.		
	12	Sales Returns and Allowances	1,200	
		Accounts Receivable – Wilson Purchasing..		1,200
		Accepted a return from a customer.		
	12	Merchandise Inventory	800	
		Cost of Goods Sold		800
		Returned goods to inventory.		
	21	Cash	27,936	
		Sales Discounts...	864	
		Accounts Receivable – Wilson Purchasing..		28,800
		Collected account receivable;		
		30,000 – 12,000 = 28,800; 28,800 x 3% = 864.		

Exercise 6-9 (30 minutes)

Merchandise Inventory

Balance, Dec. 31, 2004	27,000	Purchase discounts received	1,600
Invoice cost of purchases......	190,500	Purchase returns and	
Returns by customers	2,200	allowances received	4,100
Transportation-in	1,900	Cost of sales transactions	186,000
		Shrinkage	700
Balance, Dec. 31, 2005	29,200		

Cost of Goods Sold

Represents all entries to record the cost component of sales transactions..............	186,000	Represents all entries to record merchandise returned by customers and restored to inventory during 2005	2,200
Inventory shrinkage recorded in December 31, 2005, adjusting entry........................	700		
Balance	184,500		

Exercise 6-11 (30 minutes)

	a	b	c	d
Sales..	$ 95,200	$ 150,400	$505,800	$ 33,900
Sales discounts.......................................	1,100	1,700	2,900	950
Sales returns and allowances	3,500	14,000	4,000	0
Net sales	$90,600	$ 134,700	$498,900	$ 32,950
Cost of goods sold.................................	37,000	92,000	260,000	20,500
Gross profit from sales..........................	$ 53,600	$42,700	$ 238,900	$ 12,450
Selling expenses	26,000	12,000	92,000	16,000
Administrative expenses	34,000	28,000	105,000	28,000
Total operating expenses	60,000	40,000	197,000	44,000
Net income (loss)	($ 6,400)	$ 2,700	$ 41,900	($31,550)
Gross profit ratio....................................	59.16%1	31.70%2	47.89%3	37.78%4

Fundamental Accounting Principles, Eleventh Canadian Edition

Exercise 6-11 (*continued*)

Calculations:

1. 53,600/90,600) x 100 = 59.16%*
2. (42,700/134,700) x 100 = 31.70%*
3. (238,900/498,900) x 100 = 47.89%*
4. (12,450/32,950) x 100 = 37.78%*

*rounded to two decimal places

Exercise 6-13 (30 minutes)

*The original missing numbers are **bolded**.*

	(a)	(b)	(c)	(d)	(e)
Sales	$ 60,000	$ 42,500	$ 36,000	$78,000	$ 23,600
Cost of goods sold:					
Merch. inv. (beg.)	$ 6,000	$ 17,050	$ 7,500	$ 7,000	$ 2,560
Total cost of merch.					
purchases	36,000	1,550	33,750	32,000	5,600
Merch. inv. (end.)	(7,950)	(2,700)	(9,000)	(6,600)	(2,560)
Cost of goods sold	$ 34,050	$ 15,900	$32,250	$32,400	$ 5,600
Gross profit from sales	$25,950	$26,600	$ 3,750	$ 45,600	$18,000
Operating expenses	9,000	10,650	12,150	2,600	6,000
Net income (loss)	$16,950	$ 15,950	$ (8,400)	$ 43,000	$12,000

a. Find the merchandise inventory (ending) by subtracting cost of goods sold from the goods available for sale [$34,050 – ($6,000 + $36,000)]. Find the gross profit as the difference between the sales and cost of goods sold ($60,000 – $34,050). Find net income as the gross profit less the expenses.

b. Find the total cost of merchandise purchases by finding the number that makes the total equal the cost of goods sold. Find the gross profit as the difference between the sales and cost of goods sold.

c. Find the cost of goods sold as the difference between the sales and the gross profit. Find the cost of merchandise purchases by finding the number to make the calculation equal the cost of goods sold.

d. Calculate the cost of goods sold in the usual way. Calculate sales as the sum of the gross profit and the cost of goods sold.

e. Find the merchandise inventory (ending) by subtracting cost of goods sold from the goods available for sale. Find the gross profit as the difference between the sales and cost of goods sold. Find net income as the gross profit less the expenses.

Exercise 6-15 (30 minutes)

a) Multiple-step income statement:

COMPU-SOFT
Income Statement
For Month Ended November 30, 2005

Net sales..		$26,935*
Cost of goods sold...		14,800
Gross profit from sales		$12,135
Operating expenses:		
Wages expense	$4,200	
Utilities expense	2,100	
Amortization expense, store equipment.........	120	
Total operating expenses............................		6,420
Income from operations.................................		$ 5,715
Other revenues and expenses:		
Rent revenue...		850
Net income..		$ 6,565

Calculated as: 27,700 – 45 – 720 = 26,935

b)

2005			*Closing entries:*		
Nov.	30	Rent Revenue		850	
		Sales..		27,700	
		Income Summary			28,550
		To close temporary credit balance accounts.			
	30	Income Summary		21,985	
		Sales returns and allowances			720
		Sales discounts..			45
		Cost of goods sold...			14,800
		Amortization expense, store equipment			120
		Wages expense			4,200
		Utilities expense..			2,100
		To close temporary debit balance accounts.			
	30	Income Summary		6,565	
		Peter Delta, capital			6,565

To close income summary to capital.

30	Peter Delta, capital	3,500	
	Peter Delta, withdrawals		3,500
	To close withdrawals to capital.		

c)

Peter Delta, Capital

		1,635	(Beg. bal.)
$1,635 - $3,500 + $6,565 = \underline{$4,700}$ OR (With.)	3,500	6,565	(Net income)
		4,700	(End. bal.)

Exercise 6-17 (25 minutes)

a) $531,000 - 14,000 - 7,000 = \underline{510,000}$

b) Single-step income statement:

SABBA CO.
Income Statement
For Year Ended January 31, 2005

Revenues:		
Net sales..		$510,000
Expenses:		
Cost of goods sold...	$301,000	
Selling expenses..	117,000	
General and administrative expenses............	109,000	
Interest expense..	750	
Total expenses		527,750
Net loss		$ 17,750

*Exercise 6-19

Feb.	1	Purchases	3,500	
		Accounts Payable		3,500
		To record purchase; terms 1/10, n30.		
	5	Purchases	1,200	
		Cash		1,200
		To record purchase for cash.		
	6	Purchases	5,000	
		Accounts Payable		5,000
		To record purchase; terms 2/15, n45.		
	9	Office Supplies	450	
		Accounts Payable		450
		To record purchase; n15.		
	10	No entry.		
	11	Accounts Payable	3,500	
		Cash		3,465
		Purchase Discounts		35
		To record payment within discount period;		
		$3,500 x 1% = $35 discount.		
	24	Accounts Payable	450	
		Cash		450
		To record payment.		
Mar.	23	Accounts Payable	5,000	
		Cash		5,000
		To record payment.		

*Exercise 6-21

Jan.	5	Accounts Receivable....................................		2,000	
		Sales			2,000
		To record sale; terms 1/10, n30.			
	7	Cash...		1,800	
		Sales			1,800
		To record cash sale.			
	8	Accounts Receivable....................................		4,800	
		Sales			4,800
		To record sale; terms 1/10, n30.			
	15	Cash...		1,980	
		Sales Discounts..		20	
		Accounts Receivable.................................			2,000
		To record collection within discount period;			
		$2,000 x 1% = $20 discount.			
Feb.	4	Cash...		4,800	
		Accounts Receivable.................................			4,800
		To record collection.			

*Exercise 6-23 (15 minutes)

a)
2005

Mar. 1	Purchases		22,000	
	Accounts Payable – Raintree.............................			22,000
	Purchased merchandise on credit.			
11	Accounts Payable – Raintree..		22,000	
	Purchase Discounts			660
	Cash			21,340
	Paid account payable within the discount period;			
	22,000 x 3% = 660.			

b)
2005

Mar. 1	Accounts Receivable – Sundown Company		22,000	
	Sales...			22,000
	Sold merchandise on account.			
11	Cash...		21,340	
	Sales Discounts...		660	
	Accounts Receivable – Sundown Company....			22,000
	Collected account receivable.			

*Exercise 6-25 (35 minutes)

a.
Gross profit from sales		$145,000
Less: Operating expenses		?
Net income		$ 65,000
Therefore:		
Total operating expenses		$ 80,000

b.
Sales		$340,000
Less: Sales discounts	$ 5,500	
Sales returns	14,000	19,500
Net sales		$320,500
Less: Cost of goods sold		?
Gross profit from sales		$145,000
Therefore:		
Cost of goods sold		$175,500

c.
Merchandise inventory (beginning)		$ 30,000
Invoice cost of merchandise purchases	$175,000	
Less: Purchase discounts received	3,600	
Purchase returns received	6,000	
Net purchases	$165,400	
Add: Transportation-in	11,000	
Total cost of merchandise purchased		176,400
Goods available for sale		$206,400
Less: Merchandise inventory (ending)		?
Cost of goods sold (from b)		$175,500
Therefore:		
Merchandise inventory (ending)		$ 30,900

d. (145,000/320,500) x 100 = <u>45.24%</u> Gross Profit Ratio (rounded to two decimal places)

*Exercise 6-27 (30 minutes)

a) Net Sales:
    Sales $445,000
    Sales returns and allowances .... (25,000)

    Sales discounts .... (16,000)
    Net sales $404,000

b) Cost of goods purchased:
    Purchases $286,000

    Purchases returns and allowances .... (22,000)
    Purchase discounts .... (11,400)

    Transportation-in 8,800
    Cost of goods purchased $261,400

c) Cost of goods sold:

    Beginning inventory .... $ 15,000
    Cost of goods purchased 261,400

    Ending inventory .... (11,000)
    Cost of goods sold $265,400

d) Multiple-step income statement:

FOX FIXTURES CO.
Income Statement
For Year Ended March 31, 2005

Net sales		$404,000
Cost of goods sold		265,400
Gross profit from sales		$138,600
Operating expenses:		
Selling expenses	$69,000	
General and administrative expenses	33,500	
Total operating expenses		102,500
Income from operations		$ 36,100
Other revenues and expenses:		
Interest revenue		1,200
Net income		$ 37,300

Fundamental Accounting Principles, Eleventh Canadian Edition

*Exercise 6-29 (15 minutes)

June	1	Merchandise Inventory	2,000	
		GST Receivable	140	
		Accounts Payable		2,140

To record credit purchase;
$2,000 x 7% = 140 GST.

	5	Accounts Receivable	1,610	
		PST Payable		112
		GST Payable		98
		Sales		1,400

To record credit sale; $1,400 x 8% = 112 PST;
$1,400 x 7% = $98 GST.

	5	Cost of Goods Sold..	1,000	
		Merchandise Inventory		1,000

To record cost of sale.

PROBLEMS

Problem 6-1B (40 minutes)

Part 1

Mar.	5	Merchandise Inventory..	25,000	
		Cash...		25,000
		To record purchase of merchandise for cash.		
	6	Accounts Receivable – Tessier & Welsh	16,000	
		Sales..		16,000
		To record sales; terms 2/10, n30, FOB destination.		
	6	Cost of Goods Sold..	12,800	
		Merchandise Inventory..		12,800
		To record cost of sales.		
	7	Merchandise Inventory..	32,000	
		Accounts Payable – Janz Company......................		32,000
		To record purchase of merchandise; terms 1/10, N45, FOB shipping point.		
	8	Merchandise Inventory..	75	
		Cash...		75
		To record payment of shipping costs.		
	9	Accounts Receivable – Parker Company	28,000	
		Sales..		28,000
		To record sales; terms 2/10, n30, FOB destination.		
	9	Cost of Goods Sold..	23,000	
		Merchandise Inventory..		23,000
		To record cost of sales.		
	10	Merchandise Inventory..	7,000	
		Accounts Payable – Delton Suppliers		7,000
		To record purchase; terms 2/10, n45, FOB destination.		
	16	Cash..	15,680	
		Sales Discounts..	320	
		Accounts Receivable – Tessier & Welsh		16,000
		To record collection within discount period; $16,000 x 2% = $320 discount.		

     Fundamental Accounting Principles, Eleventh Canadian Edition

Problem 6-1B (concluded)

Mar.	17	Accounts Payable – Janz Company......................	32,000	
		Cash..		31,680
		Merchandise Inventory...............................		320
		To record payment within discount period;		
		$32,000 x 1% = $320 discount.		
	30	Accounts Payable – Delton Suppliers	7,000	
		Cash..		7,000
		To record payment.		
	31	Cash...	28,000	
		Accounts Receivable – Parker Company		28,000
		To record collection.		

Part 2

a. Net sales = $43,680 ($16,000 + $28,000 – $320)
b. Cost of goods sold = $35,800 ($12,800 + $23,000)
c. Gross profit from sales = $7,880 ($43,680 - $35,800)

Problem 6-2B (40 minutes)

May	2	Merchandise Inventory	9,000	
		Accounts Payable—Mobley Co.		9,000
		Purchased goods on credit.		
	4	Accounts Receivable—Cornerstone Co.	1,200	
		Sales		1,200
		Sold goods on credit.		
	4	Cost of Goods Sold	750	
		Merchandise Inventory		750
		To record the cost of the May 4 sale.		
	4	Merchandise Inventory	150	
		Cash		150
		Paid freight on incoming goods.		
	9	Cash	2,400	
		Sales		2,400
		Sold goods for cash.		
	9	Cost of Goods Sold	1,800	
		Merchandise Inventory		1,800
		To record the cost of the May 9 sale.		
	10	Merchandise Inventory	3,450	
		Accounts Payable—Richter Co.		3,450
		Purchased goods on credit.		
	12	Accounts Payable—Richter Co.	300	
		Merchandise Inventory		300
		Received credit memo.		
	14	Cash	1,176	
		Sales Discounts	24	
		Accounts Receivable—Cornerstone Co.		1,200
		Collected receivable within discount period;		
		1,200 x 2% = 24.		
	15	Cash	500	
		Office Equipment		500
		To record sale of office equipment at cost.		

Fundamental Accounting Principles, Eleventh Canadian Edition

Problem 6-2B *(concluded)*

May	**17**	Accounts Payable—Mobley Co.	9,000		
		Merchandise Inventory		90	
		Cash		8,910	
		Paid payable within the discount period;			
		1% × $9,000 = $90.			
	18	Cleaning Supplies	820		
		Accounts Payable–A & Z Suppliers		820	
		Purchased supplies on credit.			
	20	Accounts Receivable—Harrill Co.	1,875		
		Sales		1,875	
		Sold goods on credit.			
	20	Cost of Goods Sold	1,350		
		Merchandise Inventory		1,350	
		To record the cost of the May 20 sale.			
	22	Sales Returns and Allowances	300		
		Accounts Receivable—Harrill Co.		300	
		Issued credit memo.			
	23	Sales	75		
		Accounts Receivable—Harrill Co.		75	
		Received debit memo for error.			
	25	Accounts Payable—Richter Co.	3,150		
		Merchandise Inventory		63	
		Cash		3,087	
		Paid within the discount period;			
		3,450 – 300 = 3,150; 2% × $3,150 = 63.			
	31	Cash	1,470		
		Sales Discounts	30		
		Accounts Receivable—Harrill Co.		1,500	
		Collected receivable within discount			
		period; 1,875 – 300 – 75 = 1,500; 1,500 x 2% = 30.			
	31	Accounts Receivable—Cornerstone Co.	7,500		
		Sales		7,500	
		Sold goods on credit.			
	31	Cost of Goods Sold	4,800		
		Merchandise Inventory		4,800	
		To record the cost of the May 31 sale.			

Problem 6-3B (40 minutes)

July	3	Merchandise Inventory	15,000	
		Accounts Payable—CMP Corp.		15,000
		Purchased goods on credit.		
	4	Accounts Payable—CMP Corp.	250	
		Cash		250
		Paid freight for supplier.		
	7	Accounts Receivable—Harbison Co.	10,500	
		Sales		10,500
		Sold goods on credit.		
	7	Cost of Goods Sold	7,500	
		Merchandise Inventory		7,500
		To record the cost of the July 7 sale.		
	10	Merchandise Inventory	13,250	
		Accounts Payable—Cimarron Corporation ...		13,250
		Purchased goods on credit.		
	11	Delivery Expense or Freight-Out	300	
		Cash		300
		Paid shipping charges on July 7 sale.		
	12	Sales Returns and Allowances	1,750	
		Accounts Receivable—Harbison Co.		1,750
		Customer returned merchandise.		
	12	Merchandise Inventory	1,250	
		Cost of Goods Sold		1,250
		Returned goods to inventory.		
	14	Accounts Payable—Cimarron Corporation	2,050	
		Merchandise Inventory		2,050
		Received a credit memorandum for July 10 purchase.		
	17	Cash	8,575	
		Sales Discounts	175	
		Accounts Receivable—Harbison Co.		8,750
		Collected receivable within discount period; 10,500 – 1,750 = 8,750; 8,750 x 2% = 175.		

Problem 6-3B *(concluded)*

July	18	Cash	15,000	
		Land		15,000
		Sold land at cost.		
	19	Van	18,000	
		Cash		5,000
		Notes Payable		13,000
		To record purchase of van.		
	20	Accounts Payable—Cimarron Corporation......	11,200	
		Merchandise Inventory		112
		Cash		11,088
		Paid payable within the discount period;		
		$13,250 – 2,050 = $11,200; 11,200 x 1% = 112.		
	21	Accounts Receivable—Hess	9,000	
		Sales		9,000
		Sold goods on credit.		
	21	Cost of Goods Sold...	6,250	
		Merchandise Inventory		6,250
		To record the cost of the July 21 sale.		
	24	Sales Returns and Allowances	1,500	
		Accounts Receivable—Hess.......................		1,500
		Issued credit memo.		
	31	Cash	7,425	
		Sales Discounts...	75	
		Accounts Receivable—Hess.......................		7,500
		Collected receivable within discount		
		period; 9,000 – 1,500 = 7,500; 7,500 x 1% = 75.		
	31	Accounts Payable—CMP Corp...........................	14,750	
		Cash		14,750
		Paid payable; 15,000 – 250 = 14,750.		

Problem 6-4B (60 minutes) *Part 1*

RESOURCE PRODUCTS COMPANY
Work Sheet
For Year Ended October 31, 2005

Account	Unadjusted Trial Balance Debit	Unadjusted Trial Balance Credit	Adjusting Entries Debit	Adjusting Entries Credit	Adjusted Trial Balance Debit	Adjusted Trial Balance Credit	Income Statement Debit	Income Statement Credit	Balance Sheet and Statement of Owner's Equity Debit	Balance Sheet and Statement of Owner's Equity Credit
Cash	6,400				6,400				6,400	
Merchandise inventory	23,000			(d) 800	22,200				22,200	
Store supplies	9,600			(a) 6,300	3,300				3,300	
Prepaid insurance	4,600			(b) 3,000	1,600				1,600	
Store equipment	83,800				83,800				83,800	
Accumulated amortization, store equipment		30,000		(c) 2,800		32,800				32,800
Accounts payable		16,000				16,000				16,000
Jan Smithers, capital		80,400				80,400				80,400
Jan Smithers, withdrawals	6,000				6,000				6,000	
Sales		198,000				198,000		198,000		
Sales discounts	2,000				2,000		2,000			
Sales returns and allowances	4,000				4,000		4,000			
Cost of goods sold	74,800		(d) 800		75,600		75,600			
Amortization expense, store equipment			(c) 2,800		2,800		2,800			
Salaries expense	62,000				62,000		62,000			
Interest expense	400				400		400			
Insurance expense			(b) 3,000		3,000		3,000			
Rent expense	28,000				28,000		28,000			
Store supplies expense			(a) 6,300		6,300		6,300			
Advertising expense	19,800				19,800		19,800			
Totals	324,400	324,400	12,900	12,900	327,200	327,200	203,900	198,000	123,300	129,200
Net loss								5,900	5,900	
Totals							203,900	203,900	129,200	129,200

Problem 6-4B *(concluded)*

Part 2 Multiple-step income statement:

RESOURCE PRODUCTS COMPANY
Income Statement
For Year Ended October 31, 2005

Net sales..		$192,000
Cost of goods sold...		75,600
Gross profit from sales......................................		$116,400
Operating expenses:		
Salaries expense	$62,000	
Rent expense	28,000	
Advertising expense	19,800	
Store supplies expense	6,300	
Insurance expense	3,000	
Amortization expense, store equipment	2,800	
Total operating expenses............................		121,900
Loss from operations...		$ 5,500
Other revenues and expenses:		
Interest expense...		400
Net loss		$ 5,900

Problem 6-5B (40 minutes)

1. Net sales:

Sales	$318,000	
Less: Sales discounts	4,875	
Sales returns and allowances	21,000	
Net sales..	$292,125	

Problem 6-5B (continued)

2. Classified, multiple-step income statement:

REYNA COMPANY
Income Statement
For Year Ended May 31, 2005

Sales			$318,000
Less: Sales discounts		$ 4,875	
Sales returns and allowances		21,000	25,875
Net sales			$292,125
Cost of goods sold			123,900
Gross profit from sales			$168,225
Operating expenses:			
Selling expenses:			
Sales salaries expense	$ 43,500		
Advertising expense	27,000		
Rent expense, selling space	15,000		
Store supplies expense	3,750		
Total selling expenses		$ 89,250	
General and administrative expenses:			
Office salaries expense	$ 39,750		
Rent expense, office space	3,900		
Office supplies expense	1,200		
Total general and administrative expenses		44,850	
Total operating expenses			134,100
Net income			$ 34,125

Problem 6-5B *(concluded)*

3. Single-step income statement:

REYNA COMPANY
Income Statement
For Year Ended May 31, 2005

Net sales		$292,125
Expenses:		
Cost of goods sold	$123,900	
Selling expenses	89,250	
General and administrative expenses	44,850	
Total expenses		258,000
Net income		$ 34,125

Fundamental Accounting Principles, Eleventh Canadian Edition

Problem 6-6B (30 minutes)

2005		*Closing entries:*		
May	31	Sales	318,000	
		Income Summary		318,000
		To close temporary account with credit balance.		
	31	Income Summary	283,875	
		Sales Discounts		4,875
		Sales Returns and Allowances		21,000
		Cost of Goods Sold		123,900
		Sales Salaries Expense		43,500
		Rent Expense, Selling Space		15,000
		Store Supplies Expense		3,750
		Advertising Expense		27,000
		Office Salaries Expense		39,750
		Rent Expense, Office Space.......................		3,900
		Office Supplies Expense		1,200
		To close temporary accounts with debit balances.		
	31	Income Summary	34,125	
		Paul Reyna, capital		34,125
		To close the Income Summary account.		
	31	Paul Reyna, Capital..	24,000	
		Paul Reyna, Withdrawals		24,000
		To close the withdrawals account.		

Problem 6-7B (50 minutes)

1. Classified, multiple-step income statement:

BANDARA SALES
Income Statement
For Year Ended December 31, 2005

Sales			$946,300
Less: Sales returns and allowances		$ 7,345	
Sales discounts		1,390	8,735
Net sales			$937,565
Cost of goods sold			649,820
Gross profit from sales			$287,745
Operating expenses:			
Selling expenses:			
Sales salaries expense	$149,485[1]		
Rent expense, selling space	39,808[2]		
Amortization expense, store equipment	16,020		
Store supplies expense	4,200[3]		
Total selling expenses		$209,513	
General and administrative expenses:			
Office salaries expense	$ 64,065[4]		
Rent expense, office space	9,952[5]		
Office supplies expense	7,800[6]		
Insurance expense	6,200		
Amortization expense, office equipment	3,450		
Total general and administrative expenses		91,467	
Total operating expenses			300,980
Net loss			$ 13,235

     1. 70% × 213,550
     2. 80% × 49,760
     3. 35% × 12,000
     4. 30% × 213,550
     5. 20% × 49,760
     6. 65% × 12,000

Fundamental Accounting Principles, Eleventh Canadian Edition

Problem 6-7B *(concluded)*

2. Single-step income statement:

BANDARA SALES
Income Statement
For Year Ended December 31, 2005

Revenues:		
Net sales...		$937,565
Expenses:		
Cost of goods sold................................	$649,820	
Selling expenses...................................	209,513	
General and administrative expenses.....	91,467	950,800
Net loss...		$ 13,235

Problem 6-8B

Closing entries:

2005				
Dec.	31	Sales...	946,300	
		Income Summary.................................		946,300
		To close temporary credit balance accounts.		
	31	Income Summary......................................	959,535	
		Sales Returns and Allowances		7,345
		Sales Discounts....................................		1,390
		Cost of goods sold................................		649,820
		Salaries Expense..................................		213,550
		Rent Expense......................................		49,760
		Supplies Expense.................................		12,000
		Amortization Expense, Store Equipment....		16,020
		Insurance Expense...............................		6,200
		Amortization Expense, Office Equipment...		3,450
		To close temporary debit balance accounts.		
	31	Diego Amara, Capital...............................	13,235	
		Income Summary.................................		13,235
		To close the Income Summary account to capital.		
	31	Diego Amara, Capital...............................	102,500	
		Diego Amara, Withdrawals		102,500
		To close withdrawals to capital.		

Problem 6-9B (60 minutes)

1. Classified, multiple-step income statement:

TINKER SALES
Income Statement
For Year Ended July 31, 2005

Sales			$78,500
Less: Sales discounts			1,000
Net sales			$77,500
Cost of goods sold			47,400
Gross profit from sales			$30,100
Operating expenses:			
Selling expenses:			
Sales salaries expense	$18,000		
Advertising expense	9,900		
Rent expense, selling space	7,000		
Store supplies expense	1,600		
Amortization expense, store equipment	1,000		
Insurance expense, store	750		
Total selling expenses		$38,250	
General and administrative expenses:			
Office salaries expense	$ 5,000		
Rent expense, office space	5,000		
Amortization expense, office equipment	2,500		
Office supplies expense	1,200		
Insurance expense, office	250		
Total general and administrative expenses		13,950	
Total operating expenses			52,200
Net loss			$22,100

Fundamental Accounting Principles, Eleventh Canadian Edition

Problem 6-9B (concluded)

2. Multiple-step income statement:

TINKER SALES
Income Statement
For Year Ended July 31, 2005

Net sales..		$77,500
Cost of goods sold..		47,400
Gross profit from sales.....................................		$30,100
Operating expenses:		
Salaries expense	$23,000	
Rent expense	12,000	
Advertising expense	9,900	
Supplies expense	2,800	
Amortization expense, equipment	3,500	
Insurance expense	1,000	
Total operating expenses...........................		52,200
Net loss		$ 22,100

3. Single-step income statement:

TINKER SALES
Income Statement
For Year Ended July 31, 2005

Revenues:		
Net sales..		$77,500
Expenses:		
Cost of goods sold...	$47,400	
Selling expenses	38,250	
General and administrative expenses	13,950	
Total expenses...		99,600
Net loss		$ 22,100

*Problem 6-10B (40 minutes)

Part 1

Mar.	5	Purchases	25,000
		Cash..	25,000
		To record purchase of merchandise for cash.	

	6	Accounts Receivable – Tessier & Welsh	16,000
		Sales	16,000
		To record sales; terms 2/10, n30, FOB destination.	

	7	Purchases	32,000
		Accounts Payable – Janz Company................	32,000
		To record purchase of merchandise;	
		terms 1/10, n45, FOB shipping point.	

	8	Transportation-in or Freight-In..............................	75
		Cash..	75
		To record payment of shipping costs.	

	9	Accounts Receivable – Parker Company	28,000
		Sales...	28,000
		To record sales; terms 2/10, n30, FOB destination.	

	10	Purchases	7,000
		Accounts Payable – Delton Suppliers	7,000
		To record purchase; terms 2/10, n45, FOB	
		destination.	

	16	Cash...	15,680	
		Sales Discounts	320	
		Accounts Receivable – Tessier & Welsh		16,000
		To record collection within discount period;		
		$16,000 x 2% = $320 discount.		

	17	Accounts Payable – Janz Company......................	32,000	
		Cash..		31,680
		Purchase Discounts		320
		To record payment within discount period;		
		$32,000 x 1% = $320 discount.		

*Problem 6-10B *(concluded)*

Mar.	30	Accounts Payable – Delton Suppliers	7,000	
		Cash...		7,000
		To record payment.		
	31	Cash..	28,000	
		Accounts Receivable – Parker Company		28,000
		To record collection.		

*Problem 6-11B (30 minutes)

Date	Account	Debit	Credit
Mar. 1	Purchases...	20,000	
	Accounts Payable — Zender Holdings............		20,000
	Purchased merchandise terms 1/10, n/15.		
2	Cash	1,800	
	Sales...		1,800
	Sold merchandise for cash.		
7	Purchases...	16,000	
	Accounts Payable — Red River Co.		16,000
	Purchased merchandise terms 2/10, n/30.		
8	Transportation-in or Freight-In	350	
	Accounts Payable — Dan's Shipping..............		350
	Paid freight charges on purchase of March 7.		
12	Accounts Receivable — Bev Dole	9,000	
	Sales...		9,000
	Sold merchandise on credit, terms 2/10, n/45.		
13	Accounts Payable — Red River Co.	500	
	Purchase Returns and Allowances...................		500
	Received credit memo re purchase of March 7.		
14	Office Furniture	1,600	
	Accounts Payable — Wilson Supplies		1,600
	Purchased office furniture on credit.		
15	Accounts Receivable — Ted Smith	17,000	
	Sales...		17,000
	Sold merchandise terms 2/10, n/45.		
16	Accounts Payable — Red River Co.	15,500	
	Purchase Discounts...		310
	Cash		15,190
	Paid for merchandise purchased on March 7;		
	16,000 – 500 = 15,500; 15,500 – 2% = 15,190.		
17	Sales Returns and Allowances	1,000	
	Accounts Receivable — Ted Smith		1,000
	Issued credit memo to customer of March 15.		

*Problem 6-11B *(concluded)*

March 19	Accounts Payable — Wilson Supplies	750	
	Office Furniture		750
	To record memorandum regarding damaged		
	furniture purchased on March 14.		
24	Cash..	15,680	
	Sales Discounts...	320	
	Accounts Receivable — Ted Smith......................		16,000
	To record receipt of payment regarding March 15		
	sale less return and discount;		
	17,000 – 1,000 = 16,000; 16,000 x 2% = 320.		
27	Cash..	9,000	
	Accounts Receivable — Bev Dole......................		9,000
	Received payment from customer regarding		
	March 12 sale.		
31	Accounts Payable — Zender Holdings.....................	20,000	
	Cash		20,000
	Paid for merchandise purchased on March 1.		

*Problem 6-12B (40 minutes)

1. Net sales:

Sales..	$540,000
Less: Sales returns and allowances................................	57,000
Sales discounts..	4,700
Net sales	$478,300

2. Cost of goods purchased:

Purchases..	$ 240,000
Less: Purchases returns and allowances............................	8,100
Purchases discounts...	2,300
Transportation-in	9,700
Cost of goods purchased	$ 239,300

3. Cost of goods sold:

Beginning inventory..	$ 50,000
Cost of goods purchased (from 2).....................................	239,300
Less: Ending inventory...	32,000
Cost of goods sold	$ 257,300

*Problem 6-12B *(concluded)*

4. Multiple-step income statement:

GARNEAU COMPANY
Income Statement
For Year Ended November 30, 2005

Net Sales		$478,300
Cost of goods sold		257,300
Gross profit from sales		$221,000
Operating expenses:		
Salaries expense	$120,000	
Rent expense	72,000	
Advertising expense	6,000	
Supplies expense	10,000	
Total operating expenses		208,000
Income from operations		$ 13,000
Other revenues and expenses		
Interest expense		700
Net income		$ 12,300

5. Single-step income statement:

GARNEAU COMPANY
Income Statement
For Year Ended November 30, 2005

Revenues:		
Net sales		$478,300
Expenses:		
Cost of goods sold	$257,300	
Selling expenses	131,900	
General and administrative expenses	76,100	
Interest expense	700	
Total expenses		466,000
Net income		$ 12,300

Fundamental Accounting Principles, Eleventh Canadian Edition

*Problem 6-13B (30 minutes)

2005		Closing entries:		
Nov.	30	Merchandise Inventory	32,000	
		Sales	540,000	
		Purchases Returns and Allowances	8,100	
		Purchases Discounts	2,300	
		Income Summary		582,400
		To close temporary accounts with credit balances and record the ending inventory.		
	30	Income Summary	570,100	
		Merchandise Inventory		50,000
		Sales Returns and Allowances		57,000
		Sales Discounts		4,700
		Purchases		240,000
		Transportation-In		9,700
		Salaries Expense		120,000
		Rent Expense		72,000
		Supplies Expense		10,000
		Advertising Expense		6,000
		Interest Expense		700
		To close temporary accounts with debit balances and to remove the beginning inventory balance.		
	30	Income Summary	12,300	
		Teresa Garneau, Capital		12,300
		To close the Income Summary Account.		
	30	Teresa Garneau, Capital	20,000	
		Teresa Garneau, Withdrawals		20,000
		To close the withdrawals account.		

*Problem 6-14B (60 minutes) *Part 1*

THE DOWNTOWN STORE
Work Sheet
For Year Ended March 31, 2005

	Unadjusted Trial Balance		Adjustments		Income Statement		Balance Sheet and Statement of Owner's Equity	
	Debit	Credit	Debit	Credit	Debit	Credit	Debit	Credit
Cash	14,000						14,000	
Merchandise inventory	96,000				96,000	18,000	18,000	
Supplies	1,200			(a) 300			900	
Prepaid rent	14,000			(b) 4,300			9,700	
Store equipment	120,000						120,000	
Accumulated amortization, store equipment		28,000		(c) 3,200				31,200
Office equipment	46,000						46,000	
Accumulated amortization, office equipment		13,000		(d) 2,900				15,900
Accounts payable		32,000						32,000
Lucy Baker, capital		269,200						269,200
Lucy Baker, withdrawals	68,000						68,000	
Sales		998,000				998,000		
Sales returns and allowances	23,000				23,000			
Sales Discounts	12,000				12,000			
Purchases	692,000				692,000			
Purchases returns and allowances		5,700				5,700		
Purchases discounts		14,300				14,300		
Transportation-in	32,000				32,000			
Salaries expenses (60% selling; 40% office)	120,000				120,000			
Rent expense (80% selling; 20% office)	91,000		(b) 4,300		95,300			
Advertising expense	14,000				14,000			
Supplies expense (30% selling; 70% office)	17,000		(a) 300		17,300			
Amortization expense, store equipment	0		(c) 3,200		3,200			
Amortization expense, office equipment	0		(d) 2,900		2,900			
Totals	1,360,200	1,360,200	10,700	10,700	1,107,700	1,036,000	276,600	348,300
Net loss						71,700	71,700	
Totals					1,107,700	1,107,700	348,300	348,300

*Problem 6-14B *(concluded)* Part 2

2005   *Closing entries:*
Mar. 31   Merchandise Inventory.....................................   18,000
            Sales...   998,000
            Purchase Returns and Allowances..........................   5,700
            Purchase Discounts..   14,300
                Income Summary...   1,036,000
            To close temporary credit balance accounts.

      31   Income Summary...   1,107,700
                Merchandise Inventory....................................   96,000
                Sales Returns and Allowances   23,000
                Sales Discounts   12,000
                Purchases...   692,000
                Transportation-In...   32,000
                Salaries Expense   120,000
                Rent Expense...   95,300
                Advertising Expense   14,000
                Supplies Expense...   17,300
                Amortization Expense, Store Equipment..............   3,200
                Amortization Expense, Office Equipment.............   2,900
            To close temporary debit balance accounts.

      31   Lucy Baker, Capital..   71,700
                Income Summary...   71,700
            To close the Income Summary account to capital.

      31   Lucy Baker, Capital..   68,000
                Lucy Baker, Withdrawals   68,000
            To close withdrawals to capital.

Part 3   **Merchandise Inventory**   **Account No. 110**

Date	Explanation	PR	Debit	Credit	Balance
2004 Mar. 31	March 31, 2004 balance (brought forward)				96,000.00
2005 Mar. 31	Close out March 31, 2004 balance	G14		96,000.00	0
31	March 31, 2005 balance	G14	18,000.00		18,000.00

*Problem 6-15B

Classified multiple-step income statement:

THE DOWNTOWN STORE
Income Statement
For Year Ended March 31, 2005

Sales			$998,000
Less: Sales returns and allowances		$23,000	
Sales discounts		12,000	35,000
Net Sales			$963,000
Cost of goods sold:			
Merchandise inventory, December 31, 2004		$96,000	
Purchases	$692,000		
Less: Purchase returns and allowances	$ 5,700		
Purchase discounts	14,300	20,000	
Net purchases		$672,000	
Add: Transportation-in		32,000	
Cost of goods purchased		704,000	
Goods available for sale		$800,000	
Less: Merchandise inventory, December 31, 2005.		18,000	
Cost of goods sold			782,000
Gross profit from sales			$181,000
Operating expenses:			
Selling expenses:			
Rent expense, selling space[1]		$76,240	
Sales salaries expense[2]		72,000	
Advertising expense		14,000	
Store supplies expense[3]		5,190	
Amortization expense, store equipment		3,200	
Total selling expenses		$170,630	
General and administrative expenses:			
Office salaries expense[4]		$48,000	
Rent expense, office space[5]		19,060	
Office supplies expense[6]		12,110	
Amortization expense, office equipment		2,900	
Total general and administrative expenses		82,070	
Total operating expenses			252,700
Net loss			$ 71,700

Calculations:

1.	95,300 x 80%	4.	120,000 x 40%
2.	120,000 x 60%	5.	95,300 x 20%
3.	17,300 x 30%	6.	17,300 x 70%

*Problem 6-16B (40 minutes)

Sept.	2	Cash	8,050	
		PST Payable		560
		GST Payable		490
		Sales		7,000

To record cash sale; $7,000 x 8% = $560 PST;
$7,000 x 7% = $490 GST.

	2	Cost of Goods Sold....................................	5,800	
		Merchandise Inventory		5,800

To record cost of sale.

	3	Merchandise Inventory	8,000	
		GST Receivable	560	
		Cash		8,560

To record cash purchase; $8,000 x 7% = $560 GST.

	7	Merchandise Inventory	5,000	
		GST Receivable	350	
		Accounts Payable		5,350

To record credit purchase; $5,000 x 7% = $350 GST.

	8	Accounts Receivable	17,250	
		PST Payable		1,200
		GST Payable		1,050
		Sales		15,000

To record credit sale; $15,000 x 8% = $1,200 PST;
$15,000 x 7% = $1,050 GST.

	8	Cost of Goods Sold....................................	13,200	
		Merchandise Inventory		13,200

To record cost of sale.

	17	Accounts Payable	5,350	
		Merchandise Inventory		50
		Cash		5,300

To record payment within discount period;
$5,000* x 1% = $50.

	18	Cash	16,950	
		Sales Discounts	300	
		Accounts Receivable		17,250

To record collection within discount period;
$15,000* x 2% = $300.

*The discount applies only to the amount before tax.

*Problem 6-17B (40 minutes)

Sept.	2	Cash	8,050	
		PST Payable		560
		GST Payable		490
		Sales		7,000

To record cash sale; $7,000 x 8% = $560 PST;
$7,000 x 7% = $490 GST.

	3	Purchases	8,000	
		GST Receivable	560	
		Cash		8,560

To record cash purchase; $8,000 x 7% = $560 GST.

	7	Purchases	5,000	
		GST Receivable	350	
		Accounts Payable		5,350

To record credit purchase; $5,000 x 7% = $350 GST.

	8	Accounts Receivable	17,250	
		PST Payable		1,200
		GST Payable		1,050
		Sales		15,000

To record credit sale; $15,000 x 8% = $1,200 PST;
$15,000 x 7% = $1,050 GST.

	17	Accounts Payable	5,350	
		Purchase Discounts		50
		Cash		5,300

To record payment within discount period;
$5,000* x 1% = $50.

	18	Cash	16,950	
		Sales Discounts	300	
		Accounts Receivable		17,250

To record collection within discount period;
$15,000* x 2% = $300.

*The discount applies only to the amount before tax

Fundamental Accounting Principles, Eleventh Canadian Edition

Chapter 7   Merchandise Inventories and Cost of Sales

Exercise 7-1 (45 minutes)

(a) FIFO perpetual

Date	Purchases			Sales (at cost)			Inventory Balance		
	Units	Unit Cost	Total Cost	Units	Unit Cost	Cost of Goods Sold	Units	Unit Cost	*Total Cost*
Jan. 1	Beginning inventory								
	100 @ $10.00 =		$1,000				100 @ $10.00 = $		1,000
10				90 @ $10.00	=	$ 900	10 @ $10.00 = $		100
							10 @ $10.00 = $		100
Mar. 14	250 @ $15.00 =		$3,750				250 @ 15.00 =		3,750
				10 @ $10.00	=	$ 100			
15				130 @ 15.00	=	1,950	120 @ $15.00 = $		1,800
							120 @ $15.00 = $		1,800
Jul. 30	400 @ $20.00 =		$8,000				400 @ 20.00 =		8,000
				120 @ $15.00	=	$ 1,800			
Oct. 5				180 @ 20.00	=	3,600	220 @ $20.00 = $		4,400
Total	750		$12,750	530		$8,350	220		$4,400

Cost of goods available for sale   =   Cost of goods sold   +   Ending inventory

Gross profit calculation under FIFO:

Sales (530 units × $40)	$21,200
Cost of goods sold	8,350
Gross profit	$12,850

Exercise 7-1 *(continued)*

(b) Moving weighted-average perpetual

Date	Purchases			Sales (at cost)			Inventory Balance		
							(a)	**(b) ÷ (a)**	**(b)**
	Units	Unit Cost	Total Cost	Units	Unit Cost	Cost of Goods Sold	Total Units	Average Cost/Unit	Total Cost
	Beginning inventory								
Jan. 1	100 @ $10 =		$1000				100	$10.00	$ 1,000.00
10				90 @ $10.00 =		$ 900.00	10	$10.00	$ 100.00
Mar. 14	250 @ $15 =		$3,750				260	$14.81	$ 3,850.00
15				140 @ $14.81 =		$ 2,073.40	120	$14.81	$ 1,776.60
July 30	400 @ $20 =		$8,000				520	$18.80	$ 9,776.60
Oct. 5				300 @ $18.80 =		$ 5,640.00	220	$18.80	$ 4,136.60
Total	750		$12,750	530		$8,613.40	220		$ 4,136.60

Cost of goods available for sale = Cost of goods sold + Ending inventory

Inventory Balance Calculations

100		$ 1,000.00
−90 @	$10.00 =	−900.00
10		$ 100.00
10		$ 100.00
250 @	$15.00 =	3,750.00
260		$ 3,850.00
260		$ 3,850.00
−140 @	$14.81 =	−2,073.40
120		$ 1,776.60
120		$ 1,776.60
400 @	$20.00 =	8,000.00
520		$ 9,776.60
520		$ 9,776.60
−300 @	$18.80 =	−5,640.00
220		$ 4,136.60

Gross profit calculation under Weighted-average:

Sales (530 units × $40)	$21,200.00
Cost of goods sold	8,613.40
Gross profit	**$12,586.60**

Fundamental Accounting Principles, Eleventh Canadian Edition

Exercise 7-1 *(concluded)*

(c) LIFO perpetual

Date	Purchases			Sales (at cost)			Inventory Balance		
	Units	Unit Cost	Total Cost	Units	Unit Cost	Cost of Goods Sold	Units	Unit Cost	*Total Cost*
Jan. 1	Beginning inventory								
	100 @ $10.00 =		$ 1,000				100 @ $10.00 = $		1,000
10				90 @ $10.00 =		$ 900	10 @ $10.00 = $		100
							10 @ $10.00 = $		100
Mar. 14	250 @ $15.00 =		$ 3,750				250 @ 15.00 =		3,750
							10 @ $10.00 = $		100
15				140 @ $15.00 =		$ 2,100	110 @ 15.00 =		1,650
							10 @ $10.00 = $		100
							110 @ 15.00 =		1,650
Jul. 30	400 @ $20.00 =		$ 8,000				400 @ 20.00 =		8,000
							10 @ $10.00 = $		100
							110 @ 15.00 =		1,650
Oct. 5				300 @ $20.00 =		$ 6,000	100 @ 20.00 =		2,000
Total	**750**		**$12,750**	**530**		**$9,000**	**220**		**$3,750**

Cost of goods available for sale   Cost of goods sold   +   Ending inventory

=

Gross profit calculation under LIFO:

Sales (530 units × $40)	$21,200
Cost of goods sold	9,000
Gross profit	$12,200

Exercise 7-3 (40 minutes)

(a) Moving weighted-average perpetual

Date		Purchases				Sales (at cost)			Inventory Balance				Inventory Balance Calculations		
									(a)	(b) ÷ (a)	(b)				
	Units	Unit Cost	Total Cost		Units	Unit Cost	Cost of Goods Sold		Total Units	Average Cost/ Unit	Total Cost				
	Beginning inventory														
Jan. 1	120 @ $6.00 =		$ 720.00						120	$6.00	$ 720.00		120		$ 720.00
10					70 @	$6.00 =	$ 420.00						−70 @ $6.00 =		−420.00
									50	$6.00	$ 300.00		50		$ 300.00
													50		$ 300.00
Mar. 7	250 @ $5.60 =		$ 1,400.00										250 @ 5.60 =		1,400.00
									300	$5.67	$ 1,700.00		300		$1,700.00
													300		$1,700.00
15					125 @	$5.67 =	$ 708.75						−125 @ 5.67 =		−708.75
									175	$5.66*	$ 991.25		175		$ 991.25
													175		$ 991.25
July 28	500 @ $5.00 =		$ 2,500.00										500 @ 5.00 =		2,500.00
									675	$5.17	$ 3,491.25		675		$3,491.25
													675		$3,491.25
Oct. 3	450 @ $4.60 =		$ 2,070.00										450 @ 4.60 =		2,070.00
									1,125	$4.94	$ 5,561.25		1,125		$5,561.25
													1,125		$5,561.25
5					600 @	$4.94 =	$ 2,964.00						−600 @ 4.96 =		−2,964.00
									525	$4.95*	$ 2,597.25		525		$2,597.25
Total	1,320		$6,690.00		795		$4,092.75		525		$2,597.25				

Cost of goods available for sale　=　Cost of goods sold　+　Ending inventory

*cost/unit changed due to rounding

Exercise 7-3 (continued)

(b) FIFO perpetual

Date		Purchases Units	Unit Cost	Total Cost	Sales (at cost) Units	Unit Cost	Cost of Goods Sold	Inventory Balance Units	Unit Cost	Total Cost
Jan.	1	Beginning inventory								
		120 @	$6.00 =	$ 720				120 @	$6.00 =	$ 720
	10				70 @	$6.00 =	$ 420	50 @	$6.00 =	$ 300
								50 @	$6.00 =	$ 300
Mar.	7	250 @	$5.60 =	$ 1,400				250 @	5.60 =	1,400
					50 @	$6.00 =	$ 300			
	15				75 @	5.60 =	420	175 @	$5.60 =	$ 980
								175 @	$5.60 =	$ 980
Jul.	28	500 @	$5.00 =	$ 2,500				500 @	5.00 =	2,500
								175 @	$5.60 =	$ 980
								500 @	5.00 =	2,500
Oct.	3	450 @	$4.60 =	$ 2,070				450 @	4.60 =	2,070
					175 @	$5.60 =	$ 980	75 @	$5.00 =	$ 375
	5				425 @	5.00 =	2,125	450 @	4.60 =	2,070
Total		1,320		$6,690	795		$4,245	525		$2,445

Cost of goods available for sale =   Cost of goods sold   Ending inventory

+

Exercise 7-3 *(concluded)*

(c) LIFO perpetual

Date		Purchases			Sales (at cost)			Inventory Balance		
		Units	Unit Cost	Total Cost	Units	Unit Cost	Cost of Goods Sold	Units	Unit Cost	Total Cost
Jan.	1	Beginning inventory								
		120 @ $6.00 =		$ 720				120 @ $6.00 =		$ 720
	10				70 @ $6.00	=	$ 420	50 @ $6.00 =		$ 300
								50 @ $6.00 =		$ 300
Mar.	7	250 @ $5.60 =		$ 1,400				250 @ 5.60 =		1,400
	15				125 @ $5.60	=	$ 700	50 @ $6.00 =		$ 300
								125 @ 5.60 =		700
								50 @ $6.00 =		$ 300
Jul.	28	500 @ $5.00 =		$ 2,500				125 @ 5.60 =		700
								500 @ 5.00 =		2,500
								50 @ $6.00 =		$ 300
								125 @ 5.60 =		700
Oct.	3	450 @ $4.60 =		$ 2,070				500 @ 5.00 =		2,500
								450 @ 4.60 =		2,070
								50 @ $6.00 =		$ 300
					450 @ $4.60	=	$ 2,070	125 @ 5.60 =		700
	5				150 @ 5.00	=	750	350 @ 5.00 =		1,750
Total		1,320		$6,690	795		$3,940	525		$2,750

Cost of goods available for sale = Cost of goods sold + Ending inventory

Exercise 7-5 (30 minutes)

TROUT COMPANY
Income Statement
For year ended December 31, 2005

	Specific Identification	Moving Weighted Average	FIFO	LIFO
Sales	$11,925	$11,925.00	$11,925	$11,925
(795 units × $15 selling price)				
Cost of goods sold	4,018	4,092.75	4,245	3,940
Gross profit	$ 7,907	$ 7,832.25	$ 7,680	$ 7,985
Operating expenses	1,250	1,250.00	1,250	1,250
Net income	$ 6,657	$ 6,582.25	$ 6,430	$ 6,735

1) The LIFO method results in the highest net income with $6,735.

2) The weighted average net income of $6,582.25 does fall between FIFO net income ($6,430) and LIFO net income ($6,735).

3) If costs were rising instead of falling then the FIFO method would probably result in the highest net income.

Exercise 7-6 (15 minutes)

a. and b.

		Per Unit				LCM applied to:	
						a.	b.
Inventory Items	Units on Hand	Cost	NRV	Total Cost	Total NRV	Inventory as a Whole	Each Product
BB	22	$50	$54	$1,100	$1,188		$1,100
FM	15	78	72	1,170	1,080		1,080
MB	36	95	91	3,420	3,276		3,276
SL	40	36	36	1,440	1,440		1,440
				$7,130	$6,984	$6,984	$6,896

c. 2005
Dec. 31 Cost of Goods Sold 146
              Merchandise Inventory 146
        To write inventory down to market;
        7,130 – 6,984 = 146.

Exercise 7-7 (20 minutes)

1. $900,000 - $500,000 = $400,000

2.

	For years ended December 31, 2005, 2006, and 2007 income statement information should have been reported as:		Income statement information actually reported for years ended December 31,		
			2005	2006	2007
Sales		$900,000	$900,000	$900,000	$900,000
Cost of goods sold:					
Beginning inventory	$200,000		$200,000	$180,000	$200,000
Add: Purchases	500,000		500,000	500,000	500,000
Less: Ending inventory	200,000		180,000	200,000	200,000
Cost of goods sold		500,000	520,000	480,000	500,000
Gross profit		$400,000	$380,000	$420,000	$400,000

Exercise 7-9 (20 minutes)

	At Cost	At Retail
Goods available for sale:		
Beginning inventory	$31,900.00	$ 64,200.00
Net purchases	57,810.00	98,400.00
Goods available for sale	$89,710.00	$162,600.00
Deduct net sales at retail		130,000.00
Ending inventory at retail		$ 32,600.00

Cost ratio: ($89,710/$162,600) × 100 = 55.17%
Ending inventory at cost ($32,600 × 55.17%) $17,985.42

Fundamental Accounting Principles, Eleventh Canadian Edition

*Exercise 7-11 (20 minutes)

		Ending Inventory	Cost of Goods Sold
a.	Weighted-average cost ($3,300/1,320 = $2.50):		
	$2.50 × 50	125	
	$3,300 – $125		3,175
b.	FIFO:		
	50 × $2.20	110	
	$3,300 – $110		3,190
c.	LIFO:		
	50 × $3.00	150	
	$3,300 – $150		3,150

FIFO provides the lowest net income because it has the highest cost of goods sold due to decreasing unit costs.

*Exercise 7-13 (15 minutes)

Ending inventory:

	Units	Cost/Unit	Total Cost
Beginning inventory	80 @	$2.00 =	$160.00
March 7 purchase	22 @	2.30 =	50.60
July 28 purchase	48 @	2.50 =	120.00
	150		$330.60

Cost of goods sold:
   Cost of goods available for sale less *Ending inventory* = *Cost of goods sold*

$$\$2,208.00 - \$330.60 = \underline{\$1,877.40}$$

PROBLEMS

Problem 7-1B (40 minutes)

1) (a) FIFO perpetual

Date	Purchases			Sales (at cost)			Inventory Balance		
	Units	Unit Cost	Total Cost	Units	Unit Cost	Cost of Goods Sold	Units	Unit Cost	Total Cost
Jan. 1	Beginning inventory								
	600 @ $55.00 =		$ 33,000				600 @ $55.00 =		$ 33,000
							600 @ $55.00 =		$ 33,000
Feb. 13	200 @ $57.00 =		$ 11,400				200 @ 57.00 =		11,400
15				300 @ $55.00 =		$16,500	300 @ $55.00 =		$ 16,500
							200 @ 57.00 =		11,400
							300 @ $55.00 =		$ 16,500
							200 @ 57.00 =		11,400
Aug. 5	345 @ $59.00 =		$ 20,355				345 @ 59.00 =		20,355
10				300 @ $55.00 =		$ 16,500	165 @ 57.00 =		9,405
				35 @ 57.00 =		1,995	345 @ 59.00 =		20,355
Total	**1,145**		**$64,755**	**635**		**$34,995**	**510**		**$29,760**

Cost of goods available for sale   =   Cost of goods sold   +   Ending inventory

1) (b) LIFO perpetual

Date	Purchases			Sales (at cost)			Inventory Balance		
	Units	Unit Cost	Total Cost	Units	Unit Cost	Cost of Goods Sold	Units	Unit Cost	Total Cost
Jan. 1	Beginning inventory								
	600 @ $55.00 =		$33,000				600 @ $55.00 =		$ 33,000
							600 @ $55.00 =		$ 33,000
Feb. 13	200 @ $57.00 =		$11,400				200 @ 57.00 =		11,400
15				200 @ $57.00 =		$11,400	500 @ $55.00 =		$ 27,500
				100 @ 55.00 =		5,500			
							500 @ $55.00 =		$ 27,500
Aug. 5	345 @ $59.00 =		$20,355				345 @ 59.00 =		20,355
10				335 @ $59.00 =		$19,765	500 @ $55.00 =		$ 27,500
							10 @ 59.00 =		590
Total	**1,145**		**$64,755**	**635**		**$36,665**	**510**		**$28,090**

Cost of goods available for sale   =   Cost of goods sold   +   Ending inventory

Fundamental Accounting Principles, Eleventh Canadian Edition

Problem 7-1B (continued)

1) (c) Moving weighted-average perpetual

Date		Purchases			Sales (at cost)			Inventory Balance		
	Units	Unit Cost	Total Cost	Units	Unit Cost	Cost of Goods Sold	(a) Total Units	(b) ÷ (a) Average Cost/ Unit	(b) Total Cost	
Jan. 1	Beginning inventory 600 @ $55.00 =		$ 33,000.00				600	$55.00	$ 33,000.00	
Feb. 13	200 @ $57.00 =		$ 11,400.00				800	$55.50	$ 44,400.00	
15				300 @	$55.50	= $ 16,650.00	500	$55.50	$ 27,750.00	
Aug. 5	345 @ $59.00 =		$ 20,355.00				845	$56.93	$ 48,105.00	
10				335 @	$56.93	= $ 19,071.55	510	$56.93	$ 29,033.45	
Total	1,145		$64,755.00	635		$35,721.55	510		$29,033.45	

Cost of goods available for sale = Cost of goods sold + Ending inventory

Inventory Balance Calculations

600				$33,000.00
200	@	57.00	=	11,400.00
800				$44,400.00
800				$44,400.00
−300	@	55.50	=	-16,650.00
500				$27,750.00
500				$27,750.00
345	@	59.00	=	20,355.00
845				$48,105.00
845				$48,105.00
−335	@	56.93	=	-19,071.55
510				$29,033.45

Problem 7-1B *(continued)*

2) Specific identification

Date	Purchases			Sales (at cost)			Inventory Balance			
	Units	Unit Cost	Total Cost	Units	Unit Cost	Cost of Goods Sold	Units		Unit Cost	Total Cost
Jan. 1	Beginning inventory									
	600 @ $55.00 =		$33,000				600 @		$55.00 =	$ 33,000
Feb. 13	200 @ $57.00 =		$11,400				600 @		$55.00 =	$ 33,000
							200 @		57.00 =	11,400
15				175 @ $55.00 =		$ 9,625	425 @		$55.00 =	$ 23,375
				125 @ 57.00 =		7,125	75 @		57.00 =	4,275
							425 @		$55.00 =	$ 23,375
							75 @		57.00 =	4,275
Aug. 5	345 @ $59.00 =		$20,355				345 @		59.00 =	20,355
10				15 @ $55.00 =		$ 825	410 @		$55.00 =	$22,550
				320 @ 59.00 =		18,880	75 @		57.00 =	4,275
							25 @		59.00 =	1,475
Total	1,145		$64,755	635		$36,455	510			$28,300

Cost of goods available for sale   =   Cost of goods sold   +   Ending inventory

Fundamental Accounting Principles, Eleventh Canadian Edition

Problem 7-1B *(concluded)*

3)

	FIFO		LIFO		Moving Weighted Average		Specific Identification	
Feb. 15 Accounts Receivable.......... Sales .... *To record a credit sale; $90/unit x 300 units = $27,000.*	27,000	27,000	27,000	27,000	27,000	27,000	27,000	27,000
15 Cost of Goods Sold .... Merchandise Inventory...... *To record the sale of merchandise.*	16,500	16,500	16,900	16,900	16,650	16,650	16,750	16,750
Aug. 5 Merchandise Inventory.......... Accounts Payable............ *To record the purchase of inventory on credit.*	20,355	20,355	20,355	20,355	20,355	20,355	20,355	20,355

Problem 7-2B (40 minutes)

1) (a) FIFO perpetual

Date		Purchases			Sales (at cost)			Inventory Balance		
	Units	**Unit Cost**	**Total Cost**	**Units**	**Unit Cost**	**Cost of Goods Sold**	**Units**	**Unit Cost**	**Total Cost**
Jan. 1	Beginning inventory									
	200 @	$60.00 =	$12,000				200 @	$60.00 =	$ 12,000
Feb. 20				150 @	$60.00 =	$9,000	50 @	$60.00 =	$3,000
							50 @	$60.00 =	$ 3,000
Apr. 30	320 @	$58.00 =	$18,560				320 @	58.00 =	18,560
							50 @	$60.00 =	$ 3,000
							320 @	58.00 =	18,560
Oct. 5	250 @	$50.00 =	$12,500				250 @	50.00 =	12,500
10				50 @	$60.00 =	$ 3,000			
				320 @	58.00 =	18,560			
				130 @	50.00 =	6,500	120 @	50.00 =	$ 6,000
Total	**770**		**$43,060**	**650**		**$37,060**	**120**		**$6,000**

Cost of goods available for sale =   Cost of goods sold   +   Ending inventory

1)(b) LIFO perpetual

Date		Purchases			Sales (at cost)			Inventory Balance		
	Units	**Unit Cost**	**Total Cost**	**Units**	**Unit Cost**	**Cost of Goods Sold**	**Units**	**Unit Cost**	**Total Cost**
Jan. 1	Beginning inventory									
	200 @	$60.00 =	$ 12,000				200 @	$60.00 =	$ 12,000
Feb. 20				150 @	$60.00 =	$9,000	50 @	$60.00 =	$ 3,000
							50 @	$60.00 =	$ 3,000
Apr. 30	320 @	$58.00 =	$ 18,560				320 @	58.00 =	18,560
							50 @	$60.00 =	$ 3,000
							320 @	58.00 =	18,560
Oct. 5	250 @	$50.00 =	$ 12,500				250 @	50.00 =	12,500
10				250 @	$50.00 =	$ 12,500	50 @	$60.00 =	$ 3,000
				250 @	58.00 =	14,500	70 @	58.00 =	4,060
Total	**770**		**$43,060**	**650**		**$36,000**	**120**		**$7,060**

Cost of goods available for sale =   Cost of goods sold   +   Ending inventory

Fundamental Accounting Principles, Eleventh Canadian Edition

Problem 7-2B (continued)
1) c) Moving weighted-average perpetual

Date	Purchases Units	Unit Cost		Total Cost	Sales (at cost) Units	Unit Cost		Cost of Goods Sold	(a) Total Units	(b) ÷ (a) Average Cost/Unit	(b) Total Cost	Inventory Balance Calculations
	Beginning inventory											
Jan. 1	200 @	$60.00	=	$ 12,000.00					200	$60.00	$ 12,000.00	
												200 $12,000.00
Feb. 20					150 @	$60.00	=	$ 9,000				-150 @ 60.00 = - 9,000
									50	$60.00	$ 3,000.00	50 $ 3,000.00
												50 $ 3,000.00
Apr. 30	320 @	$58.00	=	$ 18,560.00								320 @ 58.00 = 18,560.00
									370	$58.27	$ 21,560.00	370 $21,560.00
												370 $21,560.00
Oct. 5	250 @	$50.00	=	$ 12,500.00								250 @ 50.00 = 12,500.00
									620	$54.94	$ 34,060	620 $34,060.00
												620 $34,060.00
10					500 @	$54.94	=	$ 27,470.00				-500 @ 54.94 = -27,470.00
									120	$54.92*	$ 6,590.00	120 $ 6,590.00
Total	770			$43,060	650			$36,470.00	120		$6,590.00	

Cost of goods available for sale = Cost of goods sold + Ending inventory

unit cost changed due to rounding

2)

	FIFO	LIFO	Moving Weighted-Average
Sales (650 × $80).....................	$52,000	$52,000	$52,000
Less: Cost of goods sold	37,060	36,000	36,470
Gross profit............................	$14,940	$16,000	$15,530

3) Gross profits calculated in Part 2 would increase under FIFO and decrease under LIFO if Moran Company had been experiencing increasing prices in the purchase of additional inventory. The moving weighted-average costing method would fall between FIFO and LIFO.

Problem 7-3B (40 minutes) *Part 1*

THE DENNEY COMPANY
Income Statement Comparing FIFO, LIFO, and Moving Weighted-Average Inventory Costing Methods
For Year Ended December 31, 2005

	FIFO	LIFO	Moving Weighted Average
Sales ($98 x 2,500 units)	$245,000	$245,000	$245,000
Cost of goods sold	138,440	138,200	138,363
Gross profit	$106,560	$106,800	$106,637
Operating expenses ($14 x 2,500 units)	35,000	35,000	35,000
Net income	$ 71,560	$ 71,800	$ 71,637

Calculations:

Calculate units and cost of goods available for sale:

Beginning inventory	740	@ $58	=	$ 42,920
Purchases:				
Apr. 2	700	@ $56	=	39,200
Jun. 14	600	@ $54	=	32,400
Aug. 29	500	@ $52	=	26,000
Units available	2,540			
Cost of goods available				$140,520

Fundamental Accounting Principles, Eleventh Canadian Edition

Problem 7-3B *(continued)*
1) (a) FIFO perpetual

Date	Purchases			Sales (at cost)			Inventory Balance		
	Units	Unit Cost	Total Cost	Units	Unit Cost	Cost of Goods Sold	Units	Unit Cost	Total Cost
Jan. 1	Beginning inventory								
	740 @ $58.00 =		$42,920				740 @ $58.00 =		$42,920
							740 @ $58.00 =		$42,920
Apr. 2	700 @ $56.00 =		$39,200				700 @ 56.00 =		39,200
				740 @ $58.00 =		$42,920	240 @ $56.00 =		$13,440
May 20				460 @ 56.00 =		25,760			
							240 @ $56.00 =		$13,440
Jun. 14	600 @ $54.00 =		$32,400				600 @ 54.00 =		32,400
							240 @ $56.00 =		$13,440
							600 @ 54.00 =		32,400
Aug. 29	500 @ $52.00 =		$26,000				500 @ 52.00 =		26,000
Oct. 25				240 @ $56.00 =		13,440	40 @ 52.00 =		2,080
				600 @ 54.00 =		32,400			
				460 @ 52.00 =		23,920			
Total	2,540		$140,520	2,500		$138,440	40 @ 52.00 =		$2,080

Cost of goods available for sale =   Cost of goods sold   +   Ending inventory

Problem 7-3B (continued)
1) (b) LIFO perpetual

Date	Purchases			Sales (at cost)			Inventory Balance		
	Units	Unit Cost	Total Cost	Units	Unit Cost	Cost of Goods Sold	Units	Unit Cost	Total Cost
Jan. 1	Beginning inventory								
	740 @ $58.00 =		$ 42,920				740 @ $58.00 =		$ 42,920
							740 @ $58.00 =		$ 42,920
Apr. 2	700 @ $56.00 =		$ 39,200				700 @ 56.00 =		39,200
				700 @ $56.00 =		$ 39,200	240 @ $58.00 =		$ 13,920
May 20				500 @ 58.00 =		29,000			
							240 @ $58.00 =		$ 13,920
Jun. 14	600 @ $54.00 =		$ 32,400				600 @ 54.00 =		32,400
							240 @ $58.00 =		$ 13,920
							600 @ 54.00 =		32,400
Aug. 29	500 @ $52.00 =		$ 26,000				500 @ 52.00 =		26,000
Oct. 25				500 @ $52.00 =		$ 26,000	40 @ $58.00 =		$ 2,320
				600 @ 54.00 =		32,400			
				200 @ 58.00 =		11,600			
Total	**2,540**		**$140,520**	**2,500**		**$138,200**	**40**		**$2,320**
	Cost of goods available for sale		=	Cost of goods sold		+	Ending inventory		

1) (c) Moving weighted-average perpetual

Date	Purchases Units	Unit Cost		Total Cost	Sales (at cost) Units	Unit Cost		Cost of Goods Sold	Inventory Balance (a) Total Units	(b)÷(a) Average Cost/Unit	(b) Total Cost
Jan. 1	Beginning inventory 740	@ $58.00	= $	42,920.00					740	$58.00	$42,920.00
Apr. 2	700	@ $56.00	= $	39,200.00					1,440	$57.03	$82,120.00
May 20					1,200	@ $57.03	= $	68,436.00	240	$57.02	$13,684.00
Jun. 14	600	@ $54.00	= $	32,400.00					840	$54.86	$46,084.00
Aug. 29	500	@ $52.00	= $	26,000.00					1,340	$53.79	$72,084.00
Oct. 25					1,300	@ $53.79	= $	69,927.00	40	$53.93*	$ 2,157.00
									40		$2,157.00
Total	2,540			$140,520.00	2,500			$138,363.00			

Cost of goods available for = Cost of goods sold + Ending inventory

*cost per unit changed due to rounding

Inventory Balance Calculations

```
                      740              $ 42,920.00
     700  @  56.00  =                    39,200.00
                    1,440              $ 82,120.00
                    1,440              $ 82,120.00
  –1,200  @  57.03  =                  –68,436.00
                      240              $ 13,684.00
                      240              $ 13,684.00
     600  @  54.00  =                    32,400.00
                      840              $ 46,084.00
                      840              $ 46,084.00
     500  @  52.00  =                    26,000.00
                    1,340              $ 72,084.00
                    1,340              $ 72,084.00
  –1,300  @  53.79  =                  –69,927.00
                       40              $  2,157.00
```

Problem 7-3B (concluded)

Part 2

If The Denney Company manager earns a bonus based on a percentage of gross profit, she will prefer the LIFO inventory costing method when the unit costs of merchandise inventory are decreasing.

Problem 7-4B (25 minutes) *Part 1*

Cost of goods sold

	2005	2006	2007
Reported	$205,200	$212,800	$196,030
Adjustments: Dec. 31, 2005 error	+ 17,000	− 17,000	
Dec. 31, 2006 error		− 25,000	+ 25,000
Corrected	$222,200	$170,800	$221,030

Net income:

	2005	2006	2007
Reported	$174,800	$211,270	$183,910
Adjustments: Dec. 31, 2005 error	− 17,000	+ 17,000	
Dec. 31, 2006 error		+ 25,000	− 25,000
Corrected	$157,800	$253,270	$158,910

Total current assets:

	2005	2006	2007
Reported	$266,000	$276,500	$262,950
Adjustments: Dec. 31, 2005 error	− 17,000		
Dec. 31, 2006 error		+ 25,000	
Corrected	$249,000	$301,500	$262,950

Owner's equity:

	2005	2006	2007
Reported	$304,000	$316,000	$336,000
Adjustments: Dec. 31, 2005 error	− 17,000		
Dec. 31, 2006 error		+ 25,000	
Corrected	$287,000	$341,000	$336,000

Part 2

These errors are "self-correcting" in the year following the error. Each overstatement (or understatement) of net income is offset by a matching understatement (or overstatement) in the following year. Thus, **aggregate net income for the three-year period is not affected by the errors.**

Fundamental Accounting Principles, Eleventh Canadian Edition

Problem 7-5B (30 minutes)

1)

	Incorrect Income Statement Information For Years Ended December 31				Corrected Income Statement Information For Years Ended December 31			
	2005	%	2006	%	2005	%	2006	%
Sales............................	$1,350,000	100	$1,690,000	100	$1,350,000	100	$1,690,000	100
Cost of goods sold.....	810,000	60	845,000	50	735,000*	54	937,000**	55
Gross profit................	$ 540,000	40	$ 845,000	50	$ 615,000	46	$ 753,000	45

* $810,000 – $75,000 = $735,000
** $845,000 + $75,000 – $32,000 + $49,000 = $937,000

2) The gross profit information now reflects the increasing cost of goods sold of which the owner was aware.

Problem 7-6B (50 minutes)

	Per Unit					LCM applied to:		
Inventory Items	Units on Hand	Cost	Market	Total Cost	Total Market	a. Whole	b. Major Category	c. Separately to Each Product
Office furniture:								
Desks	436	$261	$305	$113,796	$132,980			$113,796
Credenzas	295	227	256	66,965	75,520			66,965
Chairs	587	49	43	28,763	25,241			25,241
Bookshelves	321	93	82	29,853	26,322			26,322
Subtotals				$239,377	$260,063		$239,377	
Filing cabinets:								
Two-drawer	214	81	70	$ 17,334	$ 14,980			14,980
Four-drawer	398	135	122	53,730	48,556			48,556
Lateral	175	104	118	18,200	20,650			18,200
Subtotals				$ 89,264	$ 84,186		84,186	
Office Equip.:								
Fax machines	430	168	200	$ 72,240	$ 86,000			72,240
Copiers	545	317	288	172,765	156,960			156,960
Typewriters	352	125	117	44,000	41,184			41,184
Subtotals				$289,005	$284,144		284,144	
Totals				$617,646	$628,393	$617,646	$607,707	$584,444

Problem 7-7B (20 minutes)

2004 Gross margin ratio:

Sales...	$4,245,100
Cost of sales....................................	2,674,350
Gross margin....................................	$1,570,750
Gross margin ratio	37.0%

Estimated inventory:
Goods available for sale:

Inventory, December 31, 2004.....	$262,400	
Net purchases, 2005	829,800	
Goods available for sale..............		$1,092,200
Less: Estimated cost of goods sold:		
Sales...	$1,475,300	
Estimated cost of goods sold [$1,475,300 × (1 – 37%)]............		929,439
Estimated July 5, 2005 inventory lost in the flood..................................		$162,761

Problem 7-8B (25 minutes)

FOUR CORNERS EQUIPMENT CO.
Estimated Inventory
March 31, 2005

Goods available for sale:		
Inventory, January 1, 2005		$ 752,880
Purchases	$2,132,100	
Less: Purchase returns	38,370	
Add: Transportation-in	65,900	
Net cost of goods purchased		2,159,630
Goods available for sale		$2,912,510
Less: Estimated cost of goods sold:		
Sales	$3,710,250	
Less: Sales returns	74,200	
Net sales	$3,636,050	
Estimated cost of goods sold [$3,636,050 × (1 – 30%)]		2,545,235
Estimated March 31, 2005, inventory		$ 367,275

Problem 7-9B (25 minutes)

Part 1

THE R.E. McFADDEN CO.
Estimated Inventory
December 31, 2005

	At Cost	At Retail
Goods available for sale:		
Beginning inventory	$ 81,670.00	$ 114,610.00
Purchases...	502,990.00	767,060.00
Purchase returns	(10,740.00)	(15,330.00)
Goods available for sale	$573,920.00	$ 866,340.00
Sales	$786,120.00	
Sales returns	(4,480.00)	
Net sales		$781,640.00
Ending inventory at retail ($866,340 – $781,640)		$ 84,700.00
Cost ratio: ($573,920 ÷ $866,340)		66.25%
Ending inventory at cost ($84,700 × 66.25%)		$ 56,113.75

Part 2

Estimated physical inventory at cost: $78,550 × 66.25% = $52,039.38

THE R.E. McFADDEN CO.
Inventory Shortage
December 31, 2005

	At Cost	At Retail
Estimated inventory, December 31, 2005	$56,113.75	$84,700.00
Physical inventory ($78,550 × 66.25%)..........	52,039.38	78,550.00
Inventory shortage	$ 4,074.37	$ 6,150.00

Problem 7-10B (20 minutes)

	At Cost	At Retail
Goods available for sale:		
Beginning inventory..	$ 150,000	$ 250,000
Purchases	2,100,000	3,500,000
Less: Purchase returns and allowances	250,000	400,000
Add: Transportation-in.....................................	10,000	-
Goods available for sale	$2,010,000	$3,350,000
Deduct net sales at retail ($2,715,000 – $35,000)		2,680,000
Ending inventory at retail		$ 670,000
Cost to retail ratio ($2,010,000 ÷ $3,350,000):		× 60%
Estimated ending inventory at cost ($670,000 × 60%):		$ 402,000

Inventory loss = $402,000 × 20%* = $80,400

Because the insurance company covers 80% of the loss, JavCo's estimated loss is 20% (100% – 80%).

*Problem 7-11B (25 minutes) *Part 1*

Cost of units available for sale:	
6,300 units in beginning inventory @ $35	$ 220,500
10,500 units purchased @ $33	346,500
13,000 units purchased @ $32	416,000
12,000 units purchased @ $29	348,000
15,500 units purchased @ $26	403,000
57,300 units for sale	$1,734,000

Part 2

a) FIFO basis:

Total cost of the 57,300 units for sale		$1,734,000
Less: Ending inventory on a FIFO basis:		
15,500 units @ $26	$403,000	
1,000 units @ $29	29,000	432,000
Cost of units sold		$1,302,000

b) LIFO basis:

Total cost of the 57,300 units for sale		$1,734,000
Less: Ending inventory on a LIFO basis:		
6,300 beginning inventory units @ $35	$220,500	
10,200 units @ $33	336,600	557,100
Cost of units sold		$1,176,900

*Problem 7-11B *(concluded) Part 2*

c) Weighted-average cost basis:
    Total cost of the 57,300 units for sale $1,734,000
    Less: Ending inventory at weighted-average cost:
      ($1,734,000/57,300) = $30.26 × 16,500 units .... <u>499,290*</u>
    Cost of units sold .... <u>$1,234,710*</u>

*These amounts may vary if the unit cost/unit was not rounded to two decimal places.

*Problem 7-12B (25 minutes)

a) FIFO basis:

    Total cost of the 1,145 units for sale $64,755
    Less: Ending inventory on a FIFO basis:
      345 units @ $59 .... $20,355
      165 units @ $57 .... <u>9,405</u>   <u>29,760</u>
    Cost of units sold ....   <u>$34,995</u>

b) LIFO basis:

    Total cost of the 1,145 units for sale $64,755
    Less: Ending inventory on a LIFO basis:
      510 beginning inventory units @ $55 .... <u>28,050</u>
    Cost of units sold .... <u>$36,705</u>

c) Weighted-average cost basis:

    Total cost of the 1,145 units for sale $64,755.00
    Less: Ending inventory at weighted-average cost:
      ($64,755/1,145 = $56.55) × 510 .... <u>28,840.50*</u>
    Cost of units sold .... <u>$35,914.50*</u>

*These amounts may vary if the unit cost/unit was not rounded to two decimal places.

*Problem 7-13B (25 minutes)

a) FIFO basis:

Total cost of the 770 units for sale	$43,060
Less: Ending inventory on a FIFO basis:	
120 units @ $50	6,000
Cost of units sold	$37,060

b) LIFO basis:

Total cost of the 770 units for sale	$43,060
Less: Ending inventory on a LIFO basis:	
120 @ $60...	7,200
Cost of units sold	$35,860

c) Weighted-average cost basis:

Total cost of the 770 units for sale	$43,060.00
Less: Ending inventory at weighted-average cost:	
($43,060/770 = $55.92) × 120	6,710.40*
Cost of units sold	$36,349.60*

These amounts may vary if the unit cost/unit was not rounded to two decimal places.

*Problem 7-14B (45 minutes)

The Denney Company
Income Statement Comparing FIFO, LIFO and Weighted-Average Inventory Costing Methods
For Year Ended December 31, 2005

	FIFO	LIFO	Weighted Average
Sales (2,500 x $98/unit)	$245,000.00	$245,000.00	$245,000.00
COGS	138,440.00	138,200.00	138,307.20
Gross Profit	$106,560.00	$106,800.00	$106,692.80
Operating Expenses (2,500 x $14/unit)	35,000.00	35,000.00	35,000.00
Net Income	$ 71,560.00	$ 71,800.00	$ 71,692.80

Supporting calculations:

Cost of units available for sale:

740	units in beginning inventory	@	$58	=	$ 42,920.00
700	units purchased April 2	@	$56	=	$ 39,200.00
600	units purchased June 14	@	$54	=	$ 32,400.00
500	units purchased August 29	@	$52	=	$ 26,000.00
2,540					$140,520.00

a) **FIFO periodic**

Total cost of the 2,540 units for sale	$140,520.00
Less: Ending inventory on a FIFO basis:	
40 units @ 52 =	2,080.00
Cost of units sold	$138,440.00

b) **LIFO periodic**

Total cost of the 2,540 units for sale	$140,520.00
Less: Ending inventory on a LIFO basis:	
40 units @$58	2,320.00
Cost of units sold	$138,200.00

c) **Weighted-average cost basis:**

Total cost of the 2,540 units for sale	$140,520.00
Less: Ending inventory at weighted-average cost:	
($140,520/2,540) = $55.32 × 40 units =	2,212.80*
Cost of units sold	$138,307.20*

These amounts may vary if the unit cost/unit was not rounded to two decimal places.

Chapter 8   Accounting Information Systems

Fundamental Accounting Principles, Eleventh Canadian Edition

EXERCISES

Exercise 8-1 (15 minutes)

Sales Journal
Page 1

Date		Account Debited	Invoice Number	PR	Accounts Receivable Dr. Sales Cr.	Cost of Goods Sold Dr. Merchandise Inventory Cr.
2005						
Feb.	7	J. Eason	5704		1,150	700
	12	P. Lathan	5705		320	170
	25	S. Summers	5706		550	300

Exercise 8-3 (20 minutes)

Purchases Journal
Page 1

Date		Account Credited	Date of Invoice		Terms	PR	Accounts Payable Cr.	Merchandise Inventory Dr.	Office Supplies Dr.	Other Accounts Dr.
2005										
July	1	Angler, Inc.	Jul	1	n/30		8,100	8,100		
	14	Store Supplies/ Steck Company	Jul	14	2/10, n/30		240			240
	17	Marten Company	Jul	17	n/30		2,600	2,600		

Exercise 8-5 (30 minutes)

Part 1 – Wilson Purchasing

Purchases Journal

Page 1

Date	Account Credited	Date of Invoice	Terms	PR	Accounts Payable Cr.	Merchandise Inventory Dr.	Office Supplies Dr.	Other Accounts Dr.
2005								
May 11	Hostel Sales	May 11	3/10, n/90		30,000	30,000		

Cash Disbursements Journal

Page 1

Date	Ch. No.	Payee	Account Debited	PR	Cash Cr.	Merchandise Inventory Cr.	Other Accounts Dr.	Accounts Payable Dr.
2005								
May 11	84	Express Shipping	Merchandise Inv.		335		335	
20	85	Hostel Sales	Hostel Sales		27,936[1]	864		28,800

General Journal

Page: 1

Date	Account Titles and Explanations	PR	Debit	Credit
2005				
May 12	Accounts Payable – Hostel Sales................		1,200	
	Merchandise Inventory.....................			1,200
	To record return of merchandise.			

Calculations:

1. *30,000 – 1,200 = 28,800; 28,800 x 3% = 864; 28,800 – 864 = 27,936.*

Exercise 8-5 (concluded)

Part 2 – Hostel Sales

Sales Journal
Page 1

Date	Account Debited	Invoice Number	PR	Accounts Receivable Dr. Sales Cr.	Cost of Goods Sold Dr. Merchandise Inventory Cr.
2005					
May 11	Wilson Purchasing	1601		30,000	20,000

Cash Receipts Journal
Page 1

Date	Account Credited	PR	Explanation	Cash Dr.	Sales Discount Dr.	Accounts Receivable Cr.	Sales Cr.	Other Accounts Cr.	Cost of Goods Sold Dr. Merchandise Inventory Cr.
2005									
May 21	Wilson Purchasing		Wilson Purchasing	27,936[1]	864	28,800			

General Journal
Page: 1

Date	Account Titles and Explanations	PR	Debit	Credit
2005				
May 12	Sales Returns and Allowances		1,200	
	Accounts Receivable – Wilson Purchasing			1,200
	To record sales return.			
12	Merchandise Inventory		800	
	Cost of Goods Sold			800
	To record cost of merchandise returned to inventory.			

Calculations:

1. $30,000 - 1,200 = 28,800$; $28,800 \times 3\% = 864$; $28,800 - 864 = 27,936$

Exercise 8-7 (10 minutes)

a. When the schedule of accounts payable is prepared.

b. When crossfooting the Purchases Journal.

c. When the trial balance is prepared.

d. When the schedule of accounts payable is prepared.

e. When the schedule of accounts payable is prepared.

*Exercise 8-9 (30 minutes)

Part 1 – Wilson Purchasing

PURCHASES JOURNAL

Page 2

Date	Account Credited	Date of Invoice	Terms	PR	Accounts Payable Credit	Purchases Debit	Office Supplies Debit	Other Accounts Debit
2005								
May 11	Hostel Sales	May 11	3/10,n/90		30,000	30,000		

CASH DISBURSEMENTS JOURNAL

Page 2

Date	Ch. No.	Payee	Account Debited	PR	Cash Credit	Purchase Discount Credit	Other Accts. Debit	Accts. Payable Debit
2005								
May 11	84	Express Shipping	Transportation-In		335		335	
May 20	85	Hostel Sales	A/P – Hostel Sales		27,936	864		28,800

*Exercise 8-9 (continued)

General Journal

				Page: 1
Date 2005	Account Titles and Explanations	PR	Debit	Credit
May 12	Accounts Payable – Hostel Sales............. Purchase Returns and Allowances .... *To record return of merchandise purchased.*		1,200	1,200

Part 2 – Hostel Sales

SALES JOURNAL
Page 2

		Invoice Number	PR	A/R Dr. Sales Cr.
Date 2005	Account Debited			
May 11	Wilson Purchasing	1601		30,000

CASH RECEIPTS JOURNAL
Page 2

								Page 2
Date 2005	Account Credited	Explanation	PR	Cash Debit	Sales Disc. Debit	Accts. Rec. Credit	Sales Credit	Other Accts. Credit
May 21	Wilson Purchasing	Sale of May 11		27,936	864	28,800		

General Journal

				Page: 1
Date 2005	Account Titles and Explanations	PR	Debit	Credit
May 12	Sales Returns and Allowances................. Accounts Receivable – Wilson Purchasing... *To record sales return.*		1,200	1,200

*Exercise 8-11 (20 minutes)

CASH RECEIPTS JOURNAL

Page 2

Date	Account Credited	Explanation	PR	Cash Debit	Sales Disc. Debit	Accts. Rec. Credit	Sales Credit	Other Accts. Credit
2005								
Sept. 9	Notes payable	Note to bank		2,750				2,750
13	Dale Trent, capital	Owner investment		3,500				3,500
18	Sales	Cash sale		230			230	
27	J. Namal	Invoice, Sept. 7		882	18	900		

*Exercise 8-13 (20 minutes)

CASH DISBURSEMENTS JOURNAL

Page 2

Date	Ch. No.	Payee	Account Debited	PR	Cash Credit	Purchase Discount Credit	Other Accts. Debit	Accts. Payable Debit
2005								
Mar. 9	210	Narlin Corp.	Store Supplies		450		450	
17	211	City Bank	Notes Payable		1,500		1,500	
29	212	LeBaron	LeBaron		3,430	70		3,500
31	213	E. Brandon	Salaries Expense		1,700		1,700	
31	214	Pace, Inc.	Pace, Inc.		2,750			2,750

*Exercise 8-15 (30 minutes)

Part 1

ACCOUNTS RECEIVABLE SUBLEDGER

Adrian Carr			Lisa Mack		
Jan. 8	7,137		Jan. 14	23,985	

Jay Newton			Kathy Olivias		
Jan. 2	4,212		Jan. 10	15,678	
29	8,541		20	13,104	

Part 2

Jan. 31	Accounts Receivable	72,657	
	Sales..		62,100
	GST Payable		4,347
	PST Payable		6,210

Part 3

GENERAL LEDGER

Accounts Receivable			Sales		
Jan. 31	72,657			62,100	Jan. 31

Part 4

SKILLERN COMPANY
Schedule of Accounts Receivable
January 31, 2005

Adrian Carr	$ 7,137
Lisa Mack	23,985
Jay Newton	12,753
Kathy Olivas	28,782
Total accounts receivable	$72,657

*Exercise 8-17 (20 minutes)

SALES JOURNAL

Page X

Date	Account Debited	Invoice Number	PR	Accts. Rec. Debit	PST Payable Credit	GST Payable Credit	Sales Credit
2005							
Aug. 5	Jay Smith	50		25,300	1,760	1,540	22,000
11	Dee Oliver	51		19,550	1,360	1,190	17,000

CASH RECEIPTS JOURNAL

Page X

Date	Account Credited	Explanation	PR	Other Accts. Credit	Accts. Rec. Credit	PST Payable Credit	GST Payable Credit	Sales Credit	Cash Debit	Sales Discount Debit
2005										
Aug.20	A/R – Jay Smith	Inv. 50			25,300				25,300	
21	A/R – Dee Oliver	Inv. 51			19,550				19,380	170

Exercise 8-17 (concluded)

PURCHASES JOURNAL

Page X

Date	Account Credited	Date of Invoice	Terms	PR	Accts. Payable Credit	Purchases Debit	Other Accounts Debit	GST Rec'ble Debit
2005								
Aug.	1 Arden Sheet Metal	Aug. 1	2/10,n/30		5,350	5,000		350
	7 JayCee Equipment	Aug. 7	n/30		3,210		3,000	210

CASH DISBURSEMENTS JOURNAL

Page X

Date	Ch. No.	Payee	Account Debited	PR	Other Accts. Debit	GST Rec'ble Debit	Accts. Payable Debit	Pur. Disc. Credit	Cash Credit
2005									
Aug.10	28	A/P – Arden	Arden Sheet Metal				5,350	100	5,250

PROBLEMS

Problem 8-1B (20 minutes)

Date	Transaction	Special Journal	Subledger
May 1	The owner invested an automobile into the business.	G	NE
2	Sold merchandise and received cash.	CR	MI
3	Purchased merchandise inventory on credit, 1/5, n/30.	P	AP/MI
4	Sold merchandise on terms of 1/10, n/30.	S	AR/MI
5	The customer of May 4 returned defective merchandise; the merchandise was scrapped.	G	AR
6	Regarding the May 3 purchase, received a credit memorandum from the supplier granting an allowance.	G	AP/MI
15	Paid mid-month salaries.	CD	NE
17	Purchased office supplies on credit; terms n/30.	P	AP
19	Paid for the balance owing regarding the May 3 purchase.	CD	AP
22	Received payment regarding the May 4 sale.	CR	AR
25	Borrowed money from bank.	CR	NE
29	Purchased merchandise inventory paying cash.	CD	MI
30	Accrued interest revenue.	G	NE
30	Closed all revenue accounts to the income summary.	G	NE

Fundamental Accounting Principles, Eleventh Canadian Edition

Problem 8-2B (40 minutes)

Sales Journal

Page: S1

Date	Account Debited	Invoice No.	PR	A/R Dr. Sales Cr.	COGS Dr. Merchandise Inventory Cr.
2005					
June 5	Martha Stohart	347		102,000	51,000
6	Carol Larson	348		8,200	5,700
18	Lars Wilson	349		6,000	4,900
25	Nathan Blythe	350		28,000	14,500

Cash Receipts Journal

Page: CR1

Date	Account Credited	PR	Explanation	Cash Dr.	Sales Disc Dr	A/R Cr.	Sales Cr.	Other Accounts Cr.	COGS/Dr. Merchandise Inventory/Cr.
2005									
June 12	A/R – Carol Larson		Inv. 348	8,036	164	8,200			
24	A/R – Martha Stohart		Inv. 347	102,000		102,000			
27	A/R – Lars Wilson		Inv. 349	5,880	120	6,000			

Purchases Journal

Page: P1

Date	Account Credited	Date of Invoice	Terms	PR	A/P Cr.	Merchandise Inventory Dr.	Office Supplies Dr.	Other Accounts Dr.
2005								
June 1	Exeter Equip./Equipment	June 1	n30		45,000			45,000
4	Whitby Co.	June 4	1/5, n15		85,000	85,000		
8	Suppliers Unlimited	June 8	2/10, n30		1,800		1,800	

Problem 8-2B (concluded)

Cash Disbursements

Date	Ch #	Account Debited	PR	Cash Cr.	Merchandise Inventory Cr.	Other Accounts Dr.	A/P Dr.
2005							
June 11	101	Whitby Co.*		80,200			80,200
14	102	Salaries Expense		15,000		15,000	
28	103	Exeter Equipment		45,000			45,000
29	104	Salaries Expense		15,000		15,000	

*85,000 – 4,800 = 80,200

General Journal

Date	Account Titles and Explanations	PR	Debit	Credit
2005				
June 7	Accounts Payable – Whitby Co.		4,800	
	Merchandise Inventory			4,800
	To record allowance received for damages that occurred during delivery.			
26	Sales Returns and Allowances		2,800	
	Accounts Receivable – Nathan Blythe			2,800
	To record unsatisfactory goods returned by customer.			
26	Merchandise Inventory		2,200	
	Cost of Goods Sold			2,200
	Goods returned to inventory.			

Fundamental Accounting Principles, Eleventh Canadian Edition

Problem 8-3B (40 minutes)

Note: Since posting to the General Ledger was not a requirement in this problem, posting references are shown for values posted to the subledgers only.

Part 3

SALES JOURNAL
Page 3

Date		Account Debited	Invoice Number	PR	A/R Dr. Sales. Cr.	Cost of Goods Sold Dr. Merchandise Inventory Cr.
2005						
July	5	Karen Harden	918	√	18,400	10,200
	6	Paul Kane	919	√	7,500	4,100
	13	Kelly Grody	920	√	8,350	4,600
	14	Karen Harden	921	√	4,100	2,300

CASH RECEIPTS JOURNAL
Page 3

Date		Account Credited	Explanation	PR	Cash Debit	Sales Discount Debit	Accts. Rec. Credit	Sales Credit	Other Accts. Credit	Cost of Goods Sold Dr. Merchandise Inventory Cr.
2005										
July	15	Karen Harden	Sale of Jul 5	√	18,032	368	18,400			
	15	Sales	Cash sales		121,370			121,370		66,700

PURCHASES JOURNAL
Page 3

Date		Account Credited	Date of Invoice	Terms	PR	Accounts Payable Credit	Merchandise Inventory Debit	Office Supplies Debit	Other Accts. Debit
2005									
July	1	Beech Company	Jun 30	2/10, n/60	√	6,300	6,300		
	7	Blackwater Inc. /Store Supp.	Jul 7	n/10 EOM	√	1,050			1,050
	9	Poppe's Supply /Store Equip.	Jul 8	n/10 EOM	√	37,710			37,710

Problem 8-3B (continued)

CASH DISBURSEMENTS JOURNAL

Page 3

Date	Ch. No.	Payee	Account Debited	PR	Cash Credit	Merchandise Inventory Credit	Other Accts. Debit	Accts. Payable Debit
2005								
July 3	300	The Weekly Journal	Advertising Expense		575		575	
10	301	Beech Company	Beech Company	√	6,174	126		6,300
15	302	Payroll	Sales Salaries Expens		30,620		30,620	

GENERAL JOURNAL

Page 3

Date	Account Titles and Explanations	PR	Debit	Credit
2005				
July 8	Accounts Payable—Blackwater Inc.	201/√	150	
	Store Supplies...................	125		150
	Returned supplies to supplier.			

Problem 8-3B *(continued)*

Parts 1, 2, 3

ACCOUNTS RECEIVABLE SUBLEDGER

Karen Harden

Date		Explanation	PR	Debit	Credit	Balance
2005						
July	5		S3	18,400		18,400
	14		S3	4,100		22,500
	15		CR3		18,400	4,100

Kelly Grody

Date		Explanation	PR	Debit	Credit	Balance
2005						
July	13		S3	8,350		8,350

Paul Kane

Date		Explanation	PR	Debit	Credit	Balance
2005						
July	6		S3	7,500		7,500

Problem 8-3B *(concluded)*

ACCOUNTS PAYABLE SUBLEDGER

Beech Company

Date	Explanation	PR	Debit	Credit	Balance
2005					
July 1		P3		6,300	6,300
10		CD3	6,300		0

Blackwater Inc.

Date	Explanation	PR	Debit	Credit	Balance
2005					
July 7		P3		1,050	1,050
8		G3	150		900

Poppe's Supply

Date	Explanation	PR	Debit	Credit	Balance
2005					
July 9		P3		37,710	37,710

Sprague Company

Date	Explanation	PR	Debit	Credit	Balance
2005					

Fundamental Accounting Principles, Eleventh Canadian Edition

Problem 8-4B (70 minutes)
Parts 2, 3, 4

SALES JOURNAL

Page 3

Date	Account Debited	Invoice Number	PR	A/R Dr. Sales. Cr.	Cost of Goods Sold Dr. Merchandise Inventory Cr.
2005					
July 5	Karen Harden	918	✓	18,400	10,200
6	Paul Kane	919	✓	7,500	4,100
13	Kelly Grody	920	✓	8,350	4,600
14	Karen Harden	921	✓	4,100	2,300
29	Paul Kane	922	✓	28,090	15,500
30	Kelly Grody	923	✓	15,750	8,700
31	Totals			82,190	45,400
				(106/413)	(502/119)

CASH RECEIPTS JOURNAL

Page 3

Date	Account Credited	Explanation	PR	Cash Debit	Sales Discount Debit	Accts. Rec. Credit	Sales Credit	Other Accts. Credit	Cost of Goods Sold Dr. Merchandise Inventory Cr.
2005									
July 15	Karen Harden	Sale of Jul 5	✓	18,032	368	18,400			
15	Sales	Cash sales		121,370			121,370		66,700
16	Paul Kane	Sale of Jul 6	✓	7,350	150	7,500			
21	L.T. Notes Pay	Note to bank	251	20,000				20,000	
23	Kelly Grody	Sale of Jul 13	✓	8,183	167	8,350			
24	Karen Harden	Sale of Jul 14	✓	4,018	82	4,100			
31	Sales	Cash sales		79,020			79,020		43,500
31	Totals			257,973	767	38,350	200,390	20,000	110,200
				(101)	(415)	(106)	(413)	(X)	(502/119)

Problem 8-4B (continued)

PURCHASES JOURNAL

Date	Account Credited	Date of Invoice	Terms	PR	Accounts Payable Credit	Merchandise Inventory Debit	Office Supplies Debit	Other Accts. Debit
2005								
July 1	Beech Company	Jun 30	2/10, n/60	√	6,300	6,300		
7	Blackwater Inc. /Store Supp.	Jul 7	n/10 EOM	125√	1,050			1,050
9	Poppe's Supply /Store Equip.	Jul 8	n/10 EOM	165√	37,710			37,710
17	Sprague Company	Jul 17	2/10, n/60	√	8,200	8,200		
20	Poppe's Supply	Jul 19	n/10 EOM	√	750		750	
26	Beech Company	Jul 26	2/10, n/30	√	9,770	9,770		
31	Totals				63,780	24,270	750	38,760
					(201)	(119)	(124)	(X)

CASH DISBURSEMENTS JOURNAL

Date	Ch. No.	Payee	Account Debited	PR	Cash Credit	Merchandise Inventory Credit	Other Accts. Debit	Accts. Payable Debit
2005								
July 3	300	The Weekly Journal	Advertising Expense	655	575		575	
10	301	Beech Company	Beech Company	√	6,174	126		6,300
15	302	Payroll	Sales Salaries Expense	621	30,620		30,620	
27	303	Sprague Company	Sprague Company	√	5,684	116		5,800*
31	304	Payroll	Sales Salaries Expense	621	30,620		30,620	
31		Totals			73,673	242	61,815	12,100
					(101)	(119)	(X)	(201)

* $8,200 – $2,400 return = $5,800

Problem 8-4B *(continued)*

<table>
<tr><td colspan="2" align="center">**GENERAL JOURNAL**</td><td></td><td></td><td align="right">**Page 3**</td></tr>
<tr><td>**Date**</td><td>**Account Titles and Explanations**</td><td>**PR**</td><td>**Debit**</td><td>**Credit**</td></tr>
<tr><td>2005</td><td></td><td></td><td></td><td></td></tr>
<tr><td>July 8</td><td>Accounts Payable—Blackwater Inc. ....</td><td>201/√</td><td>150</td><td></td></tr>
<tr><td></td><td>   Store Supplies................................</td><td>125</td><td></td><td>150</td></tr>
<tr><td></td><td>*Returned supplies to supplier.*</td><td></td><td></td><td></td></tr>
<tr><td></td><td></td><td></td><td></td><td></td></tr>
<tr><td>24</td><td>Accounts Payable—Sprague Company......</td><td>201/√</td><td>2,400</td><td></td></tr>
<tr><td></td><td>   Merchandise Inventory........................</td><td>119</td><td></td><td>2,400</td></tr>
<tr><td></td><td>*Returned defective inventory to
merchandise supplier.*</td><td></td><td></td><td></td></tr>
</table>

Parts 1, 2, 3, 4

GENERAL LEDGER

Cash   Acct. No. 101

Date	Explanation	PR	Debit	Credit	Balance
2005					
June 30	Balance Forward				95,000
July 31		CR3	257,973		352,973
31		CD3		73,673	279,300

Accounts Receivable   Acct. No. 106

Date	Explanation	PR	Debit	Credit	Balance
2005					
July 31		S3	82,190		82,190
31		CR3		38,350	43,840

Merchandise Inventory   Acct. No. 119

Date	Explanation	PR	Debit	Credit	Balance
2005					
Jun. 30	Balance Forward				167,000
Jul. 24		G3		2,400	164,600
31		S3		45,400	119,200
31		CR3		110,200	9,000
31		P3	24,270		33,270
31		CD3		242	33,028

Office Supplies   Acct. No. 124

Date	Explanation	PR	Debit	Credit	Balance
2005					
July 31		P3	750		750

Problem 8-4B (continued)

Store Supplies   Acct. No. 125

Date		Explanation	PR	Debit	Credit	Balance
2005						
July	7		P3	1,050		1,050
	8		G3		150	900

Store Equipment   Acct. No. 165

Date		Explanation	PR	Debit	Credit	Balance
2005						
July	9		P3	37,710		37,710

Accounts Payable   Acct. No. 201

Date		Explanation	PR	Debit	Credit	Balance
2005						
July	8		G3	150		(150)
	24		G3	2,400		(2,550)
	31		P3		63,780	61,230
	31		CD3	12,100		49,130

Long-Term Notes Payable   Acct. No. 251

Date		Explanation	PR	Debit	Credit	Balance
2005						
June	30	Balance Forward				167,000
July	21		CR3		20,000	187,000

Gene Eldridge, Capital   Acct. No. 301

Date		Explanation	PR	Debit	Credit	Balance
2005						
Jun.	30	Balance Forward				95,000

Sales   Acct. No. 413

Date		Explanation	PR	Debit	Credit	Balance
2005						
July	31		S3		82,190	82,190
	31		CR3		200,390	282,580

Sales Discounts   Acct. No. 415

Date		Explanation	PR	Debit	Credit	Balance
2005						
July	31		CR3	767		767

     Fundamental Accounting Principles, Eleventh Canadian Edition

Problem 8-4B *(continued)*

Cost of Goods Sold — Acct. No. 502

Date	Explanation	PR	Debit	Credit	Balance
2005					
July 31		S3	45,400		45,400
31		CR3	110,200		155,600

Sales Salaries Expense — Acct. No. 621

Date	Explanation	PR	Debit	Credit	Balance
2005					
July 15		CD3	30,620		30,620
31		CD3	30,620		61,240

Advertising Expense — Acct. No. 655

Date	Explanation	PR	Debit	Credit	Balance
2005					
July 3		CD3	575		575

ACCOUNTS RECEIVABLE SUBLEDGER

Karen Harden

Date	Explanation	PR	Debit	Credit	Balance
2005					
July 5		S3	18,400		18,400
14		S3	4,100		22,500
15		CR3		18,400	4,100
24		CR3		4,100	0

Kelly Grody

Date	Explanation	PR	Debit	Credit	Balance
2005					
July 13		S3	8,350		8,350
23		CR3		8,350	0
30		S3	15,750		15,750

Paul Kane

Date	Explanation	PR	Debit	Credit	Balance
2005					
July 6		S3	7,500		7,500
16		CR3		7,500	0
29		S3	28,090		28,090

Problem 8-4B *(continued)*

ACCOUNTS PAYABLE SUBLEDGER

Beech Company

Date	Explanation	PR	Debit	Credit	Balance
2005					
July 1		P3		6,300	6,300
10		CD3	6,300		0
26		P3		9,770	9,770

Blackwater Inc.

Date	Explanation	PR	Debit	Credit	Balance
2005					
July 7		P3		1,050	1,050
8		G3	150		900

Poppe's Supply

Date	Explanation	PR	Debit	Credit	Balance
2005					
July 9		P3		37,710	37,710
20		P3		750	38,460

Sprague Company

Date	Explanation	PR	Debit	Credit	Balance
2005					
July 17		P3		8,200	8,200
24		G3	2,400		5,800
27		CD3	5,800		0

Problem 8-4B *(continued)*

Part 5

ELDRIDGE INDUSTRIES
Trial Balance
July 31, 2005

Account	Debit	Credit
Cash	$279,300	
Accounts receivable	43,840	
Merchandise inventory	33,028	
Office supplies	750	
Store supplies	900	
Store equipment	37,710	
Accounts payable		$ 49,130
Long-term notes payable		187,000
Gene Eldridge, capital		95,000
Sales		282,580
Sales discounts	767	
Cost of goods sold	155,600	
Sales salaries expense	61,240	
Advertising expense	575	
Totals	$613,710	$613,710

ELDRIDGE INDUSTRIES
Schedule of Accounts Receivable
July 31, 2005

Kelly Grody	$15,750
Paul Kane	28,090
Total accounts receivable	$43,840

ELDRIDGE INDUSTRIES
Schedule of Accounts Payable
July 31, 2005

Beech Company	$ 9,770
Blackwater Inc.	900
Poppe's Supply	38,460
Total accounts payable	$49,130

Problem 8-4B *(concluded)*

Part 6
Analysis component:

To find the error(s),
- re-add the account balances on the schedule of accounts payable to confirm that the addition was correct.
- trace the balances listed on the schedule of accounts payable back to the subsidiary accounts to confirm that they were listed correctly on the schedule.
- recalculate the balance of each subsidiary account to confirm that the additions and subtractions were correct.
- trace the postings from each subsidiary account and from the controlling account back to the appropriate journals.

Since the purchases and cash disbursements journals were footed and crossfooted before posting, the previous steps should disclose the error.

Fundamental Accounting Principles, Eleventh Canadian Edition

Problem 8-5B (120 minutes)

Parts 1, 2, 3

SALES JOURNAL
Page 3

Date		Account Debited	Invoice Number	P R	A/R Dr. Sales. Cr.	Cost of Goods Sold Dr. Merchandise Inventory Cr.
2005						
Oct.	6	Marge Craig	913	✓	3,300	1,800
	12	Heather Flatt	914	✓	3,650	2,000
	15	Amy Izon	915	✓	3,100	1,700
	16	Heather Flatt	916	✓	4,290	2,460
	21	Jan Wildman	917	✓	5,520	3,000
	31	Totals			19,860	10,960
					(106/413)	(502/119)

CASH RECEIPTS JOURNAL
Page 3

Date		Account Credited	Explanation	PR	Cash Debit	Sales Discount Debit	Acct. Rec. Credit	Sales Credit	Other Acct. Credit	Cost of Goods Sold Dr. Merchandise Inventory Cr.
2005										
Oct.	2	Jan Wildman	Invoice Nov 23	✓	4,116	84	4,200			
	15	Sales	Cash sales		38,830			38,830		21,400
	15	Marge Craig	Invoice, Dec 6	✓	2,401	49	2,450*			
	22	Heather Flatt	Invoice, Dec 12	✓	3,577	73	3,650			
	25	Amy Izon	Invoice, Dec 15	✓	2,842	58	2,900**			
	28	Store Supplies	Sold supplies	125	58				58	
	31	Sales	Cash sales		66,128			66,128		36,400
	31	Totals			117,952	264	13,200	104,958	58	57,800
					(101)	(415)	(106)	(413)	(X)	(502/119)

* $3,300 – $850 return = $2,450
** $3,100 – $200 return = $2,900

Problem 8-5B (continued)

PURCHASES JOURNAL

Page 2

Date		Account Credited	Date of Invoice	Terms	PR	Accounts Payable Credit	Merchandise Inventory Debit	Office Supplies Debit	Other Accts. Debit
2005									
Oct.	2	Walters Company	Oct 2	2/10, n/60	√	3,200	3,200		
	5	Green Supply Co.	Oct 3	n/10 EOM	√	1,300	1,300		
	15	Walters Company	Oct 15	2/10, n/60	√	3,990	3,990		
	15	Sunshine Company	Oct 15	2/10, n/60	√	2,650	2,650		
	16	Green Supply Co.	Oct 16	n/10 EOM	√	765		765	
	20	Green Supply Co./Store Equip.	Oct 19	n/10 EOM	165/√	7,475			7,475
	28	Sunshine Company	Oct 28	2/10, n/60	√	6,030	6,030		
	31	Totals				25,410	17,170	765	7,475
						(201)	(119)	(124)	(X)

Fundamental Accounting Principles, Eleventh Canadian Edition

Problem 8-5B *(continued)*

CASH DISBURSEMENTS JOURNAL

Page 4

Date	Ch. No.	Payee	Account Debited	PR	Cash Credit	Merchandise Inventory Credit	Other Accts. Debit	Accts. Payable Debit
2005								
Oct. 2	619	Omni Realty Co.	Rent Expense	640	2,250		2,250	
6	620	Fireside Company	Fireside Company	√	3,724	76		3,800
12	621	Walters Company	Walters Company	√	3,136	64		3,200
15	622	Jamie Ford	Sales Salaries Expense	621	2,620		2,620	
25	623	Walters Company*	Walters Company	√	3,283	67		3,350
25	624	Sunshine Company	Sunshine Company	√	2,597	53		2,650
29	625	Marlee Levin	Marlee Levin, Withdrawals	302	4,000		4,000	
30	626	Midwest Elec. Co.	Utilities Expense	690	990		990	
30	627	Jamie Ford.	Sales Salaries Expense	621	2,620		2,620	
31		Totals			25,220	260	12,480	13,000
					(101)	(507)	(X)	(201)

*3,990 – 640 return = 3,350

Problem 8-5B *(continued)*

		GENERAL JOURNAL			Page 2
Date 2005		Account Title and Explanations	PR	Debit	Credit
Oct.	4	Accounts Payable—Fireside Company..................	201/√	460	
		Merchandise Inventory	119		460
		Defective merchandise returned.			
	9	Sales Returns and Allowances..............................	414	850	
		Accounts Receivable—Marge Craig...............	106/√		850
		Returned merchandise was scrapped.			
	18	Sales Returns and Allowances..............................	414	200	
		Accounts Receivable—Amy Izon......................	106/√		200
		Returned merchandise was scrapped.			
	19	Accounts Payable—Walters Company...................	201/√	640	
		Merchandise Inventory	119		640
		Returned merchandise.			
	20	Accounts Payable—Green Supply Co.	201/√	143	
		Office Supplies...	124		143
		Returned office supplies.			

ACCOUNTS RECEIVABLE SUBLEDGER

Marge Craig

Date		Explanation	PR	Debit	Credit	Balance
2005						
Oct.	6		S3	3,300		3,300
	9		G2		850	2,450
	15		CR3		2,450	0

Heather Flatt

Date		Explanation	PR	Debit	Credit	Balance
2005						
Oct.	12		S3	3,650		3,650
	16		S3	4,290		7,940
	22		CR3		3,650	4,290

Problem 8-5B (continued)

Amy Izon

Date		Explanation	PR	Debit	Credit	Balance
2005						
Oct.	15		S3	3,100		3,100
	18		G2		200	2,900
	25		CR3		2,900	0

Jan Wildman

Date		Explanation	PR	Debit	Credit	Balance
2005						
Sept	23		S2	4,200		4,200
Oct.	2		CR3		4,200	0
	21		S3	5,520		5,520

Part 2

ACCOUNTS PAYABLE SUBLEDGER

Fireside Company

Date		Explanation	PR	Debit	Credit	Balance
2005						
Sept	28		P1		4,260	4,260
Oct.	4		G2	460		3,800
	6		CD4	3,800		0

Green Supply Company

Date		Explanation	PR	Debit	Credit	Balance
2005						
Oct.	5		P2		1,300	1,300
	16		P2		765	2,065
	20		P2		7,475	9,540
	20		G2	143		9,397

Sunshine Company

Date		Explanation	PR	Debit	Credit	Balance
2005						
Oct.	15		P2		2,650	2,650
	25		CD4	2,650		0
	28		P2		6,030	6,030

Problem 8-5B *(continued)*

Walters Company

Date	Explanation	PR	Debit	Credit	Balance
2005					
Oct. 2		P2		3,200	3,200
12		CD4	3,200		0
15		P2		3,990	3,990
19		G2	640		3,350
25		CD4	3,350		0

Parts 2, 3

GENERAL LEDGER

Cash   Acct. No. 101

Date	Explanation	PR	Debit	Credit	Balance
2005					
Sept 30	Balance				5,361
Oct. 31		CR3	117,952		123,313
31		CD4		25,220	98,093

Accounts Receivable   Acct. No. 106

Date	Explanation	PR	Debit	Credit	Balance
2005					
Sept 30	Balance				4,200
Oct. 9		G2		850	3,350
18		G2		200	3,150
31		S3	19,860		23,010
31		CR3		13,200	9,810

Merchandise Inventory   Acct. No. 119

Date	Explanation	PR	Debit	Credit	Balance
2005					
Sept 30	Balance				66,970
Oct. 4		G2		460	66,510
19		G2		640	65,870
31		S3		10,960	54,910
31		P2	17,170		72,080
31		CD4		260	71,820
31		CR3		57,800	14,020

Office Supplies   Acct. No. 124

Date	Explanation	PR	Debit	Credit	Balance
2005					
Sept 30	Balance				607
Oct. 20		G2		143	464
31		P2	765		1,229

Problem 8-5B *(continued)*

Store Supplies
Acct. No. 125

Date	Explanation	PR	Debit	Credit	Balance
2005					
Sept 30	Balance				346
Oct. 28		CR3		58	288

Store Equipment
Acct. No. 165

Date	Explanation	PR	Debit	Credit	Balance
2005					
Sept 30	Balance				42,129
Oct. 20		P2	7,475		49,604

Accumulated Amortization, Store Equipment
Acct. No. 166

Date	Explanation	PR	Debit	Credit	Balance
2005					
Sept 30	Balance				9,153

Accounts Payable
Acct. No. 201

Date	Explanation	PR	Debit	Credit	Balance
2005					
Sept 30	Balance				4,260
Oct. 4		G2	460		3,800
19		G2	640		3,160
20		G2	143		3,017
31		P2		25,410	28,427
31		CD4	13,000		15,427

Marlee Levin, Capital
Acct. No. 301

Date	Explanation	PR	Debit	Credit	Balance
2005					
Sept 30	Balance				106,200

Marlee Levin, Withdrawals
Acct. No. 302

Date	Explanation	PR	Debit	Credit	Balance
2005					
Oct. 29		CD4	4,000		4,000

Sales
Acct. No. 413

Date	Explanation	PR	Debit	Credit	Balance
2005					
Oct. 31		S3		19,860	19,860
31		CR3		104,958	124,818

Problem 8-5B (continued)

	Sales Returns and Allowances				Acct. No. 414
Date	**Explanation**	**PR**	**Debit**	**Credit**	**Balance**
2005					
Oct. 9		G2	850		850
18		G2	200		1,050

	Sales Discounts				Acct. No. 415
Date	**Explanation**	**PR**	**Debit**	**Credit**	**Balance**
2005					
Oct. 31		CR3	264		264

	Cost of Goods Sold				Acct. No. 502
Date	**Explanation**	**PR**	**Debit**	**Credit**	**Balance**
2005					
Oct. 31		S3	10,960		10,960
31		CR3	57,800		68,760

	Sales Salaries Expense				Acct. No. 621
Date	**Explanation**	**PR**	**Debit**	**Credit**	**Balance**
2005					
Oct. 15		CD4	2,620		2,620
30		CD4	2,620		5,240

	Rent Expense				Acct. No. 640
Date	**Explanation**	**PR**	**Debit**	**Credit**	**Balance**
2005					
Oct. 2		CD4	2,250		2,250

	Utilities Expense				Acct. No. 690
Date	**Explanation**	**PR**	**Debit**	**Credit**	**Balance**
2005					
Oct. 30		CD4	990		990

Problem 8-5B *(concluded)*

Part 4

STARSHINE PRODUCTS
Trial Balance
October 31, 2005

Account	Debit	Credit
Cash	$ 98,093	
Accounts receivable	9,810	
Merchandise inventory	14,020	
Office supplies	1,229	
Store supplies	288	
Store equipment	49,604	
Accumulated amortization, store equipment		$ 9,153
Accounts payable		15,427
Marlee Levin, capital		106,200
Marlee Levin, withdrawals	4,000	
Sales		124,818
Sales returns and allowances	1,050	
Sales discounts	264	
Cost of goods sold	68,760	
Sales salaries expense	5,240	
Rent expense	2,250	
Utilities expense	990	
Totals	$255,598	$255,598

STARSHINE PRODUCTS
Schedule of Accounts Receivable
October 31, 2005

Heather Flatt	$4,290
Jan Wildman	5,520
Total accounts payable	$9,810

STARSHINE PRODUCTS
Schedule of Accounts Payable
October 31, 2005

Green Supply Company	$ 9,397
Sunshine Company	6,030
Total accounts payable	$15,427

Problem 8-6B (30 minutes)

Sales Journal
Page 1

Date	Account Debited	Invoice No.	PR	A/R Dr. Sales Cr.	PR	COGS Dr. Merchandise Inventory Cr.
2005						
July 9	W. Tilden	213	√	300.00	√	108.00
15	J. Samuelson	214	√	750.00	√	270.00
22	V. Nels	215	√	600.00	√	200.60
30	M. Bains	216		810.00	√	270.81

Purchases Journal
Page 1

Date	Account Credited	Date of Invoice	Terms	PR	A/P Cr.	PR	Merchandise Inventory Dr.	Office Supplies Dr.	Other Accounts Dr.
2005									
July 4	Tulsco Supply	July 4	n/30		450.00	√	450.00		
18	Gentry Holdings	July 18	n/30		270.00	√	270.00		

NOTE: An additional PR column has been added to facilitate the referencing of inventory entries into the inventory subsidiary ledger.

Fundamental Accounting Principles, Eleventh Canadian Edition

Problem 8-6B *(continued)*

Inventory Subledger Record — Weighted-Average Perpetual

Date	PR	\<Purchases\>			\<Sales (at cost)\>			\<Inventory Balance\>		
								(a)	(b) ÷ (a)	(b)
		Units	Unit Cost	Total Cost	Units	Unit Cost	Total Cost	Total Units	Average Cost/Unit	Total Cost
July 31		Beginning inventory								
		30 @ $12.00 = $		360.00				30	$12.00	$ 360.00
4	P1	45 @ $10.00 = $		450.00						
								75	$10.80	$ 810.00
9	S1				10 @ $10.80 =		$ 108.00			
								65	$10.80	$ 702.00
15	S1				25 @ $10.80 =		$ 270.00			
								40	$10.80	$ 432.00
18	P1	30 @ $9.00 = $		270.00						
								70	$10.03	$ 702.00
22	S1				20 @ $10.03 =		$ 200.60			
								50	$10.03	$ 501.40
30	S1				27 @ $10.03 =		$ 270.81			
								23	$10.03	$ 230.59
Total		**105**		**$1,080.00**	**82**		**$849.41**	**23**		**$230.59**

Cost of goods available for sale = Cost of goods sold + Ending inventory

Inventory Balance Calculations

30				$ 360.00
45	@	10.00	=	450.00
75				$ 810.00
75				$ 810.00
−10	@	10.80	=	−108.00
65				$ 702.00
65				$ 702.00
−25	@	10.80	=	−270.00
40				$ 432.00
40				$ 432.00
30	@	9.00	=	270.00
70				$ 702.00
70				$ 702.00
−20	@	10.03	=	−200.60
50				$ 501.40
50				$ 501.40
−27	@	10.03	=	−270.81
23				$ 230.59

Note: An additional PR column has been added to the Inventory Subledger Record to facilitate referencing of inventory entries.

*Problem 8-7B (40 minutes)

Note: Since posting to the General Ledger was not a requirement in this problem, posting references are shown for values posted to the subledgers only.

SALES JOURNAL

Page 3

Date		Account Debited	Invoice Number	PR	A/R Dr. Sales Cr.
2005					
July	5	Karen Harden	918	√	18,400
	6	Paul Kane	919	√	7,500
	13	Kelly Grody	920	√	8,350
	14	Karen Harden	921	√	4,100

CASH RECEIPTS JOURNAL

Page 3

Date		Account Credited	Explanation	PR	Cash Debit	Sales Disc. Debit	Accts. Rec. Credit	Sales Credit	Other Accts. Credit
2005									
July	15	Karen Harden	Sale of July 5	√	18,032	368	18,400		
	15	Sales	Cash sales		121,370			121,370	

PURCHASES JOURNAL

Page 3

Date		Account Credited	Date of Invoice	Terms	PR	Accounts Payable Credit	Purchases Debit	Office Supplies Debit	Other Accounts Debit
2005									
July	1	Beech Company	Jun. 30	2/10,n/60	√	6,300	6,300		
	7	Blackwater Inc./Store Supplies	July 7	n/10 EOM	√	1,050			1,050
	9	Poppe's Supply/Store Equipment	July 8	n/10 EOM	√	37,710			37,710

*Problem 8-7B (continued)

CASH DISBURSEMENTS JOURNAL

Page 3

Date 2005		Ch. No.	Payee	Account Debited	PR	Cash Credit	Purchase Discount Credit	Other Accts. Debit	Accts. Payable Debit
July	3	300	The Weekly Journal	Advertising Expense		575		575	
	10	301	Beech Company	Beech Company	√	6,174	126		6,300
	15	302	Payroll	Sales Salaries Expense		30,620		30,620	

GENERAL JOURNAL

Page 3

Date 2005		Account Titles and Explanations	PR	Debit	Credit
July	8	Accounts Payable—Blackwater Inc.	201/√	150	
		Store Supplies..............................	125		150
		Returned supplies to supplier.			

Studentt Solutions Manual for Chapter 8

*Problem 8–7B *(continued)*

ACCOUNTS RECEIVABLE SUBLEDGER

Karen Harden

Date	Explanation	PR	Debit	Credit	Balance
2005					
July 5		S3	18,400		18,400
14		S3	4,100		22,500
15		CR3		18,400	4,100

Kelly Grody

Date	Explanation	PR	Debit	Credit	Balance
2005					
July 13		S3	8,350		8,350

Paul Kane

Date	Explanation	PR	Debit	Credit	Balance
2005					
July 6		S3	7,500		7,500

Fundamental Accounting Principles, Eleventh Canadian Edition

*Problem 8-7B *(concluded)*

ACCOUNTS PAYABLE SUBLEDGER

Beech Company

Date		Explanation	PR	Debit	Credit	Balance
2005						
July	1		P3		6,300	6,300
	10		CD3	6,300		0

Blackwater Inc.

Date		Explanation	PR	Debit	Credit	Balance
2005						
July	7		P3		1,050	1,050
	8		G3	150		900

Poppe's Supply

Date		Explanation	PR	Debit	Credit	Balance
2005						
July	9		P3		37,710	37,710

Sprague Company

Date	Explanation	PR	Debit	Credit	Balance
2005					

*Problem 8-8B (70 minutes)

SALES JOURNAL

Page 3

Date 2005		Account Debited	Invoice Number	PR	A/R Dr. Sales Cr.
July	5	Karen Harden	918	√	18,400
	6	Paul Kane	919	√	7,500
	13	Kelly Grody	920	√	8,350
	14	Karen Harden	921	√	4,100
	29	Paul Kane	922	√	28,090
	30	Kelly Grody	923	√	15,750
		Totals			82,190
					(106/413)

CASH RECEIPTS JOURNAL

Page 3

Date 2005		Account Credited	Explanation	PR	Cash Debit	Sales Disc. Debit	Accts. Rec. Credit	Sales Credit	Other Accts. Credit
July	15	Karen Harden	Sale of July 5	√	18,032	368	18,400		
	15	Sales	Cash sales		121,370			121,370	
	16	Paul Kane	Sale of July 6	√	7,350	150	7,500		
	21	L.T. Notes P.	Note to bank	251	20,000				20,000
	23	Kelly Grody	Sale of July 13	√	8,183	167	8,350		
	24	Karen Harden	Sale of July 14	√	4,018	82	4,100		
	31	Sales	Cash sales		79,020			79,020	
		Totals			257,973	767	38,350	200,390	20,000
					(101)	(415)	(106)	(413)	(X)

Fundamental Accounting Principles, Eleventh Canadian Edition

*Problem 8-8B (continued)

PURCHASES JOURNAL

Date	Account Credited	Date of Invoice	Terms	PR	Accounts Payable Credit	Purchases Debit	Office Supplies Debit	Other Accounts Debit
2005								
July 1	Beech Company	Jun. 30	2/10, n/60	√	6,300	6,300		
7	Blackwater Inc./Store Supplies	July 7	n/10 EOM	125/√	1,050			1,050
9	Poppe's Supply/Store Equipment	July 8	n/10 EOM	165/√	37,710			37,710
17	Sprague Company	July 17	2/10, n/60	√	8,200	8,200		
20	Poppe's Supply	July 19	n/10 EOM	√	750		750	
26	Beech Company	July 26	2/10, n/30	√	9,770	9,770		
	Totals				63,780	24,270	750	38,760
					(201)	(505)	(124)	(X)

CASH DISBURSEMENTS JOURNAL

Date	Ch. No.	Payee	Account Debited	PR	Cash Credit	Purchase Discount Credit	Other Accts. Debit	Accts. Payable Debit
2005								
July 3	300	The Weekly Journal	Advertising Expense	655	575		575	
10	301	Beech Company	Beech Company	√	6,174	126		6,300
15	302	Payroll	Sales Salaries Expense	621	30,620		30,620	
27	303	Sprague Company	Sprague Company	√	5,684	116		5,800*
31	304	Payroll	Sales Salaries Expense	621	30,620		30,620	
		Totals			73,673	242	61,815	12,100
					(101)	(506)	(X)	(201)

*$8,200 - $2,400 return = $5,800

*Problem 8-8B (continued)

GENERAL JOURNAL

Page 3

Date 2005	Account Titles and Explanations	PR	Debit	Credit
July 8	Accounts Payable—Blackwater Inc.	201/√	150	
	Store Supplies	125		150
	Returned supplies to supplier.			
24	Accounts Payable—Sprague Company	201/√	2,400	
	Purchase Returns and Allowances	507		2,400
	Returned defective inventory to merchandise supplier.			

Parts 1, 2, 3, 4

GENERAL LEDGER

Cash

Acct. No. 101

Date	Explanation	PR	Debit	Credit	Balance
2005					
June 30	Balance Forward				95,000
July 31		CR3	257,973		352,973
31		CD3		73,673	279,300

Accounts Receivable

Acct. No. 106

Date	Explanation	PR	Debit	Credit	Balance
2005					
July 31		S3	82,190		82,190
31		CR3		38,350	43,840

Merchandise Inventory

Acct. No. 119

Date	Explanation	PR	Debit	Credit	Balance
2005					
Jun. 30	Balance Forward				167,000

Office Supplies

Acct. No. 124

Date	Explanation	PR	Debit	Credit	Balance
2005					
July 31		P3	750		750

*Problem 8-8B *(continued)*

Store Supplies   Acct. No. 125

Date	Explanation	PR	Debit	Credit	Balance
2005					
July 7		P3	1,050		1,050
8		G3		150	900

Store Equipment   Acct. No. 165

Date	Explanation	PR	Debit	Credit	Balance
2005					
July 9		P3	37,710		37,710

Accounts Payable   Acct. No. 201

Date	Explanation	PR	Debit	Credit	Balance
2005					
July 8		G3	150		(150)
24		G3	2,400		(2,550)
31		P3		63,780	61,230
31		CD3	12,100		49,130

Long-Term Notes Payable   Acct. No. 251

Date	Explanation	PR	Debit	Credit	Balance
2005					
June 30	Balance Forward				167,000
July 21		CR3		20,000	187,000

Gene Eldridge, Capital   Acct. No. 301

Date	Explanation	PR	Debit	Credit	Balance
2005					
Jun. 30	Balance Forward				95,000

Sales   Acct. No. 413

Date	Explanation	PR	Debit	Credit	Balance
2005					
July 31		S3		82,190	82,190
31		CR3		200,390	282,580

Sales Discounts   Acct. No. 415

Date	Explanation	PR	Debit	Credit	Balance
2005					
July 31		CR3	767		767

*Problem 8-8B *(continued)*

Purchases   Acct. No. 505

Date	Explanation	PR	Debit	Credit	Balance
2005					
July 31		P3	24,270		24,270

Purchase Discounts   Acct. No. 506

Date	Explanation	PR	Debit	Credit	Balance
2005					
July 31		CD3		242	242

Purchase Returns and Allowances   Acct. No. 507

Date	Explanation	PR	Debit	Credit	Balance
2005					
July 24		G3		2,400	2,400

Sales Salaries Expense   Acct. No. 621

Date	Explanation	PR	Debit	Credit	Balance
2005					
July 15		CD3	30,620		30,620
31		CD3	30,620		61,240

Advertising Expense   Acct. No. 655

Date	Explanation	PR	Debit	Credit	Balance
2005					
July 3		CD3	575		575

ACCOUNTS RECEIVABLE SUBLEDGER

Karen Harden

Date	Explanation	PR	Debit	Credit	Balance
2005					
July 5		S3	18,400		18,400
14		S3	4,100		22,500
15		CR3		18,400	4,100
24		CR3		4,100	0

Kelly Grody

Date	Explanation	PR	Debit	Credit	Balance
2005					
July 13		S3	8,350		8,350
23		CR3		8,350	0
30		S3	15,750		15,750

Fundamental Accounting Principles, Eleventh Canadian Edition

*Problem 8-8B *(continued)*

Paul Kane

Date	Explanation	PR	Debit	Credit	Balance
2005					
July 6		S3	7,500		7,500
16		CR3		7,500	0
29		S3	28,090		28,090

ACCOUNTS PAYABLE SUBLEDGER

Beech Company

Date	Explanation	PR	Debit	Credit	Balance
2005					
July 1		P3		6,300	6,300
10		CD3	6,300		0
26		P3		9,770	9,770

Blackwater Inc.

Date	Explanation	PR	Debit	Credit	Balance
2005					
July 7		P3		1,050	1,050
8		G3	150		900

Poppe's Supply

Date	Explanation	PR	Debit	Credit	Balance
2005					
July 9		P3		37,710	37,710
20		P3		750	38,460

Sprague Company

Date	Explanation	PR	Debit	Credit	Balance
2005					
July 17		P3		8,200	8,200
24		G3	2,400		5,800
27		CD3	5,800		0

ELDRIDGE INDUSTRIES
Trial Balance
July 31, 2005

Account	Debit	Credit
Cash	$279,300	
Accounts receivable	43,840	
Merchandise inventory	167,000	
Office supplies	750	
Store supplies	900	
Store equipment	37,710	
Accounts payable		$ 49,130
Long-term notes payable		187,000
Gene Eldridge, capital		95,000
Sales		282,580
Sales discounts	767	
Purchases	24,270	
Purchase discounts		242
Purchase returns and allowances		2,400
Sales salaries expense	61,240	
Advertising expense	575	
Totals	$616,352	$616,352

ELDRIDGE INDUSTRIES
Schedule of Accounts Receivable
July 31, 2005

Kelly Grody	$15,750
Paul Kane	28,090
Total accounts receivable	$43,840

ELDRIDGE INDUSTRIES
Schedule of Accounts Payable
July 31, 2005

Beech Company	$ 9,770
Blackwater Inc.	900
Poppe's Supply	38,460
Total accounts payable	$49,130

*Problem 8-9B - Perpetual (100 minutes) *Part 4*

Page 2

SALES JOURNAL

Date 2005	Account Debited	Invoice Number	PR	Accts. Rec. Debit	PST Payable Credit	GST Payable Credit	Sales Credit	COGS Dr./ MI Cr.
Nov. 8	Leroy Holmes	439	√	7,429.50	635.00	444.50	6,350.00	4,445.00
10	Sam Spear	440	√	14,625.00	1,250.00	875.00	12,500.00	8,750.00
15	Marjorie Cook	441	√	4,972.50	425.00	297.50	4,250.00	2,975.00
22	Sam Spear	442	√	3,036.15	259.50	181.65	2,595.00	1,800.00
24	Marjorie Cook	443	√	3,790.80	324.00	226.80	3,240.00	2,260.00
31	Totals			33,853.95	2,893.50	2,025.45	28,935.00	20,230.00
				(106)	(224)	(225)	(413)	(502/119)

Page 3

CASH RECEIPTS JOURNAL

Date 2005	Account Credited	Explanation	PR	Cash Debit	Sales Disc. Debit	Accts. Rec. Credit	Sales Credit	Other Accts Credit	PST Payable Credit	GST Payable Credit	COGS Dr./ MI Cr.
Nov. 2	L.T. Notes Pay	Note to bank	251	86,250.00				86,250.00			
15	Sales	Cash sales		31,788.90			27,170.00		2,717.00	1,901.90	19,000.00
18	Leroy Holmes	Invoice, Nov 8	√	7,302.50	127.00	7,429.50					
19	Sam Spear	Invoice, Nov 10	√	14,375.00	250.00	14,625.00					
25	Marjorie Cook	Invoice, Nov 15	√	4,887.50	85.00	4,972.50					
30	Sales	Cash sales		41,772.51			35,703.00		3,570.30	2,499.21	25,000.00
30	Totals			186,376.41	462.00	27,027.00	62,873.00	86,250.00	6,287.30	4,401.11	44,000.00
				(101)	(415)	(106)	(413)	(X)	(224)	(225)	(502/119)

*Problem 8-9B - Perpetual (continued)

PURCHASES JOURNAL

Page 2

Date 2005	Account Credited	Date of Invoice	Terms	PR	Accts. Payable Credit	Merchandise Inventory Debit	Other Accounts Debit	GST Rec'ble Debit
Nov. 1	Jett Supply/Office Equip.	Nov 1	n/10 EOM	163/✓	5,416.34		5,062.00	354.34
4	Defore Industries	Nov 3	2/10, n/30	✓	12,198.00	11,400.00		798.00
5	Atlas Company/Store Supplies	Nov 5	n/10 EOM	125/✓	1,091.40		1,020.00	71.40
11	The Welch Company	Nov 10	2/10, n/30	✓	3,089.09	2,887.00		202.09
16	Atlas Company/Office Supplies	Nov 16	n/10 EOM	124/✓	598.13		559.00	39.13
30	Totals				22,392.96	14,287.00	6,641.00	1,464.96
					(201)	(119)	(X)	(108)

CASH DISBURSEMENTS JOURNAL

Page 3

Date 2005	Ch. No.	Payee	Account Debited	PR	Cash Credit	Merch. Inventory Credit	Other Accts. Debit	GST Rec'ble Debit	Accts. Payable Debit
Nov. 12	633	Defore Industries	Defore Industries	✓	11,970.00	228.00			12,198.00
15	634	Payroll	Sales Salaries Expense	621	8,435.00		8,435.00		
19	635	The Welch Co.*	The Welch Company	✓	2,520.00	48.00			2,568.00
30	636	Payroll	Sales Salaries Expense	621	8,435.00		8,435.00		
30			Totals		31,360.00	276.00	16,870.00		14,766.00
					(101)	(119)	(X)		(201)

*2,887 – 487 = 2,400; 2,400 x 2% = 48 discount

*Problem 8-9B - Perpetual *(continued)*

		GENERAL JOURNAL			Page 2
Date		Account Titles and Explanations	PR	Debit	Credit
2005					
Nov.	17	Accounts Payable—The Welch Company........	201/✓	521.09	
		GST Payable...	225		34.09
		Merchandise Inventory	119		487.00
		Returned merchandise.			
	26	Accounts Payable—Jett Supply........................	201/✓	986.54	
		Office Equipment	163		922.00
		GST Payable...	225		64.54
		Returned office equipment.			

*Problem 8-9B - Perpetual *(continued)*

Parts 2 and 4

ACCOUNTS RECEIVABLE SUBLEDGER

Marjorie Cook

Date		Explanation	PR	Debit	Credit	Balance
2005						
Nov.	15		S2	4,972.50		4,972.50
	24		S2	3,790.80		8,763.30
	25		CR2		4,972.50	3,790.80

Leroy Holmes

Date		Explanation	PR	Debit	Credit	Balance
2005						
Nov.	8		S2	7,429.50		7,429.50
	18		CR2		7,429.50	0.00

Sam Spear

Date		Explanation	PR	Debit	Credit	Balance
2005						
Nov.	10		S2	14,625.00		14,625.00
	19		CR2		14,625.00	0.00
	22		S2	3,036.15		3,036.15

Parts 3 and 4

ACCOUNTS PAYABLE SUBLEDGER

Atlas Company

Date		Explanation	PR	Debit	Credit	Balance
2005						
Nov.	5		P2		1,091.40	1,091.40
	16		P2		598.13	1,689.53

Fundamental Accounting Principles, Eleventh Canadian Edition

*Problem 8-9B - Perpetual (continued)

Defore Industries

Date		Explanation	PR	Debit	Credit	Balance
2005						
Nov.	4		P2		12,198.00	12,198.00
	12		CD2	12,198.00		0.00

Jett Supply

Date		Explanation	PR	Debit	Credit	Balance
2005						
Nov.	1		P2		5,416.34	5,416.34
	26		G2	986.54		4,429.80

The Welch Company

Date		Explanation	PR	Debit	Credit	Balance
2005						
Nov.	11		P2		3,089.09	3,089.09
	17		G2	521.09		2,568.00
	19		CD2	2,568.00		0.00

*Problem 8-9B - Perpetual (continued)

Parts 1 and 4

GENERAL LEDGER

Cash   Acct. No. 101

Date		Explanation	PR	Debit	Credit	Balance
2005						
Nov.	30		CR2	186,376.41		186,376.41
	30		CD2		31,360.00	155,016.41

Accounts Receivable   Acct. No. 106

Date		Explanation	PR	Debit	Credit	Balance
2005						
Nov.	30		S2	33,853.95		33,853.95
	30		CR2		27,027.00	6,826.95

GST Receivable   Acct. No. 108

Date		Explanation	PR	Debit	Credit	Balance
2005						
Nov.	30		P2	1,464.96		1,464.96

Merchandise Inventory   Acct. No. 119

Date		Explanation	PR	Debit	Credit	Balance
2005						
Oct.	31					210,000.00
Nov.	17		G2		487.00	209,513.00
	30		S2		20,230.00	189,283.00
	30		CR3		44,000.00	145,283.00
	30		P2	14,287.00		159,570.00
	30		CD3		276.00	159,294.00

*Problem 8-9B - Perpetual *(continued)*

Office Supplies   Acct. No. 124

Date		Explanation	PR	Debit	Credit	Balance
2005						
Nov.	30		P2	559.00		559.00

Store Supplies   Acct. No. 125

Date		Explanation	PR	Debit	Credit	Balance
2005						
Nov.	5		P2	1,020.00		1,020.00

Office Equipment   Acct. No. 163

Date		Explanation	PR	Debit	Credit	Balance
2005						
Nov.	1		P2	5,062.00		5,062.00
	26		G2		922.00	4,140.00

Accounts Payable   Acct. No. 201

Date		Explanation	PR	Debit	Credit	Balance
2005						
Nov.	17		G2	521.09		(521.09)
	26		G2	986.54		(1,507.63)
	30		P2		22,392.96	20,885.33
	30		CD2	14,766.00		6,119.33

PST Payable   Acct. No. 224

Date		Explanation	PR	Debit	Credit	Balance
2005						
Nov.	30		S2		2,893.50	2,893.50
	30		CR2		6,287.30	9,180.80

*Problem 8-9B - Perpetual (continued)

GST Payable
Acct. No. 225

Date		Explanation	PR	Debit	Credit	Balance
2005						
Nov.	17		G2		34.09	34.09
	26		G2		64.54	98.63
	30		S2		2,025.45	2,124.08
	30		CR2		4,401.11	6,525.19

Long-Term Notes Payable
Acct. No. 251

Date		Explanation	PR	Debit	Credit	Balance
2005						
Nov.	2		CR2		86,250.00	86,250.00

Asha Crystal, Capital
Acct. No. 301

Date		Explanation	PR	Debit	Credit	Balance
2005						
Oct.	31					210,000.00

Sales
Acct. No. 413

Date		Explanation	PR	Debit	Credit	Balance
2005						
Nov.	30		S2		28,935.00	28,935.00
	30		CR2		62,873.00	91,808.00

Sales Discounts
Acct. No. 415

Date		Explanation	PR	Debit	Credit	Balance
2005						
Nov.	30		CR2	462.00		462.00

Fundamental Accounting Principles, Eleventh Canadian Edition

*Problem 8-9B - Perpetual (continued)

Cost of Goods Sold   Acct. No. 502

Date		Explanation	PR	Debit	Credit	Balance
2005						
Nov.	30		S2	20,230.00		20,230.00
	30		CR3	44,000.00		64,230.00

Sales Salaries Expense   Acct. No. 621

Date		Explanation	PR	Debit	Credit	Balance
2005						
Nov.	15		CD2	8,435.00		8,435.00
	30		CD2	8,435.00		16,870.00

CRYSTAL COMPANY
Trial Balance
November 30, 2005

Account	Debit	Credit
Cash	$155,016.41	
Accounts receivable	6,826.95	
GST receivable	1,464.96	
Merchandise inventory	159,294.00	
Office supplies	559.00	
Store supplies	1,020.00	
Office equipment	4,140.00	
Accounts payable		$ 6,119.33
PST Payable		9,180.80
GST Payable		6,525.19
Long-term notes payable		86,250.00
Asha Crystal, capital		210,000.00
Sales		91,808.00
Sales discounts	462.00	
Cost of goods sold	64,230.00	
Sales salaries expense	16,870.00	
Totals	$409,883.32	$409,883.32

CRYSTAL COMPANY
Schedule of Accounts Receivable
November 30, 2005

Marjorie Cook	$3,790.80
Sam Spear	3,036.15
Total accounts receivable	$6,826.95

CRYSTAL COMPANY
Schedule of Accounts Payable
November 30, 2005

Atlas Company	$1,689.53
Jett Supply	4,429.80
Total accounts payable	$6,119.33

*Problem 8-9B - Periodic (100 minutes)

Part 4

SALES JOURNAL

Date 2005	Account Debited	Invoice Number	PR	Accts. Rec. Debit	PST Payable Credit	GST Payable Credit	Sales Credit
Nov. 8	Leroy Holmes	439	✓	7,429.50	635.00	444.50	6,350.00
10	Sam Spear	440	✓	14,625.00	1,250.00	875.00	12,500.00
15	Marjorie Cook	441	✓	4,972.50	425.00	297.50	4,250.00
22	Sam Spear	442	✓	3,036.15	259.50	181.65	2,595.00
24	Marjorie Cook	443	✓	3,790.80	324.00	226.80	3,240.00
31	Totals			33,853.95	2,893.50	2,025.45	28,935.00
				(106)	(224)	(225)	(413)

CASH RECEIPTS JOURNAL

Date 2005	Account Credited	Explanation	PR	Cash Debit	Sales Discount Debit	Accts. Rec. Credit	Sales Credit	Other Accts Credit	PST Payable Credit	GST Payable Credit
Nov. 2	L.T. Notes Pay	Note to bank	251	86,250.00				86,250.00		
15	Sales	Cash sales		31,788.90			27,170.00		2,717.00	1,901.90
18	Leroy Holmes	Invoice, Nov 8	✓	7,302.50	127.00	7,429.50				
19	Sam Spear	Invoice, Nov 10	✓	14,375.00	250.00	14,625.00				
25	Marjorie Cook	Invoice, Nov 15	✓	4,887.50	85.00	4,972.50				
30	Sales	Cash sales		41,772.51			35,703.00		3,570.30	2,499.21
30	Totals			186,376.41	462.00	27,027.00	62,873.00	86,250.00	6,287.30	4,401.11
				(101)	(415)	(106)	(413)	(X)	(224)	(225)

*Problem 8-9B - Periodic (continued)

Page 2

PURCHASES JOURNAL

Date		Account Credited	Date of Invoice	Terms	PR	Accts. Payable Credit	Purchases Debit	Other Accounts Debit	GST Rec'ble Debit
2005									
Nov.	1	Jett Supply/Office Equip.	Nov 1	n/10 EOM	163/✓	5,416.34		5,062.00	354.34
	4	Defore Industries	Nov 3	2/10, n/30	✓	12,198.00	11,400.00		798.00
	5	Atlas Company/Store Supplies	Nov 5	n/10 EOM	125/✓	1,091.40		1,020.00	71.40
	11	The Welch Company	Nov 10	2/10, n/30	✓	3,089.09	2,887.00		202.09
	16	Atlas Company/Office Supplies	Nov 16	n/10 EOM	124/✓	598.13		559.00	39.13
	30	Totals				22,392.96	14,287.00	6,641.00	1,464.96
						(201)	(505)	(X)	(108)

Page 3

CASH DISBURSEMENTS JOURNAL

Date		Ch. No.	Payee	Account Debited	PR	Cash Credit	Pur. Disc. Credit	Other Accts. Debit	GST Rec'ble Debit	Accts. Payable Debit
2005										
Nov.	12	633	Defore Industries	Defore Industries	✓	11,970.00	228.00			12,198.00
	15	634	Payroll	Sales Salaries Expense	621	8,435.00		8,435.00		
	19	635	The Welch Co.	The Welch Company	✓	2,520.00	48.00			2,568.00
	30	636	Payroll	Sales Salaries Expense	621	8,435.00		8,435.00		
	30			Totals		31,360.00	276.00	16,870.00		14,766.00
						(101)	(507)	(X)		(201)

*Problem 8-9B - Periodic *(continued)*

GENERAL JOURNAL

Page 2

Date 2005	Account Titles and Explanations	PR	Debit	Credit
Nov. 17	Accounts Payable—The Welch Company........	201/✓	521.09	
	GST Payable	225		34.09
	Purchases Returns and Allowances	506		487.00
	Returned merchandise.			
26	Accounts Payable—Jett Supply......................	201/✓	986.54	
	Office Equipment	163		922.00
	GST Payable	225		64.54
	Returned office equipment.			

Parts 2 and 4

ACCOUNTS RECEIVABLE SUBLEDGER

Marjorie Cook

Date		Explanation	PR	Debit	Credit	Balance
2005						
Nov.	15		S2	4,972.50		4,972.50
	24		S2	3,790.80		8,763.30
	25		CR3		4,972.50	3,790.80

Leroy Holmes

Date		Explanation	PR	Debit	Credit	Balance
2005						
Nov.	8		S2	7,429.50		7,429.50
	18		CR3		7,429.50	0.00

Sam Spear

Date		Explanation	PR	Debit	Credit	Balance
2005						
Nov.	10		S2	14,625.00		14,625.00
	19		CR3		14,625.00	0.00
	22		S2	3,036.15		3,036.15

*Problem 8-9B - Periodic *(continued)*

Parts 3 and 4

ACCOUNTS PAYABLE SUBLEDGER

Atlas Company

Date		Explanation	PR	Debit	Credit	Balance
2005						
Nov.	5		P2		1,091.40	1,091.40
	16		P2		598.13	1,689.53

Defore Industries

Date		Explanation	PR	Debit	Credit	Balance
2005						
Nov.	4		P2		12,198.00	12,198.00
	12		CD3	12,198.00		0.00

Jett Supply

Date		Explanation	PR	Debit	Credit	Balance
2005						
Nov.	1		P2		5,416.34	5,416.34
	26		G2	986.54		4,429.80

The Welch Company

Date		Explanation	PR	Debit	Credit	Balance
2005						
Nov.	11		P2		3,089.09	3,089.09
	17		G2	521.09		2,568.00
	19		CD3	2,568.00		0.00

Fundamental Accounting Principles, Eleventh Canadian Edition

*Problem 8-9B - Periodic *(continued)*

Parts 1 and 4

GENERAL LEDGER

Cash   Acct. No. 101

Date		Explanation	PR	Debit	Credit	Balance
2005						
Nov.	30		CR3	186,376.41		186,376.41
	30		CD3		31,360.00	155,016.41

Accounts Receivable   Acct. No. 106

Date		Explanation	PR	Debit	Credit	Balance
2005						
Nov.	30		S2	33,853.95		33,853.95
	30		CR3		27,027.00	6,826.95

GST Receivable   Acct. No. 108

Date		Explanation	PR	Debit	Credit	Balance
2005						
Nov.	30		P2	1,464.96		1,464.96

Merchandise Inventory   Acct. No. 119

Date		Explanation	PR	Debit	Credit	Balance
2005						
Oct.	31	Beginning balance				210,000.00

Office Supplies   Acct. No. 124

Date		Explanation	PR	Debit	Credit	Balance
2005						
Nov.	30		P2	559.00		559.00

Store Supplies   Acct. No. 125

Date		Explanation	PR	Debit	Credit	Balance
2005						
Nov.	5		P2	1,020.00		1,020.00

*Problem 8-9B - Periodic (continued)

Office Equipment   Acct. No. 163

Date		Explanation	PR	Debit	Credit	Balance
2005						
Nov.	1		P2	5,062.00		5,062.00
	26		G2		922.00	4,140.00

Accounts Payable   Acct. No. 201

Date		Explanation	PR	Debit	Credit	Balance
2005						
Nov.	17		G2	521.09		(521.09)
	26		G2	986.54		(1,507.63)
	30		P2		22,392.96	20,885.33
	30		CD3	14,766.00		6,119.33

PST Payable   Acct. No. 224

Date		Explanation	PR	Debit	Credit	Balance
2005						
Nov.	30		S2		2,893.50	2,893.50
	30		CR3		6,287.30	9,180.80

GST Payable   Acct. No. 225

Date		Explanation	PR	Debit	Credit	Balance
2005						
Nov.	17		G2		34.09	34.09
	26		G2		64.54	98.63
	30		S2		2,025.45	2,124.08
	30		CR3		4,401.11	6,525.19

Long-Term Notes Payable   Acct. No. 251

Date		Explanation	PR	Debit	Credit	Balance
2005						
Nov.	2		CR3		86,250.00	86,250.00

Asha Crystal, Capital   Acct. No. 301

Date		Explanation	PR	Debit	Credit	Balance
2005						
Oct.	31	Beginning balance				210,000.00

Fundamental Accounting Principles, Eleventh Canadian Edition

*Problem 8-9B - Periodic (continued)

Sales   Acct. No. 413

Date		Explanation	PR	Debit	Credit	Balance
2005						
Nov.	30		S2		28,935.00	28,935.00
	30		CR3		62,873.00	91,808.00

Sales Discounts   Acct. No. 415

Date		Explanation	PR	Debit	Credit	Balance
2005						
Nov.	30		CR3	462.00		462.00

Purchases   Acct. No. 505

Date		Explanation	PR	Debit	Credit	Balance
2005						
Nov.	30		P2	14,287.00		14,287.00

Purchases Returns and Allowances   Acct. No. 506

Date		Explanation	PR	Debit	Credit	Balance
2005						
Nov.	17		G2		487.00	487.00

Purchases Discounts   Acct. No. 507

Date		Explanation	PR	Debit	Credit	Balance
2005						
Nov.	30		CD3		276.00	276.00

Sales Salaries Expense   Acct. No. 621

Date		Explanation	PR	Debit	Credit	Balance
2005						
Nov.	15		CD3	8,435.00		8,435.00
	30		CD3	8,435.00		16,870.00

CRYSTAL COMPANY
Trial Balance
November 30, 2005

Account	Debit	Credit
Cash	$155,016.41	
Accounts receivable	6,826.95	
GST receivable	1,464.96	
Merchandise inventory	210,000.00	
Office supplies	559.00	
Store supplies	1,020.00	
Office equipment	4,140.00	
Accounts payable		$ 6,119.33
PST Payable		9,180.80
GST Payable		6,525.19
Long-term notes payable		86,250.00
Asha Crystal, capital		210,000.00
Sales		91,808.00
Sales discounts	462.00	
Purchases	14,287.00	
Purchases returns and allowances		487.00
Purchases discounts		276.00
Sales salaries expense	16,870.00	
Totals	$410,646.32	$410,646.32

CRYSTAL COMPANY
Schedule of Accounts Receivable
November 30, 2005

Marjorie Cook	$3,790.80
Sam Spear	3,036.15
Total accounts receivable	$6,826.95

CRYSTAL COMPANY
Schedule of Accounts Payable
November 30, 2005

Atlas Company	$1,689.53
Jett Supply	4,429.80
Total accounts payable	$6,119.33

*Problem 8-10B (30 minutes)

Sales Journal

Date	Account Debited	Invoice No.	PR	A/R Dr	PST Payable CR	GST Payable CR	Sales Cr	COGS DR Merchandise Inventory CR
2005								
May 3	Ajax Holdings	361		6,900	480	420	6,000	3,200
30	Allendale Arena	363		4,255	296	259	3,700	1,900

Cash Receipts Journal

Date	Account Credited	Explanation	PR	Cash DR	Sales Disc Dr	A/R CR	Sales CR	Other Accounts CR	PST Payable CR	GST Payable CR	COGS/DR Merchandise Inventory/CR
2005											
May 1	John Trenton, Capital			9,000				9,000			
12	A/R – Ajax			6,840	60	6,900					
13	Sales	Inv #362		2,070			1,800		144	126	1,100
15	Bank Loan Payable			5,000				5,000			

Purchases Journal

Date	Account Credited	Terms	PR	A/P CR	Merchandise Inventory DR	Other Accounts DR	GST Rec'ble DR
2005							
May 7	Moore Corporation/Off. Supplies	n/30		3,424		3,200	224
16	London Company	1/15,n/30		7,704	7,200		504

Cash Disbursements Journal

Date	Ch #	Account Debited	PR	Cash CR	Merchandise Inventory CR	Other Accounts DR	GST Rec'ble DR	A/P DR
2005								
May 5	83	Merchandise Inventory		1,712		1,600	112	
30	84	A/P – Moore Corporation		3,424				3,424

*Problem 8-11B (30 minutes)

SALES JOURNAL

Date	Account Debited	Invoice Number	PR	Accts. Rec. Debit	PST Payable Credit	GST Payable Credit	Sales Credit
2005							
May 3	Ajax Holdings	361		6,900	480	420	6,000
30	Allendale Arena	363		4,255	296	259	3,700

CASH RECEIPTS JOURNAL

Date	Account Credited	Explanation	PR	Cash Debit	Sales Discount Debit	Accts. Rec. Credit	Sales Credit	Other Accts. Credit	PST Payable Credit	GST Payable Credit
2005										
May 1	John Trenton, Capital			9,000				9,000		
12	A/R – Ajax			6,840	60	6,900				
13	Sales	Inv #362		2,070			1,800		144	126
15	Bank Loan Payable			5,000				5,000		

PURCHASES JOURNAL

Date	Account Credited	Date of Invoice	Terms	PR	Accts. Payable Credit	Purchases Debit	Other Accounts Debit	GST Rec'ble Debit
2005								
May 7	Moore Corporation/Off. Supplies	May 7	N/30		3,424		3,200	224
16	London Company	May 16	1/15,n/30		7,704	7,200		504

*Problem 8-11B *(concluded)*

CASH DISBURSEMENTS JOURNAL

PageX

Date	Ch. No.	Payee	Account Debited	PR	Cash Credit	Pur. Disc. Credit	Other Accts. Debit	GST Rec'ble Debit	Accts. Payable Debit
2005									
May 5	83	Merchandise Inventory	Purchases		1,712		1,600	112	
30	84	A/P – Moore Corporation	Lexor Suppliers		3,424				3,424

Chapter 9   Internal Control and Cash

EXERCISES

Exercise 9-1 (10 minutes)

Lombard Company's internal control system failed to require a separation of asset custody and recordkeeping. The bookkeeper should not have been allowed to sign the company's cheques. In addition, since a loss was incurred, the company apparently had not bonded its employee. Otherwise, the loss would have been insured by the bonding company. Finally, if regular, independent reviews of the accounting records had been done, the payments of salary cheques to a nonemployee may have been discovered sooner.

Exercise 9-3 (15 minutes)
a.   If a cash register cannot be used, the total sales value of the shirts and sunglasses given to the employee each day should be calculated. Then, the employee should sign a receipt for the merchandise and the amount of cash that he or she has been given. At the end of each day, the employee should be required to return cash plus remaining shirts and sunglasses equal to the amount taken to the stand.

b.   The employee should sign a receipt for the total amount of cash he or she is given each weekend. Then, each time the employee makes a purchase, he or she should obtain a signed sales receipt for the payment. The sales receipt should list the items purchased and the prices paid. When the employee returns to the business office, the total value of the signed sales receipts plus any remaining cash should equal the amount of cash originally given to the employee. Also, the merchandise brought back by the employee should be the same as the items listed on the signed sales receipts.

Fundamental Accounting Principles, Eleventh Canadian Edition

Exercise 9-5 (20 minutes)

Part 1

a.

Jan.	1	Petty Cash..	200.00	
		Cash..		200.00
		To establish the fund.		

b.

Eanes Co.
Petty Cash Payments Report
January 1 – 8, 2005

Receipts:

Postage expense	$64.00	
Merchandise inventory	19.00	
Store supplies	36.50	
Jim Eanes, Withdrawals	53.00	
Total receipts		$172.50
Fund total	$200.00	
Less: Cash remaining	27.50	
Equals: Cash required to replenish petty cash.......		172.50
Cash over/(short)...		$ -0-

Jan.	8	Postage Expense..	64.00	
		Merchandise Inventory	19.00	
		Store Supplies	36.50	
		Jim Eanes, Withdrawals	53.00	
		Cash..		172.50
		To reimburse the fund.		

Part 2

Jan.	8	Postage Expense..	64.00	
		Merchandise Inventory	19.00	
		Store Supplies	36.50	
		Jim Eanes, Withdrawals	53.00	
		Petty Cash..	300.00	
		Cash..		472.50
		To reimburse the fund and increase it by $300.		

Part 3

If the January 8 entry to reimburse the fund was not recorded, net income would be overstated.

Exercise 9-7 (20 minutes)

a.

Oct. 31	Cleaning Expense...	120.00	
	Postage Expense...	79.00	
	Delivery Expense...	60.00	
	Cash Over and Short.....................................		4.00
	Cash...		255.00
	To reimburse the fund.		

b.

Nov. 30	Computer Repair Expense..	75.00	
	Entertainment Expense..	156.00	
	Cash Over and Short..	2.00	
	Cash...		233.00
	To reimburse the fund.		

c.

Dec. 31	Gas Expense..	80.00	
	Office Supplies	140.00	
	Entertainment Expense..	62.00	
	Petty Cash...	100.00	
	Cash...		382.00
	To reimburse and increase the fund.		

Fundamental Accounting Principles, Eleventh Canadian Edition

Exercise 9-9 (30 minutes)

a.

Jan.	15	Cash	56,000	
		Sales		56,000
		To record sale of merchandise to cash customers.		
	15	Cost of Goods Sold.................................	36,400	
		Merchandise Inventory......................		36,400
		To record cost of sales.		
	17	Accounts Receivable	15,800	
		Sales		15,800
		To record sale of merchandise on terms 2/10, n30.		
	17	Cost of Goods Sold.................................	12,000	
		Merchandise Inventory......................		12,000
		To record cost of sales.		
	20	Cash	111,720	
		Credit Card Expense...............................	2,280	
		Sales		114,000
		To record sale of merchandise less credit card expense; 114,000 x 2% = 2,280.		
	20	Cost of Goods Sold.................................	74,100	
		Merchandise Inventory......................		74,100
		To record cost of sales.		
	25	Cash	71,640	
		Debit Card Expense	360	
		Sales		72,000
		To record sale of merchandise less debit card expense; 0.5% x 72,000 = 360.		
	25	Cost of Goods Sold.................................	46,800	
		Merchandise Inventory......................		46,800
		To record cost of sales.		

Exercise 9-9 *(concluded)*

b. Cash sales would be preferable, however, often it is not convenient for customers. The inconvenience of cash might prevent customers from making purchases if that was the only means of payment accepted by LenCon. Credit sales allow customers to purchase on impulse. However, two disadvantages: receipt of cash by LenCon is delayed and credit sales require administrative time to monitor the timely collection from credit customers. Debit cards have the advantage of allowing customers to make impulse purchases but only if the cash balance is available in their bank account. Debit cards are also comparable to cash (no subsequent collection required) but the bank does charge a fee for this service although it is normally significantly less than the fee charged by banks for credit card transactions. Bank credit cards have the advantages of cash being collected by LenCon immediately (positive effect on cash flow) and customers are limited only to their credit card limit (not their bank account balance); customers are buying on credit but the risk of collection is transferred to the credit card company. The disadvantage of credit cards is the fee charged by the administering bank. LenCon will likely accept all forms of payment to enhance sales and in so doing recognize the costs and risks of each.

Exercise 9-11 (25 minutes)

MEDLINE SERVICE CO.
Bank Reconciliation
July 31, 2005

Bank statement balance	$10,332	Book balance of cash	$11,352
Add:		Add:	
Deposit of July 31	2,724	Error on Ch. No. 919.......	9
	$13,056		$11,361
Deduct:		Deduct:	
Outstanding cheques	1,713	Bank service charge.......	18
Adjusted bank balance	$11,343	Adjusted book balance..........	$11,343

Fundamental Accounting Principles, Eleventh Canadian Edition

Exercise 9-13 (20 minutes)

	Bank Balance		Book Balance			Not Shown on the Reconciliation
	Add	Deduct	Add	Deduct	Must Adjust	
1. Interest earned on the account.			x		Dr.	
2. Deposit made on September 30 after the bank was closed.	x					
3. Cheques outstanding on August 31 that cleared the bank in September.						x
4. NSF cheque from customer returned on September 15 but not recorded by the company.				x	Cr.	
5. Cheques written and mailed to payees on September 30.		x				
6. Deposit made on September 5 that was processed on September 8.						x
7. Bank service charge.				x	Cr.	
8. Cheques written and mailed to payees on October 5.						x
9. Cheque written by another depositor but charged against the company's account.	x					
10. Principal and interest collected by the bank but not recorded by the company.			x		Dr.	
11. Special charge for collection of note in No. 10 on company's behalf.				x	Cr.	
12. Cheque written against the account and cleared by the bank; erroneously omitted by the bookkeeper.				x	Cr.	

PROBLEMS

Problem 9-1B (20 minutes)

1. Violates segregation of duties. It is a good internal control to segregate duties for cash receipts and cash disbursements. An employee independent of these two functions should be given the responsibility for reconciling the bank account monthly. If no employees are available, this is an acceptable duty for the owner as it allows for owner supervision which is a good internal control.

2. Violates applying technological controls and segregation of duties. It is safe to assume that Stan Spencer has knowledge of employee passwords since he implemented the system of password protection company wide. It is a potentially dangerous situation that Stan processes payroll and can now probably change employee pay rates at will, or add a fictitious employee to the file. The company should hire an outside consultant to rework the password protection system so Stan will not have the knowledge that he currently possesses.

3. Violates applying technological controls. The theatre's system needs to be backed up at least daily, not weekly. The theatre needs to change the back-up policy and make sure the back-up copies are stored off the premises.

4. Violates segregation of duties. The company needs to have three employees handle these functions instead of two. One employee should place purchase orders, one should receive merchandise, and the third should pay vendors.

5. Violates applying technological controls. The use of the cheque protector is a good internal control. However the company needs to keep the cheques and cheque protector in a locked environment to prevent unauthorized use.

Fundamental Accounting Principles, Eleventh Canadian Edition

Problem 9-2B (30 minutes) *Part 1*

July	5	Petty Cash..	200.00	
		Cash		200.00
		To establish the fund.		

Part 2

DODGE & SONS
Petty Cash Payments Report
July 5 – 31, 2005

Receipts:
 Delivery expense
  July 11 Delivery of customer's merchandise ... $ 8.75
 Auto expense
  July 30 Reimbursement for auto expense 58.80
 Postage expense
  July 28 Purchased stamps..................................   16.00
 Transportation-in (Merchandise Inventory)
  July 6 COD charges on purchased
           merchandise........................ $14.50
     27 COD charges on purchased
           merchandise........................   47.10   61.60
 Office supplies
  July 12 Purchased file folders $12.13
     14 Reimbursement for office supplies 9.65
     18 Purchased paper.............................   22.54   44.32

Total receipts		$189.47
Fund total...	$200.00	
Less: Cash remaining	11.53	
Equals: Cash required to replenish petty cash.............		188.47
Cash over/(short)..		$ 1.00

Part 3

July	31	Delivery Expense.......................................	8.75	
		Auto Expense	58.80	
		Postage Expense......................................	16.00	
		Merchandise Inventory	61.60	
		Office Supplies	44.32	
		Petty Cash..	50.00	
		Cash Over and Short		1.00
		Cash		238.47
		To reimburse fund and increase it by $50.		

Part 4

If the entry in Part 3 was not recorded, net income, assets, and owner's equity would be overstated by $82.55 ($8.75 + $58.80 + $16.00 – $1.00 = $82.55).

Problem 9-3B (20 minutes) *Part 1*

Feb.	3	Petty Cash..	150.00	
		Cash..		150.00
		To establish fund.		

	14	Postage Expenses................................	14.82	
		Repairs Expense, Computer...................	36.57	
		Merchandise Inventory	17.60	
		Office Supplies....................................	16.29	
		Cash Over and Short.............................	2.44	
		Petty Cash..	25.00	
		Cash..		112.72
		To reimburse fund and increase it by $25.		

	28	Advertising Expense..............................	40.00	
		Delivery Expense..................................	58.00	
		Office Supplies....................................	28.19	
		Petty Cash..	75.00	
		Cash..		201.19
		To reimburse fund and increase it by $75.		

Part 2

If the February 28 reimbursement is not made and no entry is recorded, the expenses would not be recognized and net income and owner's equity would be overstated by $126.19 ($40.00 + $58.00 + $28.19). Similarly, the petty cash asset and total assets would be overstated by $126.19.

Even though the February 28 entry shows a debit to Office Supplies instead of Office Supplies Expense, the expense would turn out to be understated without this entry. This result occurs because the expense equals the difference between the unadjusted Office Supplies account balance and the count of office supplies on hand at the end of the year. If the unadjusted Office Supplies account is understated, then the amount of office supplies expense will be understated.

Fundamental Accounting Principles, Eleventh Canadian Edition

Problem 9-4B (30 minutes)

a.

BURNABY COMPANY
Bank Reconciliation
November 30, 2005

Bank statement balance.............	$ 6,703.54	Book balance...................		$4,833.26
Add:				
Deposit of Nov. 29...................	1,776.58			
	$ 8,480.12			
Deduct:				
Outstanding cheques:				
No. 548 .... $949.04		Deduct:		
No. 550 .... 917.12		Bank service charges..		36.50
No. 552 .... 885.36				
No. 553 .... 931.84				
	3,683.36			
Adjusted bank balance	$ 4,796.76	Adjusted book balance ...		$4,796.76

b.

Nov. 30	Bank Service Charges Expense	36.50	
	Cash		36.50
	To record November bank charges.		

c. If the entry in (b) was not recorded, net income, assets, and owner's equity would each be overstated.

Problem 9-5B (30 minutes)

a)

ARBOUR GLEN APARTMENTS
Bank Reconciliation
June 30, 2005

Bank statement balance		$35,070	Book balance	$31,800
Add:			Add:	
Deposit of June 30 in transit		7,100	Error (A/R)	6,300
		$42,170		$38,100
Deduct:			Deduct:	
Outstanding cheques:			Service charge	200
#120	$ 520			
#127	1,700			
#131	225			
#132	1,175			
#135	650	4,270		
Adjusted bank balance		$37,900	Adjusted book balance..........	$37,900

b)

Jun. 30	Bank Service Charges Expense		200	
	Cash..			200
	To record June bank charges.			
	Cash..		6,300	
	Accounts Receivable – Darla Smith			6,300
	To correct error.			

Problem 9-6B (30 minutes) *Part 1*

BOHANNON CO.
Bank Reconciliation
December 31, 2005

Bank statement balance.............	$45,091.80	Book balance of cash	$31,743.70
Add:		Add:	
Deposit of December 31	7,666.10	Error recording Cheque No. 1267...........................	18.00
		Proceeds of note less collection charge	19,980.00
	$52,757.90		$51,741,70
Deduct:		Deduct:	
Cheques No. 1242 .. $ 370.50		NSF — Tork Ind. $749.50	
1273 .. 1,084.20			
1282... 390.00	1,844.70	Printing charge 79.00	828.50
Adjusted bank balance	$50,913.20	Adjusted book balance..........	$50,913.20

Part 2

Dec.	31	Cash	18.00	
		Office Supplies...		18.00
		To correct error.		
	31	Cash	19,980.00	
		Collection Expense...	20.00	
		Notes Receivable		20,000.00
		To record collection of note less collection fee.		
	31	Accounts Receivable—Tork Industries	749.50	
		Cash		749.50
		To record NSF cheque.		
	31	Office Supplies Expense	79.00	
		Cash		79.00
		To record cheque printing charge.		

Part 3

In a banking context, a debit memo is a notification from the bank that they have debited the depositor's account. Since the depositor's account is a liability of the bank (a credit balance account), the debit notification means they have reduced the depositor's account balance. Conversely, a credit memo is a notification that the depositor's account has been credited, which means increased in this context.

Problem 9-7B (50 minutes) *Part 1*

SAFETY SYSTEMS
Bank Reconciliation
May 31, 2005

Bank statement balance		$21,808.60	Book balance of cash			$15,270.20
Add:			Add:			
Deposit of May 31		2,526.30	Proceeds of note	$7,300.00		
		$24,334.90	Less: Collection charge ...	100.00	7,200.00	
						$22,470.20
Deduct:			Deduct:			
Cheques No. 1780	$1,325.90		NSF — Gertie Mayer		$431.80	
1786	353.10		Service charge		12.00	
1789	639.50		Error recording Cheque			
		$ 2,318.50	No. 1788		10.00	453.80
Adjusted bank balance		$22,016.40	Adjusted book balance			$22,016.40

Part 2

May	31	Cash	7,200.00	
		Collection Expense	100.00	
		Notes Receivable		7,300.00
		To record collection of note less collection fee.		
	31	Accounts Receivable—Gertie Mayer	431.80	
		Cash		431.80
		To record NSF cheque.		
	31	Bank Service Charges Expense	12.00	
		Cash		12.00
		To record bank charges.		
	31	Utilities Expense	10.00	
		Cash		10.00
		To correct error.		

Part 3

There are several possible reasons why the cancelled cheques returned with a bank statement may not be numbered sequentially. Common reasons for this include the following:
- Some of the cheques in the numbered sequence may have cleared the bank in a previous period and been returned with the bank statement in that previous period.
- Some of the cheques in the numbered sequence may remain outstanding. If so, they will be returned with the bank statement in a later period when they clear the bank.
- The issuer of the cheques may have voided one or more of the cheques in the numbered sequence, perhaps because of making an error in writing the cheques.

Problem 9-7B *(concluded)*

- Occasionally, a cheque will reach the bank but the bank will incorrectly charge the cheque to the wrong account. When the bank detects the error, it will return the cheque separately with a note of explanation.

Problem 9-8B (30 minutes) *Part 1*

MOUNTAINVIEW CO.
Bank Reconcilliation
November 30, 2005

Bank statement balance..........	$28,252	Book balance....................................		$27,013
Add:		Add:		
Deposit of November 30	2,435	Interest earned..............	$ 17	
	$30,687	Proceeds of note...........	2,150	
		Less: Collection fee......	30	2,137
				$29,150
Deduct:		Deduct:		
Outstanding cheques:		NSF—Jerry Skyles........	$905	
No. 1393....... $ 745		Error on cheque		
No. 1406....... 1,322		no. 1404......................	50	955
No. 1408....... 425	2,492			
Adjusted bank balance	$28,195	Adjusted book balance..................		$28,195

Part 2

Nov.	30	Cash...	2,120	
		Collection Expense..	30	
		Notes Receivable..		2,150
		To record collection of note less fee.		
	30	Cash...	17	
		Interest Revenue...		17
		To record interest revenue.		
	30	Account Receivable—Jerry Skyles	905	
		Cash...		905
		To record NSF cheque.		
	30	Computer Equipment	50	
		Cash...		50
		To correct error.		

Problem 9-9B (30 minutes)

EMIRATES COMPANY
Bank Reconciliation
February 28, 2005

Bank statement balance		$ 9,600	Book balance....................			$12,992
Add:			Add:			
Deposit of February 28 in transit..................................		6,300	Note Rec'ble.................	$900		
		$15,900	Less: Fee.................	20		
			Error (Office Sup)	198		
			Interest Revenue	50	1,128	
Deduct:						$14,120
Outstanding cheques:						
#200.......................	$ 330		Deduct:			
#202.......................	1,600		NSF—Tahani Ahmad...	$435		
#205.......................	110		Cheque printing...........	60	495	
#213.......................	35					
#240.......................	200	2,275				
Adjusted bank balance		$13,625	Adjusted book balance............			$13,625

Feb. 28	Accounts Receivable – Tahani Ahmad........................		435	
	Cash			435
	To reinstate customer account re NSF cheque.			
28	Cash		198	
	Office Supplies			198
	To correct error.			
28	Office Supplies Expense		60	
	Cash			60
	To record cheque printing expense.			
28	Cash		50	
	Interest Revenue			50
	To record interest earned.			
28	Cash		880	
	Collection Expense		20	
	Note Receivable...			900
	To record collection of note less collection expense.			

Problem 9-10B

Part 1

HR CAFE
Bank Reconciliation
December 31, 2005

Bank statement balance..............	$25,430	Book balance			$11,040
Add:		Add:			
Deposit of Dec. 31 in transit....	1,570	Error (480 – 345)..........	$	135	
Error...	10,000	Note Rec'ble		15,000	
	$37,000	Less: Fee.................		10	
		Interest revenue		75	15,200
					$26,240
Deduct:		Deduct:			
Outstanding cheques:		NSF – Neon Company..	$ 2,100		
#197	$4,000	Service charge.............	50		
#199	9,000	13,000	Error (930 – 840)..........	90	2,240
Adjusted bank balance		$24,000	Adjusted book balance		$24,000

Part 2

Dec. 31	Accounts Receivable – Della Armstrong...................	90	
	Cash		90
	To correct error.		
	Accounts Receivable – Neon Company	2,100	
	Cash		2,100
	To reinstate customer account re NSF cheque.		
	Cash	135	
	Accounts Payable – CT Financial		135
	To correct error.		
	Bank Service Charges Expense................................	50	
	Cash		50
	To record December bank charges.		
	Collection Expense	10	
	Cash	15,065	
	Note Receivable		15,000
	Interest Revenue		75
	To record collection of note and interest		
	less collection expense.		

Part 3

If the entries in Part 2 were not recorded, net income and owner's equity would be understated by $15 ($75 − $50 − $10 = $15); assets would be understated by $150 ($90 − $90 + $2,100 − $2,100 + $135 − $50 + $15,065 − $15,000 = $150); and liabilities would be understated by $135.

Fundamental Accounting Principles, Eleventh Canadian Edition

Chapter 10   Receivables

EXERCISES

Exercise 10-1 (20 minutes)

Apr. 6	Cash...	8,832.00	
	Credit Card Expense ($9,200 × .04).........................	368.00	
	Sales...		9,200.00
6	COGS..	5,300.00	
	Merchandise Inventory		5,300.00
10	Accounts Receivable—Colonial............................	310.00	
	Sales...		310.00
10	COGS..	160.00	
	Merchandise Inventory		160.00
17	No entry required.		
28	Cash...	5,370.40	
	Credit Card Expense ($5,480 × .02)	109.60	
	Accounts Receivable—Colonial........................		5,480.00

Exercise 10-3 (15 minutes)

a.	Oct. 31	Allowance for Doubtful Accounts	1,000	
		Accounts Receivable—Gwen Rowe.................		1,000
b.	Dec. 9	Accounts Receivable—Gwen Rowe.........................	200	
		Allowance for Doubtful Accounts....................		200
	9	Cash..	200	
		Accounts Receivable—Gwen Rowe.................		200

Exercise 10-5 (15 minutes)

a. Dec. 31   Bad Debt Expense   1,205
                      Allowance for Doubtful Accounts   1,205

Accounts Receivable		Allowance for Doubtful Accounts	
		915	Unadjusted balance
		(?) = 1,205	Adjustment
Bal. 53,000		2,120	Required Adjusted Balance
× 4%			
$ 2,120			

b. Dec. 31   Bad Debt Expense   3,452
                      Allowance for Doubtful Accounts   3,452

Accounts Receivable		Allowance for Doubtful Accounts	
		Unadjusted balance 1,332	
		(?) = 3,452 Adjustment	
Bal. 53,000		2,120	Required Balance
× 4%			
$ 2,120			

Exercise 10-7 (15 minutes)

LISTEL
Partial Balance Sheet
March 31, 2005

Assets

Current assets:

Cash		$ 29,000
Accounts receivable	$102,000	
Less: Allowance for doubtful accounts	2,100	99,900
Notes receivable, due November 30, 2005		17,000
Merchandise inventory		65,000
Supplies		4,500
Total current assets		$215,400

Note: Bad Debt Expense is an income statement account and is therefore not listed on the balance sheet. Notes Receivable due May 1, 2007, Building and Accumulated Amortization, Building are asset accounts shown on the balance sheet but they are not current assets.

Fundamental Accounting Principles, Eleventh Canadian Edition

Exercise 10-9 (30 minutes)

a.

2005			
Dec. 31	Bad Debt Expense..	1,000	
	Allowance for Doubtful Accounts......................		1,000
	To record estimate for uncollectible accounts;		
	140,000 x 2% = 2,800; 2,800 – 1,800 = 1,000.		

b.

2006		
Accounts Receivable...	1,240,000	
Sales		1,240,000
To record credit sales during 2006.		
Cost of Goods Sold	813,000	
Merchandise Inventory......................................		813,000
To record cost of sales during 2006.		
Cash...	982,600	
Sales Discounts	12,400	
Accounts Receivable...		995,000
To record collections less sales discounts.		
Allowance for Doubtful Accounts...........................	24,900	
Accounts Receivable		24,900
To record the write-off of uncollectible		
accounts.		

c.

2006			
Dec. 31	Bad Debt Expense..	29,302	
	Allowance for Doubtful Accounts......................		29,302
	To record estimate for uncollectible accounts;		
	360,100 x 2% = 7,202;		
	7,202 – 2,800 + 24,900 = 29,302.		

Exercise 10-9 *(concluded)*

d.
 Assets
  Current assets:
   Accounts receivable... $360,100
   Less: Allowance for doubtful accounts......................... 7,202 $352,898

OR

   Accounts receivable (net) $352,898

Calculations:

Accounts Receivable				Allowance for Doubtful Accounts		
Bal. Dec 31/05	140,000	2006 collections	995,000		1,800	Unadj.Bal. Dec 31/05
2006 sales	1,240,000					
		2006 write-offs	24,900		1,000	Adjustment Dec 31/05
Bal. Dec 31/06	360,100				2,800	Adj Bal Dec 31/05
		2006 write-offs	24,900		29,302	Adjustment Dec 31/06
					7,202	Adj Bal Dec 31/06

e. The main advantage of the balance sheet approach is that it adjusts the allowance for doubtful accounts to the estimated amount of uncollectibles. Like the income statement approach, it satisfies the generally accepted accounting principles of matching and conservatism. The main disadvantage is that it does require more effort in terms of calculations.

Fundamental Accounting Principles, Eleventh Canadian Edition

Exercise 10-11 (20 minutes)

Mar. 21	Notes Receivable	3,100.00	
	Accounts Receivable—Bradley Brooks		3,100.00
	To record 6-month, 10% note to replace past-due account.		

Sept. 21	Accounts Receivable—Bradley Brooks	3,255.00	
	Interest Revenue		155.00
	Notes Receivable		3,100.00
	To record dishonoured note; $\$3,100 \times .10 \times 6/12 = \$155.00$		

Dec. 31	Allowance for Doubtful Accounts	3,255.00	
	Accounts Receivable—Bradley Brooks		3,255.00
	To record write-off of Brooks' account.		

Exercise 10-13 (25 minutes)

2005

Dec. 16	Notes Receivable	8,600.00	
	Accounts Receivable—Carmel Karuthers		8,600.00
	To record 60-day, 7% note to replace past-due account.		

31	Interest Receivable	24.74	
	Interest Revenue		24.74
	To record accrued interest; $\$8,600 \times .07 \times 15/365 = \$24.74$		

31	Interest Revenue	24.74	
	Income Summary		24.74
	To record the closing of the Interest Revenue account.		

2006

Feb. 14	Cash	8,698.96	
	Interest Revenue		74.22
	Interest Receivable		24.74
	Notes Receivable		8,600.00
	To record collection of note plus interest; $\$8,600 \times .07 \times 60/365 = 98.96; 98.96 - 24.74 = 74.22.$		

Mar. 2	Notes Receivable	4,000.00	
	Accounts Receivable—ATW Company		4,000.00
	To record 90-day, 8% note to replace past-due account.		

17	Notes Receivable...	1,600.00	
	Accounts Receivable—Leroy Johnson............		1,600.00
	To record 30-day, 9% note to replace		
	past-due account.		

May 31	Cash...	4,078.90	
	Interest Revenue		78.90
	Notes Receivable		4,000.00
	To record collection of note plus interest;		
	$4,000 × .08 × 90/365 = $78.90		

*Exercise 10-15 (20 minutes)

Jan. 20	Note Receivable..	85,000.00	
	Accounts Receivable – Steve Soetart		85,000.00
	Received note in settlement of account.		

Feb. 19	Cash...	85,243.79	
	Interest Revenue		243.79
	Notes Receivable		85,000.00
	Discounted a note receivable.		

Principal of Note...	$85,000.00
Add: Interest from Note ($85,000 × 9% × 90/365)	1,886.30
Maturity Value...	$86,886.30
Less: Bank Discount ($86,886.30 × 11.5% × 60/365) ..	1,642.51
Proceeds	$85,243.79

Fundamental Accounting Principles, Eleventh Canadian Edition

PROBLEMS

Problem 10-1B (30 minutes)

July	2	Accounts Receivable—J.R. Lacey	2,780.00	
		Sales...		2,780.00
	2	COGS..	1,660.00	
		Merchandise Inventory		1,660.00
	8	Cash...	3,150.56	
		Credit Card Expense	97.44	
		Sales...		3,248.00
		$3,248 × .03 = $97.44.		
	8	COGS..	1,950.00	
		Merchandise Inventory		1,950.00
	8	Accounts Receivable—Fortune Credit Co...............	1,114.00	
		Sales...		1,114.00
	8	COGS..	665.00	
		Merchandise Inventory		665.00
	12	Cash...	2,724.40	
		Sales Discounts...	55.60	
		Accounts Receivable—J.R. Lacey		2,780.00
		$2,780 × .02		
	13	Accounts Receivable—Fortune Credit Co..............	2,960.00	
		Sales...		2,960.00
	13	COGS..	1,775.00	
		Merchandise Inventory		1,775.00
	16	No entry required.		
	23	Cash...	3,992.52	
		Credit Card Expense	81.48	
		Accounts Receivable—Fortune Credit Co.		4,074.00
		($1,114 + $2,960) × .02		

Problem 10-2B (35 minutes) *Part 1*

a. Expense is 2.5% of credit sales:

Dec.	31	Bad Debt Expense..	31,025	
		Allowance for Doubtful Accounts.....................		31,025
		$1,241,000 × .025 = $31,025		

b. Allowance is 6% of accounts receivable:

Dec.	31	Bad Debt Expense..	23,300	
		Allowance for Doubtful Accounts.....................		23,300

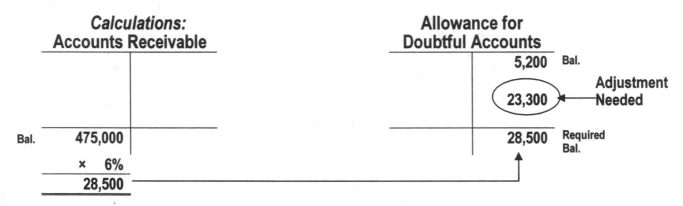

Part 2

Current assets:		
Accounts receivable..	$475,000	
Less: Allowance for doubtful accounts...............	36,225*	$438,775

OR

Accounts receivable (net of $36,225* estimated uncollectible accounts)...........................	$438,775

Calculations:

Allowance for Doubtful Accounts

	5,200	Unadjusted balance
	31,025	Adjustment
	36,225	Adjusted balance

Fundamental Accounting Principles, Eleventh Canadian Edition

Problem 10-2B (*concluded*)

Part 3

Current assets:		
Accounts receivable	$475,000	
Less: Allowance for doubtful accounts	28,500	$446,500
OR		
Accounts receivable (net of $28,500		
estimated uncollectible accounts)		$446,500

Problem 10-3B (35 minutes)

1. Calculation of the required balance of the allowance:

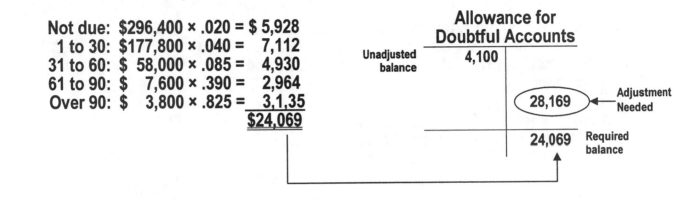

Not due: $296,400 × .020 = $ 5,928
1 to 30: $177,800 × .040 = 7,112
31 to 60: $ 58,000 × .085 = 4,930
61 to 90: $ 7,600 × .390 = 2,964
Over 90: $ 3,800 × .825 = 3,135
$24,069

Allowance for Doubtful Accounts

Unadjusted balance 4,100

28,169 — Adjustment Needed

24,069 Required balance

2.

Dec.	31	Bad debt expense..	28,169	
		Allowance for Doubtful Accounts.....................		28,169

3. Writing off the account receivable will not affect 2006 net income. The entry to write off an account involves a debit to Allowance for Doubtful Accounts and a credit to Accounts Receivable, both of which are balance sheet accounts. Net income is affected only by the annual recognition of the estimated bad debt expense, which is journalized as an adjusting entry.

Net income for 2005 (the year of the original sale) should have included an estimated expense for write-offs like this one.

Problem 10-4B (30 minutes)

Part A

1.

a)

Cash..	517,500	
Accounts Receivable...	2,932,500	
Sales		3,450,000

To record sales; 15% x $3,450,000 total sales = cash sales of $517,500.

Cost of Goods Sold	2,415,000	
Merchandise Inventory...................................		2,415,000

To record cost of sales.

b)

Sales Returns and Allowances..............................	98,000	
Accounts Receivable..		98,000

To record return of defective merchandise to be scrapped.

c)

Accounts Receivable...	58,000	
Allowance For Doubtful Accounts		58,000

To reverse write-off due to recovery.

Cash..	58,000	
Accounts Receivable..		58,000

To record recovery.

d)

Allowance For Doubtful Accounts	265,000	
Accounts Receivable..		265,000

To record write-off of uncollectible accounts.

e)

Cash..	2,949,000	
Sales Discounts...	52,000	
Accounts Receivable..		3,001,000

To record collections from credit customers less discounts of $52,000.

Part B

2.

Dec. 31	Bad Debt Expense.......................................	222,600	
	Allowance for Doubtful Accounts....................		222,600

$$2,932,500 - 98,000 - 52,000 = 2,782,500$$
$$2,782,500 \times 8\% = 222,600$$

Fundamental Accounting Principles, Eleventh Canadian Edition

Problem 10-4B *(continued)*

3.

Current assets:		
Accounts receivable	$548,000	
Less: Allowance for doubtful accounts	40,520	$507,480

OR

Current assets:	
Accounts receivable (net of $40,520 estimated uncollectible accounts)....................	$507,480

Calculation of balance in AFDA:

Calculation:

	AFDA	
		24,920
265,000		58,000
		222,600
		40,520

4. $222,600

Part C

5.

Dec. 31	Bad Debt Expense	206,740	
	Allowance for Doubtful Accounts.....................		206,740
	To record estimated uncollectible accounts receivable.		

Calculations:

Accounts Receivable

Dec. 31/04 Balance	980,000			
a)	2,932,000	98,000	b)	
c)	58,000	58,000	c)	
		265,000	d)	
		3,001,000	e)	
Dec. 31/05 Balance	548,000			

× 4.5%
= $24,660

Allowance for Doubtful Accounts

		24,920	Dec. 31/04 Balance
		58,000	c)
d)	265,000		
Unadjusted balance, Dec. 31/05	182,080	206,740	What adjustment is needed?
		24,660	Required adjusted balance

Problem 10-4B *(concluded)*

6.

Current assets:
Accounts receivable $548,000
Less: Allowance for doubtful accounts .... <u>24,660</u> $523,340

OR

Current assets:
Accounts receivable (net of $24,660
estimated uncollectible accounts).................... $523,340

7. $206,740

Problem 10-5B (35 minutes)

2005

a. Accounts Receivable.. 673,490
    Sales 673,490

   COGS 486,000
    Merchandise Inventory.. 486,000

b. Cash 437,250
    Accounts Receivable... 437,250

c. Allowance for Doubtful Accounts..................................... 8,240
    Accounts Receivable... 8,240

d. Bad Debt Expense... 10,520
    Allowance for Doubtful Accounts 10,520

Calculations:

Accounts Receivable				Allowance for Doubtful Accounts			
	0						
Credit Sales	673,490						
		437,250	Collections				
		8,240	Write-offs	Write-offs	8,240	10,520	Adjustment needed
Balance	228,000					2,280	Required Balance
	× 1%						
	2,280						

Fundamental Accounting Principles, Eleventh Canadian Edition

Problem 10-5B (concluded)

2006

e.	Accounts Receivable	927,310	
	Sales		927,310
	COGS	716,000	
	Merchandise Inventory...		716,000
f.	Cash	890,220	
	Accounts Receivable...		890,220
g.	Allowance for Doubtful Accounts.....................................	10,090	
	Accounts Receivable...		10,090
h.	Bad Debt Expense..	10,360	
	Allowance for Doubtful Accounts		10,360

Accounts Receivable				Allowance for Doubtful Accounts			
Bal.	228,000					2,280	Bal.
Credit Sales	927,310	890,220	Collections				
		10,090	Write-offs	Write-offs	10,090	10,360	Adjustment needed
Bal.	255,000					2,550	Required Balance
	× 1%						
	2,550						

Problem 10-6B (30 minutes)

a.

2005

May 31   Bad Debt Expense.. 10,500

          Allowance for Doubtful Accounts.............................   10,500

          To record estimate for uncollectible accounts;
          420,000 x 2.5% = 10,500.

b.

Assets

  Current assets:

    Accounts receivable.. $140,000

    Less: Allowance for doubtful accounts*......   13,700 $126,300

OR

    Accounts receivable (net) $126,300

*Calculations:

Allowance for Doubtful Accounts	
	Unadj.Bal.
3,200	**May 31/05**
	Adjustment
10,500	**May 31/05**
13,700	**Adj Bal May 31/05**

          Fundamental Accounting Principles, Eleventh Canadian Edition

Problem 10-6B *(concluded)*

c.

```
     2005
     May 31  Bad Debt Expense.......................................   840
                   Allowance for Doubtful Accounts...................          840
                   To record estimate for uncollectible
             accounts; 4,040* – 3,200 = 840**.
```

*Calculations:

May 31, 2005 Accounts Receivable	Expected Percentage Uncollectible	Estimated Uncollectibles
$ 98,000	1%	= 980
39,000	4%	= 1,560
3,000	50%	= 1,500
		4,040

**Calculations:

Allowance for Doubtful Accounts		
	3,200	Unadj.Bal. May 31/05
	840	Adjustment May 31/05
	4,040	Adj Bal May 31/05

d.

Assets
  Current assets:
    Accounts receivable $140,000
    Less: Allowance for doubtful accounts 4,040 $135,960

OR

    Accounts receivable (net) $135,960

Problem 10-7B (35 minutes)

Part 1

Oct. 31	Bad Debt Expense...	11,500	
	Allowance For Doubtful Accounts....................		11,500
	To record estimated uncollectible accounts;		
	2,300,000 x .005 = 11,500.		

Part 2

Nov. 30	Bad Debt Expense...	7,550	
	Allowance For Doubtful Accounts....................		7,550
	To record estimated uncollectible accounts.		

Calculations:

Accounts Receivable							Allowance for Doubtful Accounts			
Bal. Sept. 30	320,000								4,800	Bal. Sept. 30
Revenues on credit	2,300,000	2,025,000	Collection of customer accounts						65,000	Recovery
Set-up recovery	65,000	25,000	Write-off of uncollectible account	Write-off of uncollectible account	25,000		11,500[1]	Adjustment to estimate bad debts for October
Bal. Oct. 31	635,000								56,300	Bal. Oct. 31
Revenues on credit	1,975,000	1,865,000	Collection of customer accounts							
		28,000	Write-off of uncollectible account	Write-off of uncollectible account	28,000				
Bal. Nov. 30	717,000								28,300	Unadjusted bal. Nov. 30
									7,550	What adjustment is necessary to get the desired balance[3]?
									35,850[2]	Desired bal. Nov. 30

1. $2,300,000 \times \frac{1}{2}\% = 11,500$
2. $717,000 \times 5\% = 35,850$
3. $35,850 - 28,300 = 7,550$

Fundamental Accounting Principles, Eleventh Canadian Edition

Problem 10-8B (30 minutes)

a)

	Aug. + July	June	May	April	
	Not yet due	**1 to 30 days past due**	**31 to 60 days past due**	**61 to 90 days past due**	
A. Leslie	$29,000		$12,000		
T. Meston				$26,000	
P. Obrian	21,000 + 52,000 = 73,000				
L. Timms	14,000	$26,000	63,000		
W. Victor	61,000 + 32,000 = 93,000	83,000			
Totals	$ 209,000	$ 109,000	$75,000	$ 26,000	
Percent Uncollectible	× 1%	× 2%	× 5%	× 20%	
Estimated uncollectible accounts	$ 2,090	$ 2,180	$ 3,750	$ 5,200	**Total** = $13,220

b)

Aug. 31	Bad Debt Expense		19,520	
	Allowance for Doubtful Accounts.....................			19,520
	To record estimate for uncollectible accounts.			

Calculations:

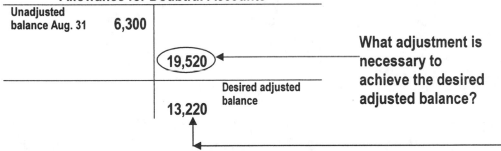

Allowance for Doubtful Accounts

Unadjusted balance Aug. 31	6,300
	19,520
	Desired adjusted balance 13,220

What adjustment is necessary to achieve the desired adjusted balance?

Problem 10-9B (30 minutes)

a.

2005
Mar. 31 Bad Debt Expense..................................... 45,865
              Allowance for Doubtful Accounts................. 45,865
              To record estimated uncollectible accounts
              using the income statement approach;
              9,173,000 x .5% = 45,865.

2006
Mar. 31 Bad Debt Expense..................................... 51,530
              Allowance for Doubtful Accounts................. 51,530
              To record estimated uncollectible
              accounts; 729,000 x 7% = 51,030;
              51,030 + 500 = 51,530.

2007
Mar. 31 Bad Debt Expense..................................... 72,500
              Allowance for Doubtful Accounts................. 72,500
              To record estimated uncollectible
              accounts; 59,000 + 13,500 = 72,500.

b.

Year	Allowance for Doubtful Accounts	Accounts Receivable	Sales
2005	$43,565*	$486,000	$9,173,000
2006	51,030	729,000	7,942,000
2007	59,000	946,000	7,500,000

*45,865 – 2,300 = 43,565

Sales are decreasing while the balance in Accounts Receivable is increasing indicating that the collection of receivables is less efficient in 2007 than in 2006 and 2005. Also, the balance in the Allowance for Doubtful Accounts account is increasing with decreasing sales confirming that the collection of receivables requires attention.

Fundamental Accounting Principles, Eleventh Canadian Edition

Problem 10-10B (30 minutes)

Note	Date of Note	Principal	Interest Rate	Term	(a) Maturity Date	(b) Days of Accrued Interest at Dec. 31, 2005	(c) Accrued Interest at Dec. 31, 2005
1	Sept. 20/04	$245,000	7%	120 days	Jan. 18/05[1]	0	0
2	Jun. 1/05	$120,000	9%	45 days	July 16/05[2]	0	0
3	Nov. 23/05	$ 82,000	9%	90 days	Feb. 21/06[3]	38 days	$768.33[5]
4	Dec. 18/05	$ 60,000	10%	30 days	Jan. 17/06[4]	13 days	$213.70[6]

Calculations as denoted by superscripts:

1. Days in September	30
Minus date of note	20
Days remaining in September	10
Add days in October	31
Add days in November	30
Add days in December	31
Add days in January	18
Period of note in days	120

2. Days in June	30
Minus date of note	1
Days remaining in June	29
Add days in July	16
Period of note in days	45

3. Days in November	30
Minus date of note	23
Days remaining in November	7
Add days in December	31
Add days in January	31
Add days in February	21
Period of note in days	90

4. Days in December	31
Minus date of note	18
Days remaining in December	13
Add days in January	17
Period of note in days	30

5. $82,000 × 9% × 38/365 = $768.33
6. $60,000 × 10% × 13/365 = $213.70

d) 2005

Dec. 31 Interest Receivable – Note 4 .... 213.70
                Interest Revenue 213.70
         To accrue interest on Note 4.

e) 2006

Jan. 17 Cash... 60,493.15
                Interest Revenue 279.45
                Interest Receivable... 213.70
                Note Receivable – Note 4................................. 60,000.00
         To record collection of Note 4 and interest;
         60,000 x 10% x 30/365 = 493.15; 493.15 – 213.70 = 279.45.

Problem 10-11B (75 minutes)

a.

2005

Nov. 16	Notes Receivable...	3,700.00	
	Accounts Receivable—Bess Parker		3,700.00

Dec.	31	Interest Receivable..	54.74	
		Interest Revenue		54.74

$3,700 × .12 × 45/365 = $54.74

	31	Interest Revenue...	54.74	
		Income Summary		54.74

2006

Feb.	14	Cash...	3,809.48	
		Interest Earned..		54.74
		Interest Receivable		54.74
		Notes Receivable		3,700.00

	28	Notes Receivable...	12,400.00	
		Accounts Receivable—The Simms Co............		12,400.00

Mar.	1	Notes Receivable...	5,100.00	
		Accounts Receivable—Bedford Holmes		5,100.00

	30	Accounts Receivable—The Simms Co	12,491.73	
		Interest Revenue		91.73
		Notes Receivable		12,400.00

$12,400 × .09 × 30/365 = $91.73

b.

Days in March	31
Minus date of note...................	1
Days remaining in March	30
Add days in April	30
Days to equal Maturity date	60

Therefore, the maturity date is <u>April 30, 2006</u>.

2006

Apr.	30	Cash...	5,183.84	
		Interest Revenue		83.84
		Notes Receivable		5,100.00

To record collection of note plus interest.
(5,100 × 60/365 × 10% = 83.84)

Fundamental Accounting Principles, Eleventh Canadian Edition

Problem 10-12B (30 minutes)

Preparation component:

2005

a. Nov. 17 Notes Receivable – RoadWorks........................... 45,000.00
                 Accounts Receivable – RoadWorks 45,000.00
                 To record acceptance of 7%, 90-day note.

b. Dec. 1 Notes Receivable – Ellen Huskey 8,000.00
                 Accounts Receivable – Ellen Huskey 8,000.00
                 To record acceptance of 7%, 4-month note.

2006

c. Jan. 31 Interest Receivable 740.59
                 Interest Revenue 740.59
                 To record accrued interest;
                 RoadWorks: 45,000 x 7% x 75/365 = 647.26;
                 Huskey: 8,000 x 7% x 2/12 = $\underline{93.33}$
                                                                          $\underline{740.59}$

d. Feb. 15 Cash 45,776.71
                 Notes Receivable – RoadWorks.................... 45,000.00
                 Interest Receivable 647.26
                 Interest Revenue 129.45
                 To record collection of note;
                 45,000 x 7% x 90/365 = 776.71;
                 776.71 – 647.26 = 129.45.

e. Apr. 1 Accounts Receivable – Ellen Huskey................ 8,186.66
                 Interest Receivable 93.33
                 Interest Revenue 93.33
                 Notes Receivable – Ellen Huskey 8,000.00
                 To record dishonour of note;
                 8,000 x 7% x 2/12 = 93.33.

f. July 15 Allowance for Doubtful Accounts...................... 8,186.86
                 Accounts Receivable – Ellen Huskey 8,186.86
                 To record write-off of accounts receivable.

Analysis component:
The credit balance in AFDA is $41,813.14 (50,000 – 8,186.86) after recording the July 15 write-off. Assuming no additional write-offs were recorded prior to year end, the large unused portion of AFDA indicates that write-offs were significantly less than expected.

*Problem 10-13B (30 minutes)

Date	Description	Debit	Credit
Mar. 1	Notes Receivable...	5,100	
	Accounts Receivable – Bolton Company.........		5,100
23	Cash..	5,050	
	Interest Expense...	50	
	Notes Receivable		5,100
June 21	Notes Receivable..	9,300	
	Accounts Receivable – Vince Soto...................		9,300
July 5	Cash..	9,100	
	Interest Expense...	200	
	Notes Receivable		9,300
Sept. 25	No entry required.		

When a business discounts notes receivable with recourse and these notes have not matured prior to year end, the business must disclose this information in the notes to the financial statements. This is a requirement because the business has a contingent liability, which means that if the maker of the note dishonours (fails to pay) the note, the business will have to pay the third party the full maturity value. This contingent liability must be disclosed to satisfy the full-disclosure principle.

*Problem 10-14B (60 minutes)

Jan.	10	Notes Receivable..	3,000.00	
		Accounts Receivable—David Huerta...............		3,000.00
Mar.	14	Accounts Receivable—David Huerta.....................	3,059.18	
		Interest Revenue		59.18
		Notes Receivable..		3,000.00

$3000 × .12 × 60/365 = $59.18

	19	Notes Receivable..	2,100.00	
		Accounts Receivable—Rose Jones..................		2,100.00
	28	Cash...	2,075.38	
		Interest Expense	24.62	
		Notes Receivable..		2,100.00

Calculations:

Principal..	$2,100.00
Interest = $2,100.00 × 0.10 × (90/365)	51.78
Maturity value..	$2,151.78
Discount = $2,151.78 × 0.16 × (81/365).....	76.40
Proceeds..	$2,075.38

June	20	No entry required

	27	Cash...	700.00	
		Notes Receivable..	1,300.00	
		Accounts Receivable—Jake Thomas		2,000.00
July	24	Cash...	1,308.86	
		Interest Revenue		8.86
		Notes Receivable..		1,300.00

Calculations:

Principal..	$1,300.00
Interest = $1,300.00 × 0.12 × (60/365)	25.64
Maturity value..	$1,325.64
Discount = $1,325.64 × 0.14 × (33/365).....	16.78
Proceeds..	$1,308.86

Aug.	29	Accounts Receivable—Jake Thomas......................	1,345.64	
		Cash		1,345.64
Sept.	4	Notes Receivable..	1,500.00	
		Accounts Receivable—Ginnie Bauer		1,500.00

*Problem 10-14B *(concluded)*

Oct.	13	Cash..		1,514.82	
		Interest Revenue			14.82
		Notes Receivable			1,500.00

Calculations:

Principal...	$1,500.00
Interest = $1,500.00 × 0.11 × (60/365)........	27.12
Maturity value...	$1,527.12
Discount = $1,527.12 × 0.14 × (21/365)......	12.30
Proceeds..	$1,514.82

Nov.	6	Accounts Receivable—Ginnie Bauer........................	1,547.12	
		Cash		1,547.12

Dec.	6	Cash..	1,561.11	
		Interest Revenue		13.99
		Accounts Receivable—Ginnie Bauer................		1,547.12

1,547.12 x 11% x 30/365 = 13.99.

	28	Allowance for Doubtful Accounts	4,404.82	
		Accounts Receivable—David Huerta................		3,059.18
		Accounts Receivable—Jake Thomas		1,345.64

Fundamental Accounting Principles, Eleventh Canadian Edition

Chapter 11   Payroll Liabilities

EXERCISES

Exercise 11-1 (15 minutes)

Regular pay (172 hours @ $12.50)		$2,150.00
Overtime premium pay (12 hours @ $6.25)		75.00
Gross pay		$2,225.00
EI deduction	$ 46.73	
CPP deduction	95.70	
Income tax deduction	383.45	
Total deductions		525.88
Net pay		$1,699.12

Exercise 11-3 (10 minutes)

Employee	Gross Pay	EI Premium	Income Taxes	United Way	CPP	Total Deductions	Net Pay	Office Salaries	Sales Salaries
				Deductions			**Pay**	**Distribution**	
Akerley, D.	1,900.00	39.90	457.05	80.00	87.39	664.34	1,235.66	1,900.00	
Nesbitt, M.	1,260.00	26.46	239.30	50.00	55.71	371.47	888.53		1,260.00
Trent, F.	1,680.00	35.28	378.30	40.00	76.50	530.08	1,149.92		1,680.00
Vacon, M.	3,000.00	63.00	858.75	300.00	141.84	1,363.59	1,636.41		3,000.00
Totals	7,840.00	164.64	1,933.40	470.00	361.44	2,929.48	4,910.52	1,900.00	5,940.00

Exercise 11-5 (25 minutes)

Employee	Gross Pay	Deductions						Payment	Distribution	
		EI Premium	Income Taxes	Medical Ins.	CPP	United Way	Total Deductions	Net Pay	Office Salaries	Sales Salaries
Crimson, L.	1,995.00	41.90	598.50	65.00	84.31	40.00	829.71	1,165.29		1,995.00
Long, M.	2,040.00	42.84	612.00	65.00	86.54	100.00	906.38	1,133.62	2,040.00	
Morris, P.	2,000.00	42.00	600.00	65.00	84.56	-0-	791.56	1,208.44		2,000.00
Peterson, B.	2,350.00	49.35	705.00	65.00	101.89	50.00	971.24	1,378.76		2,350.00
Totals	8,385.00	176.09	2,515.50	260.00	357.30	190.00	3,498.89	4,886.11	2,040.00	6,345.00

*$3,500 exemption ÷ 12 months = $291.67 exempt

1. 1,995 × 2.1% = 41.90
2. 2,040 × 2.1% = 42.84
3. 2,000 × 2.1% = 42.00
4. 2,350 × 2.1% = 49.35
5. 1,995 × 30% = 598.50
6. 2,040 × 30% = 612.00
7. 2,000 × 30% = 600.00
8. 2,350 × 30% = 705.00
9. (1,995 − 291.67) × 4.95% = 84.31
10. (2,040 − 291.67) × 4.95% = 86.54
11. (2,000 − 291.67) × 4.95% = 84.56
12. (2,350 − 291.67) × 4.95% = 101.89

Fundamental Accounting Principles, Eleventh Canadian Edition

Exercise 11-7 (15 minutes)

Aug. 25	Salaries Expense	65,950.00	
	EI Payable		1,384.95
	CPP Payable		3,097.93
	Employees' Income Taxes Payable		22,458.75
	Medical Insurance Payable		1,150.00
	United Way Payable		1,319.00
	Salaries Payable		36,539.37

Exercise 11-9 (10 minutes)

Sept. 15	EI Payable (1,384.95 + 1,938.93)	3,323.88	
	CPP Payable (3,097.93 x 2)	6,195.86	
	Employees' Income Taxes Payable	22,458.75	
	Cash		31,978.49

Exercise 11-11 (20 minutes)

	CPP Contribution	EI Contribution	Retirement Fund Contributions	Health Insurance
Doherty ($36,000 – 3,500) × 4.95% = $1,608.75		$36,000 × 2.1% = $ 756.00	$ 3,600.00	$1,440.00
Fane......	1,801.80	819.00	6,100.00	1,440.00
Kahan...	1,801.80	819.00	5,900.00	1,440.00
Martin ... ($37,000 – 3,500) × 4.95% = 1,658.25		$37,000 × 2.1% = 777.00	3,700.00	1,440.00
Poon	1,801.80	819.00	4,800.00	1,440.00
Totals....	$8,672.40	$ 3,990.00	$24,100.00	$7,200.00

Payroll taxes and fringe benefits as a percentage of salaries:

$$\frac{\$8,672.40 + (\$3,990.00 \times 1.4) + \$24,100 + \$7,200}{\$241,000} = 18.90\%$$

Exercise 11-13 (30 minutes)

Jan. 31	Benefits Expense	22,507	
	Estimated Vacation Payable		22,507

$ 96,000	× (2/50)	=	$ 3,840
224,000[1]	× (4/48)	=	18,667
$320,000			$22,507

1. 320,000 x 70% = 224,000

ALTERNATE PROBLEMS

Problem 11-1B (55 minutes)

Payroll Register

Employees	Employee No.	M	T	W	T	F	S	S	Total Hours	O.T. Hours	Reg. Pay Rate	Regular Pay	O.T. Premium Pay	Gross Pay	
Ben Amoko	31	8	8	8	8	8	0	0	40	0	17.00	680.00	0.00	680.00	1
Auleen Carson ..	32	7	8	8	7	8	4	0	42	2	18.00	756.00	18.00	774.00	2
Mitale De	33	8	8	8	0	8	4	4	40	0	18.00	720.00	0.00	720.00	3
Gene Deszca.....	34	8	8	8	8	8	0	0	40	0	15.00	600.00	0.00	600.00	4
Ysong Tan.........	35	0	6	6	6	6	8	8	40	0	15.00	600.00	0.00	600.00	5
												3,356.00	18.00	3,374.00	6

Week Ended November 21, 2003

	CPP*	Employment Insurance	Income Tax	Hospital Insurance	Union Dues	Total Deductions	Net Pay	Office Wages Expense	Service Wages Expense
1	0.00	0.00	136.00	30.00	12.00	178.00	502.00		680.00
2	0.00	0.00	154.80	30.00	12.00	196.80	577.20	774.00	
3	32.31	15.12	144.00	30.00	12.00	233.43	486.57		720.00
4	26.37	12.60	120.00	30.00	12.00	200.97	399.03		600.00
5	26.37	12.60	120.00	30.00	12.00	200.97	399.03		600.00
6	85.05	40.32	674.80	150.00	60.00	1,010.17	2,363.83	774.00	2,600.00

*$3,500 exemption ÷ 52 weeks = $67.31 exempt

Problem 11-1B (concluded)

Part 2

Nov. 21	Office Wages Expense......................................	774.00	
	Service Wages Expense	2,600.00	
	EI Payable...		40.32
	CPP Payable..		85.05
	Employees' Income Taxes Payable...........		674.80
	Employees' Hospital Insurance Payable...		150.00
	Employees' Union Dues Payable..............		60.00
	Wages Payable...		2,363.83
21	EI Expense..	56.45	
	CPP Expense..	85.05	
	EI Payable ($40.32 x 1.4)..........................		56.45
	CPP Payable..		85.05

Problem 11-2B (20 minutes) *Part 1*

Jan. 10	Sales Salaries Expense....................................	23,400.00	
	Office Salaries Expense..................................	5,820.00	
	Employees' Income Taxes Payable...........		6,180.00
	EI Payable...		613.62
	CPP Payable..		1,296.46
	Employees' Hospital Insurance Payable...		920.00
	Employees' Union Dues		490.00
	Salaries Payable.......................................		19,719.92

Part 2

Jan. 10	EI Expense...	859.07	
	CPP Expense..	1,296.46	
	EI Payable ($613.62 × 1.4)..........................		859.07
	CPP Payable..		1,296.46

Problem 11-3B (30 minutes)

Part 1

Oct. 17	Sales Salaries Expense	1,250.00	
	Office Salaries Expense	720.00	
	Shop Salaries Expense	1,740.00	
	EI Payable		31.08
	CPP Payable		66.60
	Employees' Income Taxes Payable		882.65
	Employees' Medical Insurance Payable		185.50
	Employees' Union Dues Payable		74.20
	Salaries Payable		2,469.97

Part 2

Oct. 17	EI Expense	43.51	
	CPP Expense	66.60	
	EI Payable ($31.08 × 1.4)		43.51
	CPP Payable		66.60

Part 3

Oct. 17	Benefits Expense	704.90	
	Employees' Medical Insurance Payable		185.50
	Employees' Retirement Program Payable ($3,710 × 8%)		296.80
	Estimated Vacation Pay Liability ($3,710 × 6%)		222.60

Fundamental Accounting Principles, Eleventh Canadian Edition

Problem 11-4B (40 minutes)

Mar.	14	Employees' Income Taxes Payable	1,212.00	
		EI Payable	347.76	
		CPP Payable	595.58	
		Cash		2,155.34
	28	Office Salaries Expense.....................................	2,300.00	
		Shop Salaries Expense......................................	4,600.00	
		Employees' Income Taxes Payable...........		1,212.00
		EI Payable..		144.90
		CPP Payable...		297.79
		Employees' Medical Insurance Payable....		345.00
		Salaries Payable..		4,900.31
	31	Benefits Expense	759.00	
		Employees' Medical Insurance Payable....		345.00
		Estimated Vacation Pay Liability		414.00
	31	EI Expense...	202.86	
		CPP Expense	297.79	
		EI Payable ($144.90 × 1.4).........................		202.86
		CPP Payable...		297.79
Apr.	13	Employees' Income Taxes Payable	1,212.00	
		EI Payable (144.90 + 202.86)	347.76	
		CPP Payable (297.79 x 2)	595.58	
		Cash		2,155.34
	13	Employees' Medical Insurance Payable...........	2,070.00	
		Cash (1,380 + 345 + 345)...........................		2,070.00